W9-AEH-055

Beyond Socialist Realism

Soviet fiction since *Ivan Denisovich*

Geoffrey Hosking

Beyond Socialist Realism

Soviet fiction since *Ivan Denisovich*

HOLMES & MEIER PUBLISHERS, INC.
New York

First published in the United States of America 1980 by
Holmes & Meier Publishers, Inc.
30 Irving Place, New York, N.Y. 10003

Copyright © 1980 by Geoffrey Hosking

Library of Congress Cataloging in Publication Data

Hosking, Geoffrey A
    Beyond socialist realism.

    Bibliography: p.
    Includes index.
    1. Russian fiction – 20th century – History and criticism.
I. Title.
PG3098.4.H67 1979   891.7'3'4409   78-31891
ISBN 0-8419-0484-7

Printed in Great Britain

Contents

Acknowledgements

In putting together this work, I owe a great debt to many people. Deming Brown, Martin Dewhirst, Ronald Hingley and Michael Nicholson read the whole of an earlier draft and made invaluable comments on it. Nikolai Andreyev read several draft chapters and showed me new directions, drawing on his endless knowledge and insight in the culture and history of Russia. Angela Livingstone and Diana Hughes helped me with individual chapters. I have benefited much also from discussions with Katerina Clark (to whom I am most grateful for the chance to read her unpublished work), Priscilla Meyer, Boris Shragin, and my colleagues in the Soviet Literature Study Group which meets regularly in Oxford. The Russian Institute, Columbia University, gave me a Senior Fellowship in the spring semester 1976, which was a vital interval of leisure and stimulating company in which to begin turning the fruits of years of reading into the present study. Above all I am indebted to my wife, Anne, who has kept telling me I ought to write this book (even when I wasn't certain) and ensured me the domestic tranquillity to do so. The mistakes and misconceptions which remain in spite of everybody's help are, of course, entirely my own responsibility.

I am grateful to the publishers for permission to reproduce ideas or material from the following articles, which I wrote at earlier stages in the gestation of this book:

'The Russian peasant rediscovered: "village prose" of the 1960s', *Slavic Review,* Vol. 32, no. 4 (December 1973), pp. 705–24.

'Vasily Belov – chronicler of the Soviet village', *Russian Review,* Vol. 34, no. 2, pp. 165–85.

'The search for an image of man in contemporary Soviet fiction',

Forum for Modern Language Studies, Vol. 11, no. 4 (October 1975), pp. 349–65.

'The good soldier Chonkin', *Times Literary Supplement,* 23 January 1976.

'The fiction of Vasilii Shukshin', in D. M. Fiene (editor), *Vasilii Shukshin: Snowball Berry Red,* Ann Arbor, Michigan: Ardis Press, 1978.

No list of acknowledgements would be complete without a special word of thanks to Stuart Rees and the staff of Essex University Library, whose rich collection of Soviet and émigré Russian literature supplied almost all the material I needed for this study.

*   *

– © Copyright 1973, 1975 by Nordland Publishing Company.

Frederick A. Praeger, Inc. and Mr Solzhenitsyn: *One Day in the Life of Ivan Denisovich* by Alexander Solzhenitsyn, translated by Max Hayward and Ronald Hingley – © 1963 by Frederick A. Praeger, Inc.

Random House, Inc. Alfred A. Knopf, Inc. and Weidenfeld (Publishers) Ltd: *The Seven Days of Creation* by Vladimir Maximov, passages quoted in Geoffrey Hosking's translation – © Possev-Verlag, V. Gorachek K.G. 1971; English translation © Alfred A. Knopf, Inc. 1974.

Collins Publishers and Doubleday & Company, Inc.: *Karantin* by Vladimir Maximov, passages quoted in Geoffrey Hosking's translation before the appearance of the official English translation to be published by Collins and Doubleday – © Possev-Verlag, V. Gorachek K.G. 1973.

Farrar, Straus & Giroux, Inc. and Jonathan Cape Ltd: *The Life and Extraordinary Adventures of Private Ivan Chonkin* by Vladimir Voinovich, passages quoted slightly adapted from the translation by Richard Lourie – Translation Copyright © 1977 by Farrar, Straus & Giroux, Inc.

Jonathan Cape Ltd and Simon & Schuster, Inc.: *Faithful Ruslan* by Georgy Vladimov, passages quoted in Geoffrey Hosking's translation instead of the official English translation published by Cape and Simon & Schuster – Copyright © 1978 by Possev-Verlag; Translation copyright 1979 by Michael Glenny.

Ardis/rlt, Ann Arbor: *Snowball Berry Red and other stories* by Vasily Shukshin, edited by D. M. Fiene – © 1979 by Ardis.

Introduction

This work has arisen out of the need that I, and I think many students of Soviet affairs, have felt to understand what has been happening in Soviet fiction in the last fifteen to twenty years, roughly speaking since the publication of Solzhenitsyn's *One Day in the Life of Ivan Denisovich*. The so-called 'thaw' of 1953–63 made a big impact on western observers, and much was written at that time about contemporary Soviet fiction. Then, however, a new phenomenon, *samizdat*, engrossed western attention, and it came to be implied, or even openly stated, that little or nothing published in the Soviet Union itself was worth reading, because of the restrictions imposed by the censorship. Living there myself for quite extended periods during these years, and keeping up, whenever possible, with the literary journals, I have come to feel that this dismissive attitude is unjustified Much that is of great interest and probably literary value has been published by Soviet publishing houses in the last two decades. The best writers have not retreated into the well-tried Socialist Realist stereotype: they have pursued further the questions raised by the 'thaw' – and sometimes their probing has taken them over the uncertain boundary into *samizdat*. Sometimes, on the other hand, they have been able to say much that they wanted to in officially published form. It is true that *samizdat* works are usually more outspoken and unequivocal: but what they say is being reiterated in Soviet publications in ways that the informed and sensitive reader cannot fail to understand.

I do, then, regard *samizdat* and published literature as part of the same phenomenon – as part of one Soviet literature. Probably neither Soviet critics nor many émigré ones will approve of this view, and it is, of course, true that the operation of the censorship makes a big difference to the way the two types of literature are produced. Nevertheless, I think the boundary between them has been persistently overstressed: a number of works have in fact crossed it – *Ivan Denisovich,* for example, in one direction, and Bulat Okudzhava's *Poor Avrosimov* (or *A Gulp of Freedom*) in the other.

I have deliberately been selective in my approach to recent fiction. Probably more novels and short stories are published in the Soviet Union than anywhere else in the world, and any general survey of them could do no more than list names. I have chosen just nine authors for close examination. They are all representative of the renewed realism, springing from concern to portray Soviet society faithfully, which, I argue, has constituted the mainstream of Soviet fiction in the sixties and seventies. Even in dealing with these nine, I have concentrated on works which display particular awareness of the spiritual and philosophical issues raised by the Soviet experience.

This study attempts to interpret in intellectual, social and spiritual terms the works with which it deals; it does not attempt to evaluate their literary worth. Anxious questions about the 'validity' of a literary work do much to impede a sympathetic response to it. In the case of Soviet literature, because of the peculiar problems it raises, a purely aesthetic approach is especially unfruitful. I have approached the texts rather as the historian does, for the light they throw on the author, his spiritual and intellectual world, and on the society in which he lives. I have tried to let the authors, wherever possible, speak more or less for themselves, while ordering and explaining what they say. All the same, I have endeavoured not to be insensitive to literary values, and certainly believe that most of the works dealt with here at any length can stand on their own merit and, if translated, would be appreciated in the west. The conditional mood is perhaps unnecessary: many of them are already known and valued in continental western Europe, where publishers and readers seem to have quicker responses than Anglo-Americans.

Colchester
May 1979

1

The Socialist Realist Tradition

Soviet literature faces us, as western readers, with unusual challenges –
the Soviet literature, that is, which is written, not for private
circulation or for smuggling out to the west, but by ordinary writers for
publication in ordinary Soviet journals and publishing houses. We
have great difficulty in classifying these writers. We are reluctant to
acknowledge their *bona fide* status, since they accept through their
professional organisation, the Union of Soviet Writers, a charter
which appears to subordinate literature to explicitly extra-literary
goals. Their work, moreover, passes through the mincer of a
censorship whose first priority is state security (very broadly
interpreted) and whose second is propaganda favourable to the
interests of the Soviet Communist Party. When Nadezhda
Mandel'shtam was asked recently what was happening on the Soviet
literary scene, she is reported to have retorted: '*What* literary scene?'[1]
Many western critics would second her implied opinion. To the
sophisticated literary scholar, brought up on a complex and highly
individualized diet in the west, nothing could be more oppressively
uninviting than the thick, dusty volumes of the Soviet classics,
especially those published during the high Stalin era, with their
crudely confident heroes, their contrived conflicts, their omniscient
narrators, their uplifting sentiments and their compulsory happy
endings. Are these works really literature in any sense of the word?

The authors of these formidable tomes (and their post-Stalin
successors, for that matter) profess to practise a method which they
call Socialist Realism. This is a doctrine which the party imposed, and
which the first congress of the Soviet Writers' Union (1934) accepted,
as an appropriate set of guiding principles for literary creativity in the

1

first society building socialism. Most western commentators, however, deny any literary standing whatever to Socialist Realism, seeing it as a purely political doctrine. Edward J. Brown, for example, speaks of 'this meaningless authoritarian term', while Gleb Struve calls adherence to it 'tantamount in practice to an undeviating toeing of the current party line.'[2] And in a recent general work on Soviet literature, Marc Slonim comments acidly: 'Had the theoreticians of Communist aesthetics said that a "good" work of art is one that supports Communism, and a "bad" work one that either does not do it or does it half-heartedly, they would have avoided many further troubles.'[3]

These diagnoses are, of course, quite correct, as far as they go. The extent to which the party manipulates literary output can be judged by the merest glance at the long list of independently thinking writers who were forced to devote themselves to journalism or translation, to fall silent, or were even physically liquidated: Babel', Zamyatin, Pil'nyak, Olesha, Bulgakov, Mandel'shtam, Pasternak, Akhmatova, Zosh-chenko – most of the major names of the twenties and thirties. But as an explanation of what Soviet literature actually said, even during the Stalin period, such judgements are very negative. A political line cannot determine the actual content even of bad fiction: it can only establish the frontiers within which that content takes shape. A country's landscape cannot be adequately grasped by surveying its borders alone, but in our approach to Soviet literature, we are often like hostile frontier guards, peering suspiciously at the few landmarks discernible from our vantage point. We reproach it for what it has not done, instead of trying to analyse what it actually says and wherein lies its appeal. Brown, for example, evokes the 'monotonous uniformity in the content and form of Russian literature during the Stalin period',[4] without telling us very much *about* that content and form, except in a few unusual works which, by his own admission, do not conform to the stereotype. Slonim, likewise, focusses mainly on the confusions in the theory, denying that Stalinist literature can have a coherent aesthetic or deal seriously with the important questions of man's existence: 'Basically, Socialist Realism negated human limitations and avoided the problem of death and the human condition in the universe.'[5] Rufus Mathewson makes broadly the same point: a continuing theme of his book is that official Soviet literature is aesthetically invalid because it excludes both psychological complexity and the possibility of tragedy. He does at least describe something of the positive content of Socialist

Realist fiction in tracing the tradition of the 'monolithic, functional, political man' from Chernyshevsky's Rakhmetov to Ostrovsky's Pavel Korchagin, but denies that such a figure can be the hero of a successful novel. 'The novelist's obligation to reveal the whole of man in all his meaningful relations runs full tilt against any pressure to advocate or celebrate virtue in fiction.'[6] Western readers may agree that novelists do have such an obligation, but then why in blockaded, starving, wartime Leningrad did people queue up to buy Ostrovsky's *How the Steel was Tempered*? Were they just puppets responding to propaganda, or was there some real spiritual hunger driving them on? That is what is so difficult for westerners to understand.

If we want to achieve this kind of understanding, we should perhaps begin by making the effort to imagine what Socialist Realist writing means to its sincere practitioners, and to its – possibly naïve and poorly educated, but nevertheless sometimes enthusiastic – audience.

Perhaps official statements of the doctrine would help us to comprehend what at least the Soviet writer is *trying* to do:

Socialist Realism, the basic method employed by Soviet artistic literature and literary criticism, demands from the writer an authentic, historically specific depiction of reality in its revolutionary development. This authenticity and historical specificity in the depiction of reality should be combined with the task of ideologically reshaping and educating the toilers in the spirit of socialism.

Socialist Realism guarantees the creative artist exceptional opportunities for the manifestation of his creative initiative, for the choice of various forms, styles and genres.[7]

So Socialist Realism does not define a genre, style or school: it is much more all-embracing than that. It is, apparently, a 'method', which has been adopted in numerous and diverse works enjoying the imprimatur of Soviet publishing houses. Such generosity of definition obscures as much as it explains.

In authoritative commentaries certain other terms are regularly used, which may help us to understand the 'method'. The Socialist Realist work is described as being *narodnyi* (loosely: 'popular'), both in the sense that its subject-matter reflects the life of ordinary people, and in the sense that it is readily comprehensible to them. It is *ideinyi*: that is, it reflects a mature, correct and fully formed ideology on the part of the author, for otherwise it could not play its educative role. And it is *partiinyi*: it is imbued with the ideals of the party and accords with the party's current policy, for art is not an autonomous activity, but has civic responsibilities to fulfil, and works closely with the party in order to achieve this. Lenin formulated this requirement as early as 1905 in a much-quoted article, 'Party organization and party literature'. Above all, though Socialist Realism is a realist method, it does not reflect reality *tout court*, but 'in its revolutionary development'. At the First Congress of Soviet Writers in 1934 Zhdanov called this approach to reality 'revolutionary romanticism', and urged that it 'must become a constituent part of literary creativity, because the whole life of our party, the whole life of the working class and its struggle combines the most stern and sober practical work with a supreme spirit of heroic deeds and magnificent future prospects.'[8] In practice, this combination of 'sober practical work' with 'magnificent prospects' was to be the chief aesthetic problem of official Soviet literature, and much hangs on how each writer has solved it for himself.

All these keywords tell us something, then, but as they stand they are capaciously ambiguous, and they are certainly open to considerable modification and reinterpretation. The party's policy, and even its ideology, can and does change a good deal in the long term. The life of the common people also changes, and so does their comprehension of art, so that forms deemed too obscure or recherché at one stage may become acceptable at another. Even the term 'realism', though associated with the practices of the nineteenth-century Russian fictional mainstream, is by no means immutable, as indeed is suggested by its being linked with the notion of 'revolutionary romanticism'. One recent authoritative commentator has stated:

Faithfulness to reality . . . does not restrict writers either in their choice of themes, plots and conflicts in all their most unexpected twists, nor in their techniques for communicating living impressions, nor in their investigation of the most modern techniques for the artistic rendering of their characters. The reproduction of life in its objective forms has nothing in common with copying it. On the contrary it requires daring flights of the imagination, poetic invention . . . creative transformation of tried formulae for the artistic depiction of reality, and the creation of new ones.[9]

Whatever else it may be, then, Socialist Realism is pre-eminently flexible. Nowadays, with the Soviet reading public growing ever more aware of western experimental techniques, this flexibility (or what Brown would call its 'meaninglessness') is seen to full advantage.[10] The doctrine may be said to play the same sort of role as the Thirty-Nine Articles in the history of the Church of England: as an all-embracing formula which enabled warring factions to live together – and, incidentally, the state to take them all over in a single umbrella organization. That being so, meticulously interpreting the concept of *ideinost'* may get us no further than debating the attributes of the Holy Spirit.

The official proclamation of Socialist Realism in 1932, with the formation of the Union of Soviet Writers, did in fact bring to an end a long period of in-fighting between literary groups, each with its own programme, and each hoping with the party's blessing to establish its own hegemony in the literary world. The twenties had been a time of variety and experimentation in Russian literature. In part this was a matter of genre and technique, but the variety and experimentation also arose out of the need, felt even by such a non-political writer as Mandel'shtam, to answer the fundamental question: what is the meaning of the Revolution? It is difficult for us now, knowing where communist rule was to lead, to see just how open the question was then. Even the political and economic, let alone the spiritual and cultural effects of the Revolution had still not fully revealed themselves. The Futurists and Constructivists declared that it had cleared the way for a daring, experimental art of the future, which would play a decisive part in building a new society. The various Proletkul't groups argued, on the other hand, that it made possible a specifically proletarian art, distinct from the aristocratic and bourgeois art of the past, and drawing its strength from the experience of ordinary people. The Serapion Brothers and other 'fellow travellers' maintained, against both tendencies, that the Revolution did not of its nature make any particular demands on the artist, but simply created a society in which he would be free to follow the laws of his own craft, learning from and developing the best traditions of the past.[11]

None of these groups or programmes directly generated 'Socialist Realism', but all the same some individual works of the twenties do stand out as potential exemplars of the doctrine, prior to its official formulation, and it is perhaps from these that we can best begin to study what the term means in practical application. Much as the Church Councils of the fourth century AD defined Christianity in part by establishing which writings were to be included in the sacred canon, so too the ideological statements of the period 1932–34 (from the initial designation of the doctrine to the first Writers' Congress) defined Socialist Realism more by listing works held to constitute its exemplars than through any elucidation of the doctrine's character-istics. The works most frequently mentioned included Gor'ky's

Mother (of 1907, as an original fountainhead, to which some would add Chernyshevsky's *What is to be Done?* from the 1860s), F. Gladkov's *Cement* (1925), D. Furmanov's *Chapaev* (1923), A. Serafimovich's *The Iron Flood* (1924), A. Fadeev's *The Rout* (1927), and the first parts of M. Sholokhov's *The Quiet Don* (1928-33). If one excludes the last (which is simply a very good Cossack regional novel, and an exception to most generalizations about Socialist Realism), these novels had quite striking features in common: a hero appears from among the people, he is guided and matured by the party, which tempers his 'spontaneity' with its 'consciousness', and then he leads his brethren to great victories over enemies and natural obstacles in the name of the Great Future which the party is building. This characteristic outline could not be deduced from any of the official definitions of Socialist Realism, but it was in fact to become the archetypal plot of the novels of the Stalin period, and to some extent afterwards. The official doctrine was essentially non-committal, a more or less empty shell whose content was to be provided by the writers themselves. Socialist Realism may have been imposed by politicians, but it was *created* by writers, a fact which scarcely any western study of the phenomenon has yet recognized.[12] In effect, the party put together from among the available models a synthetic prototype suited to its purpose and then tried to impose it on everyone.

The proclamation of Socialist Realism was, then, part of an *administrative* process which terminated the group conflicts of the twenties by closing down the most militant and successful of these groups, RAPP (the Russian Association of Proletarian Writers). The doctrine was consciously framed in such a way as to exclude too narrow an interpretation of the 'method'. With the completion of the First Five-Year Plan (1928-32), and the elimination of the kulaks as a class, the party declared that the 'dictatorship of the proletariat' was now entering its later or 'socialist' stage, when the sharpest class battles were past and the remnants of once hostile classes could be called upon to take their place in the common work of national construction. For that reason, terms like 'proletarian realism', 'communist realism' or 'the dialectical materialist creative method' were rejected as too narrow.[13] Socialist Realism was declared to be the culmination of literary traditions which had originated long before the October Revolution, not only in Russia, but all over the world. Elements of it could, indeed, it was stated, be found in every great writer of the past: they were all in some sense *narodnyi*, and all in some sense depicted reality faithfully. Some of course – Stendhal, Balzac, Dickens, Tolstoy, Zola – were closer to the standard than others. Then, through Chernyshevsky and Gor'ky, the world heritage, it was argued, flowed on to reach its high point in the postrevolutionary Russian works now in the process of being canonized. The Gorky Institute of World Literature was set up to train potential writers through the study of this cosmopolitan heritage; and a number of established foreign writers were invited to the First Congress of the Union of Soviet Writers to consecrate these links with international culture.

What was being emphasized, in fact, at the time of the formulation of the doctrine was not so much its *revolutionary* or *proletarian* nature as its identification with the party, as the indwelling spirit of the established socialist state, and its perceived links with the 'best' literary traditions of all times and of all nations. This reflected the overall aspiration of the Stalinist state, increasingly evident in the early thirties, to project itself as a great empire – of a new and higher kind, to be sure, but possessing all the positive attributes of the great civilizations of the past. Despite the obvious differences, one might compare the new Soviet Russia with seventeenth-century France, where the state of the Sun King also tried to lay the foundations of a great literary tradition, through the Académie Française, by prescribing norms of taste derived from the classical past. It is probably no accident that Mikhail Bulgakov, as his difficulties with the literary establishment grew, turned to the figure of Molière as a subject close to his heart.

It was in the same monolithic imperial spirit that the Union of Soviet Writers was established. The Central Committee resolution of 23 April 1932 asserted that 'the framework of the existing proletarian literary and artistic organizations is becoming too narrow and is hindering the proper development of artistic work.' The new Union was to 'unite all writers supporting the platform of Soviet power and aspiring to participate in the building of socialism':[14] and in fact former 'fellow travellers' were at least as prominent in it as the self-proclaimed 'revolutionary' and 'proletarian' writers. The Union offered its members security, material resources, privileges and access to publication on a scale undreamt of by all but the most successful writers in capitalist societies. Most journals and publishing houses in the field of artistic literature came under its authority, so that all doubting or dissenting writers could be squeezed out of the literary world. The whole structure signified an unprecedented institutionalization of literature, as a result of which the greater part of the party's supervisory role was assumed by the writers themselves (in consultation, where necessary, with the cultural department of the party Central Committee). The ultimate sanctions for the less compliant lay of course elsewhere, with the NKVD and with Stalin himself – and they were to be of the utmost brutality – but the routine policing of literature was undertaken first of all by the author himself, in self-censorship, then by the editorial boards of journals, and by the secretariat of the Writers' Union and its various commissions. Not even the formal state censorship needed to be involved all that often. As Arkady Belinkov has testified: 'The overwhelming majority of books not published in the Soviet Union were not destroyed by the censor, but were ruined during the very process of their creation, either at the manuscript stage, or when they reached the editor's desk.'[15]

The Union surrounded the writer with solicitous care not only in his professional life. It usually found him a comfortable apartment to live in, a dacha for his rest, a sanatorium in which to take a holiday or health cure, a hospital and a doctor better than those available to most Soviet citizens if he should fall ill. It secured him advances on his work, arranged journeys for him to 'collect material', assured him peace and quiet in a 'creative retreat' for writing, and provided secretarial staff to prepare his manuscript. It suggested themes for new works and organized regular seminars in which to discuss their progress. In short, the Writers' Union was – and still is – a way of life. Its norms became part of the writer's bloodstream and conformity to them a scarcely questioned habit, as is normal in corporate professional life the world over.

Acceptance of the doctrine of Socialist Realism was not only a matter of security and a quiet life. It also offered certain definite, if meretricious, spiritual rewards of its own. The intellectual who had known the intense but isolated and fissiparous literary life of the 1910s–20s now found himself part of a great national movement, subscribing to a credo accepted at least nominally by the whole reading public, and participating in tasks which were to bring a glorious future to everybody (nobody could believe all of this all the time, but if even one-tenth of it were true . . . !). The writer felt himself again part of society, a useful person. This might involve some pressure on his conscience, which had been nurtured in a more fastidious epoch, but, after all, much of his previous literary activity had probably consisted in denouncing this and that aspect of 'bourgeois' culture, so why should he not go the whole hog and join those who promised to get rid of the bourgeoisie for ever? No Soviet writer has left us candid reflections on this period of his life, but the Polish émigré Czeslaw Milosz has described the characteristic mixture of idealism and vengefulness:

The intellectual's eyes twinkle with delight at the persecution of the bourgeoisie, and of the bourgeois mentality. It is a rich reward for the degradation he felt when he had to be part of the middle class, and when there seemed to be no way out of the cycle of birth and death. Now he has moments of sheer intoxication when he sees the intelligentsia, unaccustomed to rigorously tough thinking, caught in the snare of the revolution. The peasants, burying hoarded gold and listening to foreign broadcasts in the hope that a war will save them from collectivization, certainly have no ally in him. Yet he is warm-hearted and good: he is a friend of mankind. Not mankind as it is, but as it *should* be. He is not unlike the inquisitor of the middle ages: but whereas the latter tortured the flesh in the belief that he was saving the individual soul, the intellectual of the New Faith is working for the salvation of the human species in general.[16]

Nor is this only a Polish view. Nadezhda Mandel'shtam, who has had ample occasion to observe the underside of the Soviet literary establishment, also considers that the Symbolist and Modernist *gruppovshchina* of the 1910s–20s, with their overweening manifestos and their ruthless feuds, killed the roots which bound the writer to tradition and morality, and thereby plunged him into an isolationism – or vicious sectarianism – which rendered him vulnerable to the monolithic appeal of the New Faith:

The roots binding us together were cut in the twenties, and henceforth the tacit rule was 'All is permitted', the principle which Dostoevsky fought all his life. The peculiar feature of this society – after it had been gripped in an iron vice and reduced at breakneck speed to a state of what is called here 'unanimity' – was the fact that it proved to consist of individuals working for their own self-advancement either singly or in small groups. Groups sprang up whenever there was someone to lead them, and they fought among themselves to get a monopoly from the government.[17]

Nadezhda Mandel'shtam is not alone in regarding the Soviet experiment in the light of Dostoevsky's categories: as we shall see, even some established Soviet writers of today would agree with her, having paused to reflect on the life which they themselves lead.

Writers of the thirties were not just under external pressure, in fact: they had their own internal reasons for writing as they did. They may have been captives, but they were in part willing captives. The image of the 'straitjacket', sometimes employed to describe party control over literature, is not wholly appropriate. Perhaps a more suitable image would be that of a hothouse, where the party and the literary institutions cultivate talents of a certain type, in protected and artificial conditions, where an illusion of real life can be sustained away from the harsh blasts of real criticism or the frosty indifference of a book-buying public with a genuine choice.

Socialist Realism was not so much a set of aesthetic principles as an institutional membership card, a password that guaranteed admission to privileged quarters. But for that very reason the empty spaces in the theory had to be filled out by writers themselves. How did they do this?

One might imagine that it would be sufficient to turn to the Marxist-Leninist theory of history and of literary creativity to discover the kind of content or message which writers would be expected to communicate to their audience, and perhaps the kind of technique best suited to the job. However, as Mathewson has shown, Marxism-Leninism does not offer much that could serve as the basis for a positive aesthetic. It is materialist and determinist, and in its Leninist form (whatever may have been true of Marx's own position) regards man unequivocally as part of the material and phenomenal world. Man's consciousness, his beliefs, his values are seen as secondary: there can be no autonomous meaning to them, because they are merely derivative.[18]

A philosophy of this kind contains nothing from which the writer can create inspiring literary figures. Nor, in fact, does it offer much to the political propagandist who needs to inspire the public. For this reason, there has always been a certain tension in official Marxism-Leninism between the 'scientific' theory and the 'voluntarist' practice. *Someone* has to stand above the grey, doomed present-day world, Milosz's 'cycle of birth and death', and see forward into the shining (if inevitable) future. *Someone* has to elude the rigid destiny which engulfs his fellow men, in order to inspire them to struggle for that future. In fact, therefore, in the image of man which Marxist-Leninist propaganda projects, there tends to arise a kind of 'company of the elect' (approximate to, but never wholly synonymous with, the party), consisting of the few who are not subject to the otherwise universal predestination, but are able to prepare everyone else for ultimate release from it. These are the guardians of the Purpose, the guarantors of those 'magnificent prospects' of which Zhdanov spoke, and in the light of which reality can legitimately be corrected and embellished. These are the guides and mentors for the spiritually elevated life of the new Soviet man, who in imitation of them can discover and consolidate his identity as a loyal servant of the people, a defender of the fatherland and a builder of socialism. These few, in fact, were to be the positive heroes of Socialist Realist fiction.

Mathewson has shown how, in the absence of a Marxist tradition of positive heroes, the writers and critics of the twenties and thirties, searching for an officially acceptable aesthetic, found a source for these 'voluntarist' heroes in earlier Russian models: in the criticism of Belinsky, Dobrolyubov and Chernyshevsky, and in the fictional heroes of Chernyshevsky and Gor'ky. From these prototypes came a hero with his face set towards the future, committed to the destruction of the present fallen world, gripped by his own vision of life as it ought to be, and bound to the closely knit group that shared this vision. All enjoyment or pleasure in existence, all personal relationships not found within the group and subordinated to the Purpose, were eschewed as unworthy.

Of course the party's accession to power changed the nature of this hero from his prerevolutionary prototype, since his ascetic commitment was now harnessed to the needs of the powers-that-be, a less attractive attitude than the determination of the revolutionary. As Mathewson says, this kind of personality 'is manipulated from above, and in turn manipulates those beneath him'.[19] It is not surprising, then, that the most attractive positive heroes have played their roles at times and places where Soviet power was not secure, as in the Civil War, or more recently in the Second World War. Such figures are able to stand out as genuine popular leaders, not as mere rungs in a hierarchy of manipulators. Prerevolutionary life and war will always be popular themes in Socialist Realist fiction. For the same reason there has been the persistent tendency to turn even peace time into a succession of campaigns and battles, in which leaders and heroes are needed.

To understand fully the appeal of these figures, one must remember the relative youthfulness of the Russian fictional tradition, and its relative closeness to preliterary culture – which has been, in the main, a source of great strength. Krylov and Pushkin stand in Russian literature almost where Langland and Chaucer do in English: they were the first masters to take the rich oral tradition and remould it in literary forms. Foreign readers have often found Pushkin elusive because they cannot sense, under the Byronic surface of *Evgeny Onegin*, the equivalent of the *Canterbury Tales* providing continuous subterranean nourishment. The major works of the nineteenth

century draw on the same underground streams. The novels of Gogol'
and Tolstoy have, in their different ways, something of the epic about
them: hence the otherwise puzzling appellation of *Dead Souls, poema*,
or narrative poem. Dostoevsky's sources of inspiration are much more
complex, but, as Bakhtin has shown, it is clear that oral and early
literary forms figure prominently among them.[20]

These works were written for a relatively small audience. Soviet
authors have been able to reach a much wider circle of readers, thanks
to the way in which the late Tsarist and Soviet educational systems
have set about eliminating illiteracy. Soviet literature has been
addressed to a different kind of readership: to newly literate peasants
coming into the towns during the first Five-Year Plans, to the new
class of 'Red specialists' moving into skilled, administrative and
managerial jobs, to the students of the *rabfaki* (workers' faculties) and
the reformed universities, to Komsomol and party members often of
modest social origin and meagre cultural background. It was the
writer's task to create the culture of a new intelligentsia and a new
narod. Literature had to give them a sense of their own identity, to
provide a meaning for the unaccustomed harsh urban work discipline,
the authoritarian political structure and the high standard of personal
ethics and political consciousness which the party, ostensibly at least,
demanded. It was meant, in a word, to socialize them.

Faced with their audience of raw but eager readers, it is not
surprising that Soviet writers, in explaining Soviet reality, have drawn
upon genres and myths which were preliterary or at least, on the
European scene, preceded the widespread appearance of the novel. In
the west the novel was the product of a long heritage of cultural and
intellectual development. It usually implied the apprehension of
immediate individualized reality through the eyes of a single person,
rather than of the community, and so rested on an individualized and
original plot.[21] In contrast to this, the Socialist Realist novel often
strikes one as springing from some kind of common experience of the
people, with a generalized and stereotyped plot, and dealing with an
ideal or transcendental reality (reality 'in its revolutionary development'): the author seems more like the *skazitel'*, the man who mediates
the heritage by fashioning it in the most appropriate words. Valentin
Kataev, in *Forward, oh Time* (*Vremya, vperëd!*, 1932) portrays the
narrator as a consciously craftsmanlike journalist, the modern
equivalent, perhaps, of the *skazitel'*, collating the experiences of all
the workers on the building project.

Consciously or unconsciously, then, Soviet novelists seeking to flesh out the bare framework of Socialist Realism have been attracted to earlier literary and folk genres. One model which seems to have been particularly influential is the *bylina,* the folk epic. Both in the *bylina* and in the Socialist Realist novel the hero is portrayed against the background of the people, with whom he is identified, and his actions gain strength from their support. He is strong, determined, decisive and ready for all situations and opponents; they are cheerful and simple, good followers, though often confused and sometimes brutal. The plot usually concerns a battle, a journey or an ordeal through which he leads them to triumph. The narrative is partly ritualized, involving much use of hyperbole and the frequent repetition of epithets. A Soviet folklorist's characterization of the *bylina* may help to bring out the features it shares with the Socialist Realist novel·

The knowledge of the diverse material and spiritual life of ancient Russia, of the various phenomena of national culture, also gave the composers of the popular *byliny* an opportunity to express with poetic vividness, in the figures of the knights, the heroic features of the Russian people, and equipped them with that wealth of colours and poetic devices by the aid of which they delineated the favourite *figures* of the *byliny.* The creative imagination of the folk-singers, with all its hyperbole in the description of events and the delineation of heroes, was nevertheless based on a true understanding of historical, or typical characteristics of the Russian people, of their hopes and expectations.[22]

Elements of the *bylina* are to be found in a large number of novels accepted into the Socialist Realist canon, especially in those concerning the Civil War or the Second World War. But the genre rarely appears in a simple form: the modern world is too complicated for that, the underlying historical movement is now more purposeful and conscious, and anyway the external form being adopted *is* now the novel. The hero has to spend far more time and energy than would be expected of the hero of the *bylina,* the *bogatyr'*, learning about himself and the social reality around him. He has to learn to identify the objective disposition of forces in society, and his own place in them. He has to tame personal feelings under the guidance of his mentors and in accordance with the Theory, which guarantees total understanding of history and therefore ultimate victory. A very large number of such novels hinge around the resultant struggle in the hero between 'spontaneity' and 'consciousness'. This struggle for personal maturity and self-mastery has something about it of the *zhitie* (life of the saint), and even more perhaps of the western Puritan spiritual biography of the *Pilgrim's Progress* type.[23] In the *zhitie* the saint learns through prayer and devotional exercises, and often too through communal discipline, to subdue what is unworthy in his own nature and to cultivate what brings him closer to God's image and enables him to be an example to other men. On the other hand, the Russian hagiographical tradition usually idealizes a modesty, humility and acceptance of the existing order quite foreign to the Socialist Realist hero. In this respect the active and questing Puritan believer is a much closer model: the pilgrim who has before him the goal of salvation, the 'magnificent city', which he can only reach by avoiding temptation, understanding God's laws, gaining self-mastery and working within the community to confirm the good, uproot the evil and vindicate God's providence. The Puritan biographer normally strove to present this example for edification as simply and comprehensibly as possible, eschewing what the seventeenth-century divine William Perkins called 'poetical fictions, Talmudical dreams and Schoolmen's quiddities' (the equivalent of highly sophisticated, experimental or modernist art in the eyes of the Socialist Realist) to make himself understood by all whose souls might be saved. Simple truths need unadorned explanation, as Bishop Downame exhorted the would-be preacher: 'Whereas men in their writings affect the praise of flowing eloquence and loftiness of phrase, the holy Ghost . . . hath used great simplicity and wonderful plainness, applying himself to the capacity of the most unlearned . . .'[24] The Socialist Realist novel has on the whole adopted the same 'simplicity' and 'plainness', and for similar reasons. Both genres seek to put before the reader a model or image of man as a means of reorienting his moral and spiritual life. The lives of saints (and positive heroes) are intended for everyday meditation, like icons, so that one's whole view of humanity, and hence of one's own nature, can be penetrated by them.

It is precisely in this respect that Chernyshevsky's *What is to be Done?* is a model for Socialist Realism. As Lenin said, 'Under its influence, hundreds of people became revolutionaries . . . It is a work which gives one inspiration for a lifetime.'[25] The very motif of a seamstresses' cooperative centred on a sexless marriage suggests a kind of secular monasticism very reminiscent of the Puritan ideal. Vera Pavlovna, as she learns about life (especially about society) and attains some degree of mastery over her own laziness and self-indulgence, is the Puritan heroine seen from the inside; while Rakhmetov, who divides out his time systematically between eating, sleeping, exercise, study and seeing people, is the secular saint observed from the outside, the 'new man', devoted to the cause, who has reached a degree of perfection accessible, so far, only to a tiny band of the elect.

Most Soviet positive heroes go through some kind of process of discovery, both of themselves and of the laws by which the world around them operates. They do it in different ways, through suffering and humiliation, through struggle, through ordeals, through weakness experienced, understood and conquered. Often they are guided by an elder or mentor, usually from the party. In the end they find themselves united, or reunited, with the ordinary people, able to reproduce their simple wisdom at a higher level where it joins with party doctrine and becomes the driving force of history. 'Spontaneity' and 'consciousness' are synthesized at this higher stage, and the hero is then able to assume the role of the *bylina* hero leading his men to triumph. Davydov, the Leningrad worker sent to collectivize a Cossack village in Sholokhov's *Virgin Soil Upturned,* has to learn to rethink his political training in the light of his rural experience, to temper his impetuosity and avoid insulting the feelings of the Cossacks; but when he manages to do this, he is able to win them over, and his death at the hands of conspirators is an inspiration to them, a stage on what the reader is bound to see as the triumphal progress to complete collective agriculture. Pavel Korchagin, in Ostrovsky's novel *How the Steel was Tempered,* learns, first from the sailor Zhukhrai, then from senior Komsomol and party workers, the meaning of his sufferings in the old world, and the nature of the struggle being conducted to create a new society. He has to overcome not only inner impatience, but also a series of crippling physical injuries incurred in the course of that struggle. These take him several times virtually through death itself, and thence to rebirth and to a transfigured existence in which he makes the fruits of his experience available to the next generation. The analogies with the Puritan biography are particularly strong in this work, and its essentially religious overtones may help to account for its evident popularity at periods of crisis in Soviet history. In Alexei Tolstoy's *The Road to Calvary* (note the religious overtones of the title), the two sisters, Katya and Dasha, and their eventual husbands, begin as doomed souls in the idle, rootless ennui of prewar St Petersburg, but move towards redemption through the ordeals of international and civil war (where they have to live alongside the *narod* in considerable hardship), and gradually discover their love for each other in unity with the Russian people and the emerging socialist system. Their final union takes place at a great public meeting in Moscow where Lenin and Krzhizhanovsky are explaining the plan for the electrification of Russia (electrification, thanks perhaps to Lenin's slogan 'Communism equals Soviet power plus electrification of the whole country', has always been a particularly evocative symbol of progress for the Soviets).

As the Stalin period advanced, and especially under Zhdanov's tightened literary controls from 1946, the elements of struggle and heroism became more subdued, and tended to give way to a more static and majestic view of the evolution of society. Since historical inevitability had already incarnated itself in the Soviet state, it came to be implied, there was no place for fundamental struggle and conflict any more. The literary model which began to make itself felt was the official, imperial mode of eighteenth-century Russia, especially of Lomonosov and Derzhavin. It is no accident that it was Catherine the Great who made perhaps the first attempt in Russian literature to define the ideal author and his positive hero:

[The good-hearted author] sets an example in the person of a man embellished with various perfections, that is, with virtue and fairness; he describes a devout observer of faith and law, praises the son of the fatherland burning with love for and loyalty to his sovereign and society, delineates the peace-loving citizen, the true friend, the faithful guarantor of a secret word once given ... Here is the finest way to correct human frailties! Reading such a composition each person feels an inner exultation, adheres to virtue, having disdain neither for himself nor for the author.[26]

This is of course a profoundly unrevolutionary hero. His personality belongs to handbooks of etiquette rather than to the necrology of saints, martyrs and rebels. His virtues are those of an established, even conservative society. He knows of no inner conflicts, because he has been brought up to the social and spiritual precepts by which he is expected to live, and he has never dreamt of challenging them. External conflicts are no longer a matter of life and death because the chief battles have already been won. This is the aesthetic of a confident, powerful Empire, already imbued with a sense of order and tradition, and proud of having risen, as it proclaims, to a new and higher level of civilization. This is the picture which Stalin, like Catherine, liked to paint, especially in his later years. Laws on the family and inheritance came to reward stability; the Academy of Sciences and the old universities drove out the various upstart communist academies; monolithic official organizations took over all the arts; architecture and sculpture became monumental; the ode became the most natural poetic form, and the epic took over as the dominant mode in fiction. This was an era in which it seemed natural and appropriate to name a novel about collective agriculture *The Cavalier of the Golden Star*.[27] 'Socialist classicism' would, as Abram Terts commented already in the late fifties, be a more appropriate term for this aesthetic than Socialist Realism.[28]

A characteristic example of this 'socialist classicism' is Vsevolod Kochetov's novel *The Zhurbins* (*Zhurbiny*), first published in 1952, just before the thaw, and worth dwelling on as an example of what later writers have been reacting against. The hero here is collective: the hereditary working-class family of the shipyards whose surname forms the title. They are shown, in effect, as a new aristocracy, superior to the old because modern and progressive. They began as a *noblesse d'épée*: Grandfather Matvei stormed the Winter Palace in 1917, and his sons Il'ya and Vasily wore the peakless cap of the Baltic Fleet through the battles of the Civil War. Resuming their working life at the party's summons, they became, one might say, a 'nobility of the hammer', as they rebuilt the old shipyard and prepared it for its modern tasks. More than thirty years later, at the time of the action of the novel, their life, and that of their families, is still firmly centred on the shipyard. The Zhurbin clan has by now its own collections of medals, its songs and ceremonies: only a coat of arms is lacking. The novel opens solemnly with the birth, symbolically on the First of May, of the latest scion of the dynasty, greeted by a salute of rifle shots.

The course of the novel shows that the family is capable of meeting a challenge and keeping up with the paramount demands of progress. Riveting is being replaced by continuous welding: the old skills are falling into disuse, and new ones have to be learned. The members of the family respond each in their own way, but all of them, even the older members, succeed in adapting to the new techniques. Furthermore, it is one of the Zhurbins, Anton, who is responsible for the innovations: he is a graduate of the Leningrad Shipbuilding Institute, and in his person the family is in the vanguard of technological change. A new *noblesse de robe* is in the making.

Unlike the old aristocracy, this one is not exclusive: it is in the process of raising the entire people to its level, in order ultimately to dissolve among them. Il'ya understands this less well than his son, Anton:

'Zhurbins are needed everywhere, son.'

'They *are* everywhere already, father,' Anton retorted cheerfully. 'Only they have different surnames. One is called Alexeev, another Vasil'ev, a third Stepanov.'[29]

'Have you met them?'

'Yes.'

'Ah, you've no family pride, son.'

'Yes, I have, but it's broader. I'm proud of all the Zhurbins, including the ones called Stepanov and Vasil'ev.'

'You diplomat! Avoiding the question! Why did princes and counts have the right to be proud of their family names, and we don't?'

'Well, they've been thrown out now, haven't they?'

'Yes, and it's obvious why. They were thrown out because they had nothing *but* their names.'

'Right, and it follows from that that the name is not what really matters.'[30]

The leaven of this aristocracy is of course the party. Zhukov, the Central Committee delegate from Moscow, is an essential enabler, who brings people together, holds meetings and smooths out conflicts – not that there are real conflicts: in fact the author brings in a flood at the end, to provide the dramatic interest which the novel otherwise rather lacks. Zhukov gives the whole process of re-equipping the yard a direction, and his reflections constitute the guiding vision for the whole novel:

The mighty party – once a mere handful of people grouped round Lenin – had come a long way. It had destroyed the old society and the old order, had created a new order and a new society, and its great ideas had flooded like an ocean over the country, and indeed across its frontiers. What mammoth tasks had been accomplished! Now it was no longer a handful bearing these ideas, but millions of people, mutually educating and renewing each other. The party was leading them on and on, scooping out a channel through which that ocean could flow ever on into the future. [31]

The Socialist Realist novel and its characters have thus gone through a number of stages, from the ascetic, desperately struggling heroes of the twenties and much of the thirties to the righteous and confident aristocrats of the late forties and early fifties. All these figures have, however, something in common. They know, or discover, the laws governing their social existence, and the ultimate outcome of those laws in a Great Society of the future. This is the Purpose to which everything is subordinated. The positive characters have overcome, or they learn to overcome, their personal weaknesses, anything that stands in the way of unremitting struggle on behalf of this vision. Personal and private life is strictly regulated to the requirements of these public goals. Once knowledge and self-mastery have been attained, the hero is iron-willed, resolute, resourceful, able unfailingly to sum up situations at a glance and decide exactly how to act. The narrator is an Olympian figure, who understands completely the laws of history, and knows where each character fits into them and where he is going; he has, moreover, a privileged right of entry into the hearts and minds of each one of them, so that he can analyse as well as judge them. His language – especially in the late Stalin period – is correct, formal, even semi-bureaucratic, and increasingly the characters too have a tendency to express themselves in this way. Slang, dialect, jargon, obsolete words and neologisms are rigidly shunned as unworthy of the high subject-matter being presented, a situation reminiscent of the linguistic divisions in Russian literature of the eighteenth century. Above everything else towers the Purpose in whose service the narrator stands, and towards which all the characters are moving. Things and people are valued not for themselves, but for the extent to which they contribute to the Purpose or help us to see it. Reality is viewed exclusively in the light of its 'revolutionary development', for what it tells us about the 'magnificent prospects' and the 'great new world' that is to come. Realism in effect gives way to what Katerina Clark has called an 'idiosyncratic neo-Platonism',[32] in which the mere here-and-now is seen only as a figure of the greater and more real reality that is to come.

*   *

Today, a quarter of a century later, it is not always appreciated in the west just how different Soviet fiction looks from the stereotype that has just been sketched. The period 1953 63, the so-called 'thaw' (in fact a succession of 'thaws' and 'freezes'), has received a good deal of attention, and this is obviously merited, for it was a time of rapid change, of moving back – though not eliminating – barriers, of asking new questions, raising new subjects, and to some extent experimenting with new techniques. After 1963, however, official tolerance in the field of literature narrowed, and the attention of western commentators shifted more and more to *samizdat* works. Their assumption seems to have been that, once the external controls on literature began to tighten once more, then officially permitted material would cease to develop any further, or would even regress towards the old stereotype.

However, as has been argued above, even in the most rigid Stalinist times, external controls did not wholly determine the form and content of fiction. There was an intrinsic literary rationale in the directions taken by Soviet fiction in the thirties and forties: Socialist Realism was (and is) a hollow frame which the writer filled out with the products of his own imagination. That being so, there is no reason why the tightening of political controls should necessarily prevent writers from pursuing, within those ever-present but vacillating frontiers, genuinely literary concerns. In fact, as it is the concern of this book to show, though novelists have on the whole found their freedom of operation becoming more restricted,[33] they have continued to work out their own solutions: some of them have found themselves in the process crossing the frontier into *samizdat* (often without wishing to) while others have been able to remain in the official community of Soviet writers. Official tolerance, though perceptibly less than in 1962, is still much broader than at any time between 1932 and 1953, and Soviet society is somewhat more open and pluralist, more exposed to information from outside than under Stalin. As a result even officially published writers have been able to take up and continue the explorations begun in the 'thaw' period, often going much deeper in their historical, anthropological and philosophical insights than in the relatively superficial works published then. The break with the classical Socialist Realist model as outlined above has widened, not narrowed, since 1963.

The 'thaw' was a period of uncertainty, not only in literature, but in all aspects of Soviet life, when the death of Stalin, the denunciation of the 'cult of personality', the easing of terror and the amnestying of prisoners left many questions bewilderingly open. For if the Great Leader and Benefactor of Humanity had not only made mistakes, but committed crimes on a huge scale, then what was to be said about the current leaders, who had reached the top under him, about the party in whose name they all ruled, or indeed about the revolution which had conferred popular legitimacy on that rule? These questions were not directly raised in published literature, but they soon began to appear in *samizdat,* and they increasingly lay behind much that was actually published. The censorship did not cease to operate, but its implementation became less predictable. Party supervision over culture changed direction so many times that it became questionable whether the party any longer had a coherent view of the role it expected culture to fulfil in society. Above all, reflecting this external confusion, writers' policing of their own and each others' work became less rigid, and the attitudes of editors and publishers towards submitted material became more relaxed and enterprising. The first result of this was actually a *strengthening* of Socialist Realism, as writers sought to restore some authentic meaning to concepts like 'faithfulness to reality', 'spirit of socialism' and *narodnost'*, and to create some genuine and human heroism in place of the artificial striking of poses characteristic of the late Stalin period. The *Zeitgeist* no longer suggested self-restraint, integration into existing society, submission to civic command and the dutiful embellishment of reality, but rather self-expression, individuality, independence, frankness and a degree of experimentation. 'Sincerity' became the watchword of a literary generation, following a maverick critical article in the monthly *Novy Mir*.[34]

This was the reason for the popularity of Ehrenburg's novel *The Thaw* (*Ottepel'*, 1956), the work that gave its name to the period. It is a kind of fictional tract on sincerity. It begins with a society in deep freeze, dominated by authoritarian, plan-fulfilling factory directors and smug, established, insincere artists. Social institutions function and families survive, but they do so by inertia: real human feelings have somehow been drained out of them. People are afraid to be spontaneous, to say what they think: 'consciousness' and fear of authority have triumphed everywhere.

Gradually, in the course of the novel, warmth and creativity return. Lovers discover and avow their feelings for one another. Artists rediscover the capacity to infuse their work with delight at the outline of a tree or a woman's face. But this is a renewal, not a repudiation, of the Socialist Realist myth. Warmth and spontaneity are seen as contributing to the progress towards the Purpose, removing, as it were, the ice floes which have obstructed this progress in the recent past. Ehrenburg is changing the imagery associated with man's social advances, but he is not abandoning the teleogical thrust, indeed if anything he is reinforcing it. Towards the end of the first part, one of the main characters, Dmitry Koroteev, reflects on the changes taking place:

It's easy to take a machine to bits and replace the faulty parts. But what can you do with a man? If you had asked me a year ago, I would probably have said that Zhuravlëv [the overbearing factory director] was not a bad workman. True, I could see the other side of him even then, but I tried not to think about it. I must have changed. I feel as though I've just climbed out of a rubbish pit. . . .

We need different people. . . . We need romantics. It's a steep climb, the air is thin, and weak lungs can't stand it. . . . If a man has a certain nobility in him, he won't get lost, he'll find the high road. But what should we do with the others? It's not enough to educate them, we have to train their feelings. . . . It's going to be difficult. It's all right growing grapes in the Crimea . . . but what we have to do is to take the wild shoots, the budding Zhuravlëvs, and graft a conscience onto them. Like growing grapes in Yakutiya: difficult, but possible with devotion, will-power and sensitivity.[35]

This excerpt, with its succession of mixed metaphors, conveniently encapsulates the ambiguities of Ehrenburg's position. The transition from mechanical to horticultural imagery is significant: that shift in the view of man is partly what the thaw was about – treating man no longer as a cog, but as a living being.[36] In spite of that shift, however, the imagery still implies that men are to be manipulated by those who know best – by agronomists rather than engineers, perhaps, but still manipulated. Furthermore, the notion of a goal to be reached with great difficulty (here it seems to be the top of a mountain) is still very much present. Man can now afford to work in harmony with nature, and to trust his own feelings, but the dominance of the Purpose remains unchanged. The transformation that Dmitry feels in himself is not a revulsion against the party's authority, but a renewed and more profound dedication to the party's programme.

Real, ascetic, struggling heroism returned to fashion again: indeed there was a reversion to the early Socialist Realist prototypes of the twenties and early thirties. The young Vladimir Tendryakov, for example, asked:

Why in recent years have there been few positive heroes like Pavel Korchagin, Makarenko in *A Pedagogue's Epic*, or Davydov in *Virgin Soil Upturned*? Perhaps it is a coincidence. I think an important factor is that we have often been inclined to underplay negative phenomena doomed to extinction – that is to say, the very things against which the positive hero has to struggle.[37]

The implication of reviving the positive hero in his full glory was that there were still serious evils in Soviet society for him to struggle against, nearly two generations after the Revolution. This is why these renewers of the Socialist Realist myth were so controversial (and why western observers gained the misleading impression that they represented a new departure in Soviet literature). None more so than Vladimir Dudintsev and his novel *Not by Bread Alone* (*Ne khlebom edinym*, 1956).

This is a Socialist Realist novel in the grand manner. Even the religious associations of the title are not unusual, as we can see from reference to Alexei Tolstoy's novel above. The work portrays a struggle between good and evil: it is a folk epic in which an ordinary schoolmaster – a member of the common people without privileges, money, specialist qualifications or power – triumphs over the highly placed and learned, using native wit, determination, stamina, faith in the future, and the help of those members of the real *narod* who share his faith. He even wins the wife of his leading antagonist. The only difference is that evil is actually represented by Soviet officials and academics: here the Socialist Realist myth is turned against the Soviet establishment itself. The ending, it is true, also, has disquieting traces of uncertainty about it: though Lopatkin's invention eventually wins through and is a great success, his bureaucratic opponents appear merely to reshuffle jobs and hence presumably survive to block the next bright idea that comes along. Nevertheless, the Purpose still shines bright ahead, and there are still good people both in the party and outside it, so that there is no reason in principle why the great journey should not be resumed.

Much controversy was also caused by so-called 'youth prose', centred in the journal *Yunost'*. At first sight the works of writers like Kuznetsov, Aksënov and Gladilin look like a complete break with the past: not only the characters, but the narrators as well, use a language which deliberately sets out to shock with its slang expressions drawn from sport, fashion, pop music, science, space research and western life. Their heroes appear cynical, sophisticated and world-weary: they reject the values of their elders, and sometimes any values at all, and go off to do their own thing in their own way. 'There's no such thing as love, that's an old-fashioned fairy tale. There's only the satisfaction of sexual need,' declares one of the blasé young men in Aksënov's *Ticket to the Stars* (*Zvëzdnyi bilet*, 1961).[38] Their travels take them, initially at least, not east to the virgin lands or the great industrial sites of Siberia, but west, to the 'decadent' Baltic coast, as near to the longed-for outside world as a Soviet citizen can get without an exit visa. How could anything be less like the stately, patriotic, right-thinking heroes of Babaevsky and Kochetov?

Yet on closer examination all this effervescence usually turns out to be the old myth in a new form. After working their way through their youthful rebellion, these young people return to the old values, having dusted off the late Stalinist patina which initially made those values seem dim and unexciting. Having drawn what nourishment they can from the western extremities of the Soviet Union, they finish up at a Siberian hydroelectric power station after all, having restored some 'revolutionary romanticism' to the prospect of constructing it and dedicating it to the future. Disciplined work, devotion to the collective, the struggle for a brighter, cleaner, more technological future – these are the ideals which always lie deep in them, subconsciously motivate their rebellion, and then guide them towards the constructive work which follows it. Sashka Zelenin, when he gets out to the remote northern village where he has unexpectedly chosen to be sent after graduation from medical institute, is not interested in preserving the past (as his equivalent ten or even five years later would be): on the contrary, he is horrified by the abject poverty and the old-fashioned unproductive techniques he has occasion to observe there. He longs to drag the place into the future: 'In three years Kruglogor'e will be a town'[39] is his succinct comment on the patriarchal way of life. These young people are apostles of the modern. What they reject in their parents' way of life is its conservatism and conformism. In *Ticket to the Stars* the generation gap actually runs between two brothers, the younger of whom tells the elder:

'Do you really think I dream of following in your footsteps? Do you think your life is an ideal for me? Huh, your life was planned out by Mama and Papa when you were still in your cradle. Top of the class at school. Distinction at the institute, then graduate student, junior scientific worker, doctor, academician. . . . And what then? The much respected, late lamented. . .? You've never taken a really serious decision in your life, you've never risked anything. To hell with that! . . . Better to be a tramp and suffer failures than to live one's whole life as a boy carrying out other people's decisions.'[40]

Finding one's own way in life, dedicating oneself with fresh zeal to the great future in the name of the people: this is the ideal which inspires Sashka Zelenin and his colleagues. They see all life's tribulations as a battle of the new against the old, with the people on the side of the new. When Sashka gets stabbed by a village lout and is operated on, one of his colleagues reflects:

There they were, workers, loaders, lumberjacks, drivers, policemen, going into attack on the old world! The world where knives were used, where life was not valued at a kopeck, where people were consumed by murky passions. We had been on the offensive, attacking frontally for forty years. Our front line could be found all over the world. We were attacking not only what was outside us, but also the things that rise up inside us sometimes. Doubt, despondency and cynicism come from that world too. They still live within us, and at times they may seem to have taken over altogether. But no. We are new people precisely because we fight against all that and win, taking our place in the world-wide front line.[41]

'New people': the words and the spirit directly recall Chernyshevsky's *What is to be Done?*. For Aksënov at this stage in his career, the battleground in the human heart is not (as for Dostoevsky) between good and evil, between God and the Devil, it is between the old and the new, and the division corresponds exactly to a social division. All political, social and moral categories relate ultimately to the Purpose and must be presented and analysed in that light.

The heightened subjectivity of 'youth prose', then, was originally intended to reinvigorate the old myth, to restore the full splendour of the Purpose. But the outlook which these young writers adopted, and the style in which they put it across, had implications which, in the long run, made that myth more difficult to sustain. In their rejection of the monolithic and Olympian, they deliberately cultivated a style that was as informal as possible, and often conducted their narration in the first person (Aksënov even adopted a multi-personal narrative stance in his *Oranges from Morocco – Apel'siny iz Marokko*, 1963). The briefer, more inconclusive fictional genres, *povest'* and *rasskaz*, took the place of the *roman*.[42] Narrators increasingly attempted to achieve vividness, intimacy and immediacy, presenting situations and action as though in a conversation or in a letter to a close friend.

'Youth prose' exposes the reader to a less certain world. The narrator's thoughts are often expounded not logically or discursively, but abruptly, impressionistically, sometimes confusedly, with afterthoughts and extra detail thrown in at the end. Occasionally this manner of exposition approaches stream of consciousness. Words and expressions are often employed which come from a specific professional or intellectual milieu: the narrator assumes that the reader will understand them, implying that he is a close associate, someone in whom strong personal interest and identity of outlook and values can be taken for granted. There is no trace of the pompous expository tone which often figured in earlier fiction.

At the same time the language tends to be deliberately emotionally restrained, indeed almost bald, that of young people not yet sure of their feelings, and anxious not to make fools of themselves by overstatement. The dominant attitude is one of scepticism combined with openness to experience. Expressions of political or philosophical opinion are avoided. Dialogue – and often narration too, even when conducted in the third person – is clipped and allusive. The characters are usually highly literate young people, well versed in Russian and to some extent world literature, familiar with political jargon and journalese, so that, when they are uncertain how to describe their feelings or thoughts, they can always couch them in some readily available cliché, implying a certain coolness and detachment from their own experience. The resulting tone of gentle irony towards oneself and one's associates is very different from the caustic satire of, say, the twenties; it implies rather the bantering mutual affection of raw, untried people taking their first steps in a complicated world. Everyone, narrator, characters, reader too, is assumed to be on the same level: no one has superior knowledge to anyone else. Historical laws may exist, but each person must find them for himself. Everyone is in the same general uncertainty, moved by a common humanity, and always ready to listen to a good human interest story.

Take the opening of Anatoly Kuznetsov's *Continuation of a Legend* (*Prodolzhenie legendy*, 1957):

Who invented the word 'maturity'? Who first had the idea of handing out 'certificates of maturity' to green youngsters when they leave school? As if a piece of paper could revolutionize your life in one day! Maturity indeed! I have just finished the tenth grade, but I've never in my life felt so lost. Helpless. Like a puppy. I've no idea what's to happen next. . . .[43]

Increasingly narrators get into the habit of moving from one narrative voice to another without transition, or from indirect to direct speech:

I pulled out a fresh 100-ruble note. The waitress assured me that – certainly, right away – she would run to the cashier's desk and change it – just one moment, please.[44]

Characters are seen both from inside and outside in swift succession, as in the opening of Andrei Bitov's *The Loafer* (*Bezdel'nik*, 1962/8):

My supervisor said to me: 'No, Vitya, this won't do. It just won't. I can't make out, Vitya, what your head is stuffed with. You create the impression of such a reliable person, but look more closely and what do you find? Let us see. Your probationary period is running out, isn't it? And when it has, what will you have to show for it? Damn all, eh? (That's his little joke.) Now just listen carefully to me . . .'
He's right, of course, I do create that sort of impression. I create a lot of different impressions. Even that of being reliable. But what kind of person I really am, I can't say. Take the mirror now. Surely the mirror should tell us how we look to other people. That's why we look in it. But often I don't even recognize myself in the mirror. . . .[45]

In the long run, of course, this sustained tone of irony, detachment, uncertainty and non-commitment carries its own implications. The most important, perhaps, is that there is no single monolithic, objective truth which can be understood by everybody in exactly the same way, but rather that there are several approaches to the truth –

perhaps even several truths – and that the personality who perceives them is an important factor in interpretation. In other words, truth is, partly at least, subjective. We shall see this implication of the techniques of 'youth prose' explored further in the work of Voinovich, Vladimov, Shukshin and Trifonov. But even in 1961–62 the scepticism of these writers seemed subversive enough for Il'ichev, the Central Committee secretary responsible for culture, to attack Aksënov, and for the party authorities to exert pressure for the removal of Valentin Kataev, chief editor of *Yunost'*.[46]

One writer who stands rather alone in the thaw period, yet made an important contribution to the national self-image, was Yury Kazakov. His work seems recently to have run into the sands, but in the fifties and early sixties he anticipated a number of the themes which are now dominant in Soviet fiction. He was perhaps the first writer to discern and give expression to Soviet man's need for a deeper understanding of himself as an individual, his need to detach himself somewhat from the collective, to retreat into isolation, into nature or the past. In his short stories about life in the distant villages and fishing settlements of the Far North, he portrays men as loners, remote from urban civilization, attentive to the depths within themselves, and receptive to the hush of the forest, the swell of the sea and the bewitching cold light of the white nights. Characters who are drunken and destructive in the town change completely when they can get back to their 'remote, black-earth water meadows, where Old Believers live' and take part in the annual haymaking.[47] An idle, drunken buoy-keeper proves to have a rich interior world when he can tell tales of his days in the Northern Fleet and sing old Russian folksongs.[48] Kazakov admires the austere and self-reliant piety of the Old Believers. In *Pomorka* (a title which can imply either a White Sea coastal dweller or a member of a particular branch of the Old Belief) he portrays a ninety-year-old woman, her hard and lonely but self-sufficient life, her prayers in front of the icon, and her readiness for death and reunion with her family:

'The grave has long waited for me,' she said good-naturedly, as though about something pleasant, looking over my head with her dim eyes. 'My mother and father lie there. . . . And my sons, all of them are there. They must be looking forward to my coming.'[49]

His urban dwellers, for the most part, have no such reserves of faith and spiritual strength, no sense of being organically united with others. They are wilful and unhappy loners, like the artist

Ageev in *Adam and Eve* (*Adam i Eva*, 1962).

Kazakov's work is full of haunting reminders of what Soviet fiction had been lacking for more than a generation. If one excepts him, and the two writers to whom the next chapter is devoted, one could say that most of the fiction of the thaw period moved within the concepts and myths already accepted as the artistic embodiment of the Socialist Realist formulae. If anything it attempted to revivify those myths by restoring youthfulness, self-sacrifice, devotion and 'revolutionary romanticism' to literary forms which had become routinized and bureaucratized. But in this process of revival, writers struck attitudes, tried out techniques and raised questions which, in time, were to take them well beyond the safe, inherited stock of themes, images and solutions which had up to now done duty for the otherwise undefined literary method called 'Socialist Realism'.

2

Two Key Works: *Doctor Zhivago* and *One Day in the Life of Ivan Denisovich*

What most of the 'thaw' writers lacked was, first of all, any real understanding of the non-Chernyshevskian, non-Marxist currents in the Russian intellectual tradition, and secondly any capacity to draw upon the genuine *narodnyi* folk culture which enjoyed a strange underground renaissance in Stalin's 'pre-Gutenberg' Russia. It is the rediscovery of these buried philosophical and cultural riches which has made the real difference to post-'thaw' literature.

The tendency of Stalinist Socialist Realist fiction to create a kind of substitute mythology, increasingly celebratory and classical in form, probably distanced literary creativity from genuine folk art,[1] and certainly made it more difficult to render authentically the life of the common people. Yet, strangely enough, folk culture was, unperceived, preparing its own countervailing genres, in the form of the political anecdote and the labour-camp ballad. 'The future of Russian literature, if it is destined to have a future at all, has been nourished on political jokes, just as Pushkin grew up on the fairy tales told by his nanny.'[2] So wrote Abram Terts (a little belatedly, perhaps) in 1974, mentioning also the 'troubadours and minstrels' who had married the cabaret song with that of the labour camp to produce a new genre, the 'author's song', as it is known, to distinguish it from the anonymous folk songs of old. During the sixties the new minstrels, Okudzhava, Galich, Vysotsky and others, became the most popular entertainers in Russia, distilling popular speech and attitudes, and using the semi-permitted, semi-prohibited medium of the tape recorder to disseminate works that no Soviet publishing house or recording company would have dared to take on.[3]

The characteristic tone of both anecdotes and songs is laconic, ironic, off-the-cuff: they present a brief, revealing 'slice of life' without explicit comment, making their points through juxtaposition, through play on familiar words and phrases, and by pointing up discrepancies between ideal and reality. If the language parodies bureaucratese or one of the established literary styles, it is always firmly anchored in popular speech, to which it descends in moments of joyful bathos. In these respects, anecdote and ballad did much to prepare the way for the tone of a good deal of recent fiction. ('Youth prose', though more self-conscious and westernized, helped to start the process.)

The penetration of popular speech and of these distinctively twentieth-century folk forms into written literature resembles, in a highly compressed manner, the processes which Erich Auerbach and Mikhail Bakhtin have described as constituting the challenge that was presented by folk culture and the 'creativity of laughter' (*smekhovoe tvorchestvo*) to established genres and to the hierarchy of styles in late antiquity and in the renaissance.[4] Both authors see these processes as an essential part of the prehistory of the novel as a literary genre.

Laughter destroys fear and piety in the face of the object and of the world, makes them available for familiar contact and thus prepares the way for an absolutely free investigation of their nature. . . . The familiarization of the world through laughter and through the use of popular language is an important and necessary stage in the evolution of scientific-cognitive and aesthetically realist creativity among the peoples of Europe.[5]

It is as if the 'high culture' of a society still not sure of itself, still subject to rigid authority, and still not accustomed to the egalitarianism and mass literacy of its own stated ideals, were now giving way to a more confident, robust and genuinely popular art coming from a nation who, whatever they had suffered under Stalin, *had* learnt to read. A comic and truly *narodnyi* art also made possible greater distance and objectivity in attitudes to Soviet society, and thus facilitated the emergence of an authentic and critical realism, such as Soviet culture desperately needed in the face of its long-established cosmetic myths.

From the philosophical point of view the crucial development was the gradual rediscovery, during the sixties, of Dostoevsky, not just as a novelist, but as a thinker, and of the Russian religious and philosophical renaissance of the early twentieth century, especially the trends associated with the seminal symposia *Problems of Idealism* (*Problemy idealizma*, 1902) and *Landmarks* (*Vekhi*, 1909).

The importance of the main *Vekhi* thinkers, Struve, Bulgakov, Berdyaev and Frank, was that they had all gone through Marxism and then rejected it, and with it the rest of the Russian revolutionary tradition. In each case their rejection was stimulated by the encounter with Kant, from whom they drew the insight that man was not primarily a causally generated material phenomenon, to be explained in a 'science of society' generated by pure reason, but above all a free spirit, the subject and creator of history. They rejected Marx's attempt to amalgamate explaining and changing society as based on an inadequate metaphysics, as a confusion of pure reason and practical reason, and as a misguided fusing of two incompatible elements, sociology and prophecy.

The four main *Vekhi* thinkers each went his own individual way, but it may be said of all of them that, starting from a Kantian re-examination of Marx, they proceeded to the view that man was primarily *noumenon* (rather than *phenomenon*), spirit, free and creative, and only secondarily matter, phenomenon, and bound by causality. It followed from this that the primary reality in society was personality, or spirit, not matter or aggregates of persons, classes. God was the highest manifestation of personality, and the individual had his deepest roots not in the human collective, but beyond it in God Himself. Bulgakov, Berdyaev and Frank all believed, in their different ways (and they elaborated their views in emigration after the revolution), that history was advancing, not towards proletarian revolution and the introduction of socialism, but towards the ultimate reunion of God and man in Godmanhood.

These thinkers were attractive to Soviet intellectuals for a number of reasons. Their revival coincided roughly with the final failure of Khrushchev's attempts to introduce a reformist communist system in the Soviet Union. Disillusionment with the regime was fast becoming disillusionment with communism and even with Marxism as a philosophy and world outlook. Hence the attraction of thinkers who had been enthusiastic Marxists and then abandoned the doctrine for reasons which in a sense prophesied the disasters of Soviet history. Secondly, many Soviet intellectuals found in their writings the whole range of western philosophy and theology reopened to them in a way that was lively, penetrating and always conscious of Marxist categories while also highly critical of them. Soviet intellectuals came out of the narrow sectarian cocoon in which their speculative thinking had been confined, and rediscovered Plato, Aristotle, St Augustine, the early church fathers, and the whole array of medieval, renaissance and reformation thinkers. Even Locke, Kant and Hegel looked very different when no longer seen through a Leninist focus. Alexander Piatigorsky has written of the 'strange profusion' of metaphysical thinking in the Soviet Union today, and of private seminars at which lecturers in electronics or dialectical materialism pass their leisure hours discussing 'Plato, Hegel, Christianity and our life'.[6]

Thirdly, these thinkers were *Russian*, and their intellectual and spiritual development brought them ultimately to the Russian Orthodox Church. It is not surprising that, at least among the Russian citizens of the Soviet Union, disillusionment with Marxism and the party should stimulate a revival of interest both in religion and in Russian national traditions. Indeed, that has been a process much broader and encompassing more classes of the population than the relatively narrow revival of metaphysical concerns among the intellectuals. We shall see that in fiction the rise of 'village prose', often with muffled religious undertones, became a major feature of the literary scene, even without philosophical implications. It was all the more exciting, then, for those with a philosophical bent to discover a serious and profound critique of Marxism, well grounded in the whole of western thought, but nevertheless unmistakably Russian.

At any rate, any foreigner in regular contact with Soviet literary intellectuals, certainly in Moscow and Leningrad, in the sixties, must have been aware of the growing influence of Dostoevsky and the *Vekhi* thinkers. This became such a problem to the guardians of orthodoxy that it was the subject of a heated discussion at a Writers' Union critical seminar in April 1969.[7] All the same, it is difficult to estimate exactly what the influence has been on individual Soviet writers. Most never refer directly to it, though some do so at least by implication. All that can be said with certainty is that these thinkers have changed the climate of opinion in which all writers work, and have contributed to the increasing confidence which we shall find in our novelists that *personality* (not the party or the state, not History or progress) is the fundamental reality of all social life, and that the categories of the personality are the ones that should suggest the form and content of a work of fiction.

*   *

The rediscovery of philosophy and of folk culture was the work of Pasternak and Solzhenitsyn, which is why their writings stood out from most of what was published in the late fifties and early sixties, and pointed towards the future. They completed the movement away from Marxism-Leninism and pseudo-*narodnyi* culture back to real philosophy and real contact with the language and outlook of the people.

Pasternak's *Doctor Zhivago*, of course, was published abroad in 1957, and it seems clear that its reception inside the Soviet Union, even among intellectuals who considered themselves opposed to the establishment, was not enthusiastic. Certainly, it was very different from anything that any of the major 'thaw' figures was attempting at the time. It was in fact in virtually every respect what Kierkegaard would have called an 'offence' to the Socialist Realist outlook and aesthetics. To begin with, the hero is on principle politically passive. He becomes a doctor so that he can serve others, but at vital moments in the plot, he takes the inactive (not necessarily the easier) option, or the one that preserves him best from involvement in politics. When the Revolution breaks out, his main preoccupation is not how to further it, or for that matter how to fight against it, but how to ensure some kind of security for his family. When he does get involved in the Revolution, it is only because he is captured by Red partisans. In his private life, which he regards as more important than public activity, he is no less inconsistent, not to say irresponsible. In the end, he even gives up his profession and lives almost as a tramp, doing odd jobs round Moscow until disease finally strikes him down. His life is, in fact, one of continual retreat and failure.

That this was the light in which leading Soviet literary figures of the time regarded the novel we can see from the letter the editors of *Novyi Mir* write to Pasternak about it in 1956. Their verdict on Zhivago is that 'under cover of superficial sophistication and morality, a character arises of an essentially immoral man who refuses to do his duty by the people and who is interested only in his own rights, including the alleged privilege of a superman to betray with impunity.'[8] They recognize the Christian imagery surrounding him, but dismiss it as specious:

Did not the Golgotha of Zhivago consist in that the Doctor-poet, prophesying his 'second advent' and last judgement, in life scorned the man of reality, raising himself to a pedestal inaccessible to a mortal? Did not the vocation of this intellectual Messiah consist in that he killed, betrayed, hated man, falsely sympathizing with him for the sake of saving his own 'spirit', and raising himself to self-idolization?[9]

Yury's rejection of the Revolution they attribute entirely to self-interest, to distaste for the 'discomforts and privations' it brings him.[10]

What is interesting about this reaction is that it is a wholly plausible, even perceptive reading of the novel if looked at from the viewpoint of the revised Socialist Realism current in the 'thaw'. Pasternak, however, was operating on another plane altogether. What was at issue was a whole way of seeing the world and man's place in it. Born a generation earlier than any of the other writers to be explored in detail in this book, he rejected Soviet ideology and aesthetics not only as a result of having lived through their consequences, but also on the basis of his prerevolutionary education and culture. In particular he was influenced by the neo-Kantianism current in Marburg when he studied there as a young man, and by the Russian artistic, religious and philosophical revival of the early twentieth century, especially the current of thought associated with *Problems of Idealism* and *Vekhi*.

Personality, then, occupies the central position in Pasternak's outlook: it is free and follows its own nature, which is creativity and love.[11] Its home is not the phenomenal universe (which can, at least in principle, be explained by objective laws, pure reason), but in history (which can be understood – not explained – only by reference to subjective values, to practical reason). Vedenyapin, we are told, publishes books which see 'history as another universe – a universe built by man with the help of time and memory in answer to the challenge of death. Inspired by a new understanding of Christianity, [these books] resulted in a new conception of art.'[12] Vedenyapin puts this directly in his confrontation with the Marxist Voskoboinikov:

'What you don't understand is that it is possible to be an atheist, it is possible not to know if God exists or why He should, and yet to believe that man does not live in a state of nature but in history, and that history as we know it now began with Christ, it was founded by Him on the Gospels. Now what is history? Its beginning is that of the centuries of systematic work devoted to the solution of the enigma of death, so that death itself may eventually be overcome. This is why people write symphonies and why they discover mathematical infinity and electromagnetic waves. Now, you can't advance in this direction without a certain upsurge of spirit. You can't make such discoveries without spiritual equipment, and for this, everything necessary has been given us in the Gospels. What is it? Firstly, the love of one's neighbour – the supreme form of living energy. Once it fills the heart of man it has to overflow and spend itself. And secondly, the two concepts which are the main part of the make-up of modern man – without them he is inconceivable – the ideas of free personality and of life regarded as sacrifice.... It was not until after the coming of Christ that time and man could breathe freely. It was not until after Him that men began to live in their posterity and ceased to die in ditches like dogs – instead, they died at home in history, at the height of the work they devoted to the conquest of death. . . .'[13]

Voskoboinikov has no immediate answer to this, yet throughout the novel the Marxist and the personalist concepts of history are in continued conflict. Yury takes his philosophy more or less complete from his uncle, and although he does not develop it, he applies it to his own life, and hands it on to posterity in the books he publishes in the twenties and in the verse manuscripts which form the final part of the novel. Confronted with the Revolution, even in its Marxist form, he at first admires its freshness, the ruthlessness with which the old world has been destroyed, and sees it as a product of the creative spirit:

'The revolution broke out willy-nilly, like a breath that's been held too long. Everyone was revived, reborn, changed, transformed. You might say that everyone has been through two revolutions – his own personal revolution as well as the general one. It seems to me that socialism is the sea, and all these separate streams, these private, individual revolutions are flowing into it – the sea of life, of life in its own right. I said life, but I mean life as you see it in a work of art, transformed by genius, creatively enriched. Only now people have decided to experience it not in books and pictures but in themselves, not in theory but in practice.'[14]

Later, however, he (or at least his father-in-law, with whom he entirely agrees) comes to see this directness of the Revolution's early edicts as having been 'turned inside out' by the 'Jesuitism of politics'. The Revolution falls, by its own dynamic, into the hands of the hard men, who are incapable of experiencing real creativity through their own private revolutions, but merely abuse the public revolution to clear the way for their own assumption of power. Among them are even some fine people, like Pasha Antipov/Strel'nikov, 'a shy, girlish mocking boy full of mischief and obsessed with purity', who loves Lara with the calf love of the enduring schoolboy, and who goes into war and then revolution in order to avenge her sufferings and to make the world a more worthy place for her and their little daughter to live in:

He had an unusual power of clear and logical reasoning, and he was endowed with great moral purity and sense of justice: he was ardent and honourable.

But to the task of a scientist breaking new ground, his mind would have failed to bring an intuition for the incalculable: the capacity for those unexpected discoveries which shatter the barren harmony of empty foresight.

And in order to do good to others he would have needed, besides the principles which filled his mind, an unprincipled heart – the kind of heart that knows of no general cases, but only of particular ones, and has the greatness of small actions.[15]

Antipov is a man who sees in the world, and in people, only laws and principles (pure reason), not individual things and persons (practical reason). He is the soul of purity and honesty, whom Lara loves out of what she feels to be the depth of her degradation. She says of him: 'He has a wonderful, upright, shining personality. I am very much at fault that our marriage went wrong. . . . he is so outstanding, so big, he has such immense integrity – and I'm no good at all, I'm nothing in comparison with him. That's where my fault lies.'[16] He was the dream of 'purity' which had haunted her since early childhood.[17] What she does not understand, and indeed tries to deny, is that it is these very qualities which make him a fit hero for the era of wars and revolutions. He is the romantic, ascetic kind of Socialist Realist hero seen in the light of the narrator's Christian personalist philosophy.

The pure, idealist revolutionaries like Pasha Antipov are destined to be destroyed by the other kind of revolutionary leader, the devotees of power for its own sake, like Liberius Mikulitsyn, whose Roman name and entourage ('two silent youths' with 'fine, stone faces' which 'revealed nothing except blind loyalty to their chief and readiness to serve him at whatever cost') suggest the 'pock-marked Caligulas' whose 'boastful dead eternity of bronze monuments and marble columns' preceded the Christian era, in Vedenyapin's philosophy.[18] The climax of Liberius's campaign is the execution of thirteen conspirators from his partisan band on what appears to be an ancient pagan tumulus erected in enormous slabs of rock.[19]

Both kinds of revolutionaries, in Yury's eyes, are men who suffer from a basic incapacity for life:

'it turns out that those who inspired the revolution aren't at home in anything except change and turmoil: that's their native element; they aren't happy with anything that's less than on a world scale. For them, transitional periods, worlds in the making, are an end in themselves. They aren't trained for anything else, they don't know about anything except that. And do you know why there is this incessant whirl of never-ending preparations? It's because they haven't any real capacities, they are ungifted. Man is born to live, not to prepare for life. Life itself – the gift of life – is such a breathtakingly serious thing!'[20]

What *is* this 'life' that Yury counterposes to the narrow-mindedness of revolutionaries? His reflections on poetry at Varykino give us a clue to his conception:

art always serves beauty, and beauty is the joy of possessing form, and form is the key to organic life since no living thing can exist without it, so that every work of art, including tragedy, witnesses to the joy of existence.[21]

Personality is one kind of form: in his published works Yury describes it as 'the biological basis of the organism'.[22] It is not synonymous with individuality, since it is not confined by the boundaries of the individual. 'You in others are yourself, your soul,' as Yury tells Tonya's mother, lying seriously ill and afraid of the self-extinction which she thinks will follow death.[23] Immortality of the soul is not the indefinite perpetuation of the individual's existence beyond death, but his continued existence as a constituent element of personality in the broader sense.

'So what will happen to your consciousness? *Your* consciousness, yours, not anyone else's. Well, what are *you*? That's the crux of the matter. Let's try to find out. What is it about you that you have always known as yourself? What are you conscious of in yourself? Your kidneys? Your liver? Your blood vessels? – No. However far back you go in your memory, it is always in some external, active manifestation of yourself that you come across your identity – in the work of your hands, in your family, in other people. And now look. You in others are yourself, your soul. This is what you are. This is what your consciousness has breathed and lived on and enjoyed throughout your life.... And what now? You have always been in others and you will remain in others. And what does it matter to you if later on it is called your memory? This will be you – the you that enters the future and becomes a part of it.'[24]

Art is the expression of human personality in this overarching of death. It 'has two constant, two unending preoccupations: it is always meditating upon death and it is always thereby creating life.'[25] When Yury's poetic creativity reaches its most fruitful, he feels art to be something independent which has taken over, as though at the roots of his personality is something beyond his individuality.

At such moments the correlation of the forces controlling the artist is, as it were, stood on its head. The ascendancy is no longer with the artist or the state of mind which he is trying to express, but with language, his instrument of expression. Language, the home and dwelling of beauty and meaning, itself begins to think and speak for man and turns wholly into music, not in the sense of outward, audible sounds but by virtue of the power and momentum of its inward flow. . . .

At such moments Yury felt that the main part of his work was not being done by him but by something which was above him and controlling him: the thought and poetry of the world as it was at that moment and as it would be in the future. He was controlled by the next step it was to take in the order of its historical development; and he felt himself to be only the pretext and the pivot setting it in motion.[26]

The devices of language, therefore, are not simply tools of writing, but determinants of consciousness and creativity. Metaphor, in particular, the device which runs right through Pasternak's poetry and prose, is no mere figure of speech, but a fundamental outlook on life, the ever-ready sensitivity to the inter-relatedness of things. Metaphor is both form and content, if you like, since the content of the novel is precisely this inter-relatedness. It is apparent in the way in which people's fates constantly cross and recross in the course of the narrative (coincidences which appear dangerously improbable in the light of nineteenth-century realism), in the narrator's vivid sense of *things* participating in human life, and feelings, so that 'flowers talk philosophy at night, stone houses hold meetings', a rowan tree becomes a mother to the birds and a mistress to Yury,[27] and the evening landscape of Lara's departure becomes a close participant in his grief, 'as if . . . the trees had only now taken up their places, rising out of the ground on purpose to offer their condolences.'[28]

The love of Yury and Lara is depicted in close relation to everything in their world. When he is recovering from typhus, Lara appears to Yury as 'Not he, but something bigger than himself', that 'wept and complained in him'.[29] Her generous white arms are the wings of an angel, or the branches of the rowan tree. Their mutual understanding is easy and penetrating, 'as full of meaning as the Dialogues of Plato'.[30] As Lara – and the narrator – understand it afterwards:

It was not out of necessity that they loved each other, 'enslaved by passion', as lovers are described. They loved each other because everything around them willed it, the trees and the clouds and the sky over their heads and the earth under their feet. Perhaps their surrounding world, the strangers they met in the street, the landscapes drawn up for them to see on their walks, the rooms in which they lived or met, were even more pleased with their love than they were themselves.

Well, of course, it had been just this that had united them and had made them so akin! Never, never, not even in their moments of richest and wildest happiness, had they lost the sense of what is highest and most ravishing – joy in the whole universe, its form, its beauty, the feeling of their own belonging to it, being part of it.[31]

It is at the height and greatest concentration of this feeling that Yury is in closest touch with the 'organic key to existence', composes his poems and lays the foundations for his philosophical works.

Pasternak thus intends us to take metaphor not just as an expressive device, but as actual meaning. This is a very different aesthetic and attitude to the world from that of both the Symbolists and the Socialist Realists, who saw fundamental reality ('reality in its revolutionary development') as *hidden behind* appearances. It is much more akin to the outlook of the Acmeists (whatever may have been Pasternak's youthful poetic allegiances), who saw fundamental reality as *revealed* to us in the given world. That is why the Acmeists reproached the Symbolists with being 'bad householders' who did not appreciate 'this world, the God-given palace'.[32] It is significant that Yury sees Symbolism along with Tonya and the family as part of the limited, ordered world of his childhood, while the new aesthetic currents of 1912–14 (including presumably Acmeism) are 'signs of the new', of the time when 'revolution' would really mean revolution, suffering would be in earnest, and love would be the elemental, healing but also destructive Lara.

This perception of the literalness of the figurative is what Yury's two surviving comrades, Gordon and Dudorov, learn from their lives in wars and labour camps, and what they emphasize in their conversation with each other, which ends the novel:

'This has happened several times in the course of history. A thing which has been conceived in a lofty, ideal manner becomes coarse and material. Thus Greece became Rome, and the Russian enlightenment became the Russian revolution. Take that line of Blok's, "We, the children of Russia's terrible years," and you can see the difference between the two epochs at once. When Blok said it, he meant it to be understood figuratively, metaphorically. The children were not children, but the sons and heirs, the intelligentsia, and the terrors were not terrible but providential, apocalyptic – quite different. Now the figurative has become literal, the children are children and the terrors are terrible. There you have the difference.'[33]

'The figurative has become literal': that might almost be a summary both of Pasternak's aesthetic and of the epiphany which is the subject of his novel. This is the outlook of the survivor of the extremities which man's Promethean experiment has brought upon himself. As Terrence des Pres has said in his study of the experience of the concentration camps, 'in extremity symbolism *as symbolism* loses its autonomy . . . meaning no longer exists above and beyond the world; it re-enters concrete experience, becomes immanent and invests each act and moment with urgent depth.' The man who has hidden in the Warsaw sewers has experienced defilement in a sense which is not metaphorical.[34]

That is perhaps the greatest difference between the fiction of Stalinist Socialist Realism and the best Soviet fiction of today. The former is written by the victors, those who claim to see Ultimate Reality, the Purpose, concealed behind everybody and everything; the latter is written by the survivors, those who have been through the worst, absorbed and learnt from their experience. They see reality no longer in the light of 'its revolutionary development', of the Purpose above and beyond it, but simply for itself, for the meaning it carries within itself. As observers and narrators they are no longer confident about the final goal of history, and they replace that goal with openness to experience, with close, even loving attention to things and people immediately around them.

Of no work is this more true than it is of Solzhenitsyn's *One Day in the Life of Ivan Denisovich* (*Odin den' Ivana Denisovicha*, 1962), in appearance so different from *Doctor Zhivago*, yet united with it by an analagous affectionate care in the depiction of immediate reality. Whereas Pasternak worked his way towards this approach from the prerevolutionary cultural and intellectual tradition, and from his own early highly experimental poetry, Solzhenitsyn came to it more directly, through the life of ordinary people in the labour camps. Pasternak's search is a metaphysical one. Solzhenitsyn's is humbler, but no less important: simply to re-establish the literal truth about Stalinist society, a truth hitherto obscured by the radiance of the 'magnificent prospects' ahead. Ivan Denisovich is very different as a person from Yury Zhivago, but his perceptions likewise open up a whole new literary world, based on an epistemology close to Pasternak's.

What first strikes the reader of *Ivan Denisovich* is the dense everyday detail that fills every page of it. The narrator dwells on every circumstance of the day: arranging the bedding so as to sleep warmly, covering draughty window embrasures with roofing felt, laying breeze blocks on a frosty day when the mortar freezes as soon as applied. The layout of the camp compound, the mess hut, the barracks is described with as much obsessive detail as in any work of Robbe-Grillet. But the detail is not arbitrary or theoretical: the fat content of the gruel, the state of the fish-bones in the watery soup are a matter of life and death. It is the trivia which often decide whether a man will survive or not in a universe which has deliberately been made harsh for him. In these circumstances a man's sensitivity to the ordinary and everyday is immeasurably heightened: whether a guard searches in two mittens or only one, whether a neighbour has received a food parcel, whether a cook at the service hatch has taken his hands off two full bowls.

The same minute attention extends to social relationships within the camp. Much about man is revealed sharply here which is only dimly observable in ordinary social life. Social relationships are vital to survival: each prisoner must build up for himself what one might call an anthropologist's guide to the institution. These relationships are not simple. The camp is both a penal institution and also an economic enterprise. The penal authorities have interests which do not at all points coincide with those of the economic management. Thus the escort guards will allow a certain amount of pilfering of firewood from the building site for the prisoners' stoves, since they get a kickback from it. Besides, the higher authorities must rely on ordinary human beings to carry out the lower level operations, and these have their own interests to protect. The warders are poorly paid and conduct a black market trade in grain, filched from the unfortunate prisoners' daily ration.

The prisoner has to rumble such formal and informal arrangements before he can begin to work the system for whatever advantage – or even momentary absence of disadvantage – it can yield him. The key to his social existence is the brigade, which is both a blessing and a curse. The authorities invented the brigade for their own purposes:

You might well ask why a prisoner worked so hard for ten years in a camp. Why didn't they say to hell with it and drag their feet all day long till the night, which was theirs?
But it wasn't so simple. That's why they'd dreamed up these brigades. It wasn't like brigades 'outside', where every fellow got paid separately. In the camps they had these brigades to make the prisoners keep each other on their toes. So the fellows at the top didn't have to worry. It was like this – either you all got something extra or you all starved. ('You're not pulling your weight, you swine, and I've got to go hungry because of you. So work, you bastard!')[35]

On the other hand, this same enforced mutual dependency also generates mutual aid and even a certain genuine intimacy. Ivan Denisovich assumes, when taken to the guardroom by a warder, that the rest of the brigade will save him some breakfast – and they do. The prisoners' worst enemy is other prisoners, but the brigade provides a limit to the universal struggle of man against man. Competition between brigades, for easy work, for a place at the mess table, or near the stove, is absolute, but within the brigade it is moderated by the common need for survival. The brigade leader is the key figure:

In a camp, your brigade leader is everything. A good one can give you a new lease on life, but a bad one will finish you off. . . . Shukhov never had any dealings with the Commandant, the PPS [Production Planning Section], the work-supervisors, and the engineers. The leader took care of all that sort of thing. He was like a rock. But he only had to raise an eyebrow or point a finger and you ran off to do what he wanted. You could cheat anyone you liked in the camp, but not Tyurin. That way you'd stay alive.[36]

Tyurin's success in averting the brigade's transfer to the bleak, windswept Socialist Community Development project, and in finding them a job where they can take shelter, may literally mean survival for the physically weaker members. Similarly his fiddling the work rates so that the team gets more food to eat. Naturally all this adroit manoeuvring means establishing good relations with the work supervisors. Hence the yield from individual food parcels – the most individual things in the prisoner's life – often becomes the property of the whole brigade:

The leader needed a lot of [lard] to slip to the people in the PPS and still have enough left for his own belly. He didn't get any packages from home, but he was never short of [lard]. It was always handed over to him right away by anyone in the brigade who got some.[37]

The brigade, in fact, functions as a kind of collective, its members living together, working together, economically and spiritually dependent on one another. Besides, after so long together in such an enclosed and peculiar existence, the prisoners have far more in common with one another than with their families outside.

Like all social systems, the camp depends on a complex set of hierarchies and conventions for its functioning. Some of these, of course, are the formal hierarchies and regulations established by the authorities for the smooth running of the place. But not all. Some prisoners, because of their skills, their connections, or their abundant food parcels, become obviously more influential than many of the warders and guards, or even the NCOs of the camp command. Thus Caesar, well provided with food parcels, gets a cushy office job, can discuss recent films in comfort and can afford to look down on the likes of Ivan Denisovich. A separate and different kind of hierarchy is formed by the *stukachi* (squealers), because of the information they provide for the security services, which may damage anyone, from ordinary prisoners to the camp commandant himself; they are universally regarded with caution and loathing, but have as a rule to be tolerated.

Within the brigade itself there also exists an unofficial but nonetheless generally acknowledged hierarchy. The brigade leader, of course, is unrivalled, and even his assistant is a minor feudal lord in the eyes of most members. These two are *the* authority figures and protectors in most of life's incidents. Apart from that, those members who are skilled in certain ways (for example, Shukhov and Kilgas as carpenter and mason) or who are particularly experienced in camp enjoy a certain prestige. Those who, like Caesar, receive a lot of food parcels have strong bargaining power and can get others to do little services for them. The weaker and less skilled, on the other hand, and even those with too little self-respect, sink to the bottom of the pile. The 'goners' are treated as Spartans treated weakling children, with ruthless contempt: when Shukhov finds a couple in the way, he simply shooes them off.[38] Fetyukov, who cannot restrain himself from begging favours, enjoys little respect, though a factory director in life outside: when he spills the mortar, Shukhov has no compunction in prodding him and mocking, 'You lazy slob. I bet you really took it out on the fellows in that factory you managed!'[39] In the furnace of the camp, as on the Calvinist day of judgement, all the hierarchies of this world are rendered meaningless, everyone is abruptly reduced to equal status and has to find his own level, depending on the qualities within him, and drawing what sustenance he can from the limited but sometimes genuine personal relationships he forges with his colleagues.

All this is presented as a closed system, perverted, but complete and self-sufficient. Nobody expects it to change, and to fight against it would be patently absurd (though occasionally squealers are murdered). The man who learns its laws and conventions must simply adapt himself to them. He must find the will to survive and hence the meaning of his life not in a new and better world which he is struggling to build, but in the primary sensations that remain to him, laying bricks skilfully, squeezing grains of gruel between his tongue and teeth. This is all that can be salvaged from existence at the extreme, and the rediscovery of these primary sensations is a basic feature distinguishing the contemporary hero from his Socialist Realist predecessor.

Ivan Denisovich is far from being a fighter. His motto is *kryakhti da gnis'; a upräsh'sya – perelomish'sya* ('groan and bend your back; if you fight them, they'll break you'). Furthermore, the narrator is in obvious agreement with him on this point. Perhaps most important of all, the language in which the new hero and the new morality are presented is very close to that of Ivan Denisovich himself. Pasternak had broken away from the 'doublethink' language of classical Socialist Realism by evoking the echoes of prerevolutionary culture. Solzhenitsyn does it by drawing on the powerful underground stream of folklore and popular language, which had virtually disappeared from literature during the 'imperial' period of Stalinism. Instead, the novel is full of sayings which embody the popular wisdom driven underground but not destroyed by the Stalinist literary-beaucratic steamroller.

Kto kogo smozhet, tot togo i glozhet. ('Every man for himself' or 'he who can devours his neighbour').

Tëplyi zyablogo razve kogda poimët? ('How can a warm man understand a cold one?')

Bryukho – zlodei, starogo dobra ne pomnit. ('The belly is an ungrateful bastard, doesn't remember past services.')

These are the sayings of the zeks as a nation, the fruits of their long experience in this harsh land with its impenetrable frontiers. These truths, wrung from extremity, are true in a much more direct sense than official statements, expressed in bureaucratic euphemisms which steer round the truth rather than coming to grips with it.

In longer stretches the language often takes on the character of folk narration, with the rhythms, repetitions, parallelisms and word inversions of the *skazka* (fairy tale):

A bylo vot kak: v fevrale sorok vtorogo goda na Severo-Zapadnom okruzhili ikh armiyu vsyu, i s samolëtov im nichego zhrat'ne brosali, a i samolëtov tekh ne bylo. (It was like this: in February '42 their whole army had been surrounded on the North-Western front, and nobody had parachuted supplies to them from aeroplanes, in fact there weren't any aeroplanes.)

The basic narrative language, in fact, is one which might well be that of Shukhov himself, were he capable of the written transcription of his experiences. At times the reader may even get the impression that Shukhov himself is telling the story. In actual fact this is not the case, but the ambiguity surrounding the narrator is another profoundly influential feature of this work. What the author has done is to take his narrative stance very close to Ivan Denisovich, at times letting his narrative voice merge with his, at times withdrawing a little from him, occasionally even reporting events which Ivan Denisovich could not see or thinking thoughts a little beyond his capacities. One might say that this is, in a sense, the 'generalized voice of the prisoners . . . including Shukhov's voice as the dominant one within the general blending.'[40]

What Solzhenitsyn achieves by this technique is immediacy of presentation combined with enough flexibility to be able to distance himself and make short-term judgements through juxtaposition, irony and comment. The old-fashioned Socialist Realist objective narrator was too distant from events to feel their impact on his skin, and saw them as part of an intellectual pattern whose outcome he knew in advance. Shukhov, by contrast, apart from being illiterate, has not the capacity to generalize in more than the most primitive way outside his own immediate experience. By combining the two narrative modes, Solzhenitsyn accepts subjectivity and indeed uncertainty as part of the lot of mankind, including the writer, but at the same time is able to draw on a common stock of experience and reflection. The Olympian narrator has definitely been banished, but he is not replaced by the mere individual, prisoner of his own consciousness.

The stylistic technique that Solzhenitsyn uses to give form to his viewpoint is third person direct speech or *erlebte Rede*. It was much used in the nineteenth-century novel to illuminate psychological and mental processes, but perhaps no writer before Solzhenitsyn had made it so much the central structural feature of his work – and this is a characteristic in which he has been followed by a number of subsequent Soviet prose-writers, Abramov, Belov, Vladimov, Voinovich, Trifonov, and for the same reason: to gain vividness, open-endedness, the sense of personal values being at stake that comes from using direct speech, without altogether forfeiting the capacity to make statements that reflect more than just one person's stock of wisdom. The Russian language is unusually well adapted to this function, through its variety of impersonal and infinitive constructions, its ability to dispense with a verb in the present tense, and above all the absence of any differentiated sequence of tenses for indirect speech. All this means that direct and indirect speech are often indistinguishable from one another, and for quite long passages it remains ambiguous who is speaking. By the same token, gradual unmarked transitions can be made from the narrator's stance to that of one or more of his characters. In translation the ambiguity usually has to be cleared up, and the effect is lost. That such transitions are being made appears very obviously in one or two passages where even the Russian cannot remain ambiguous:

Shukhov could see what it was all about when the column cleared a rise they'd been passing. Way over on the plain there was another column heading for the camp, right across our path. These fellows must've spotted us too and put a spurt on.

The abrupt transition from third to first person narration was too much here for the English translators, who replaced 'our' with 'their' and 'us' with 'them'.[41]

What sort of man is it whose outlook is so close to that of the narrator? Can the reader really learn anything from Ivan Denisovich?

He is experienced in camp life and far from stupid, but on the other hand he is a very ordinary peasant, not really even a traditional peasant, heir to a centuries-old folk culture. On the contrary, this culture has already been half destroyed. Odd vestiges of it, and of both pagan and Christian religion, crop up in his mind, but he treats them half-sceptically, as though conscious that they do not hang together any more. 'The old people at home used to say that God breaks the old moon up into stars.'[42] God, for him, if He exists at all, is a projection of earthly authority figures, and – unlike the West Ukrainians, only recently annexed to the Soviet Union – he is one of the Russians who 'didn't even remember which hand you cross yourself with'.[43] He prays desperately and briefly to God when he thinks his piece of metal is going to be discovered in the search, but normally he has no faith in prayer: 'all these prayers are like the complaints we send in to the higher-ups – either they don't get there or they come back to you marked "Rejected".'[44]

In the few passages that reflect life outside the camp, the work contains clear hints about what has destroyed Russia's peasant culture. Tyurin, the brigade leader, was cashiered from the Red Army in 1930 as a kulak's son, and when he got home he found the following scene:

'I got home late one night and entered by the back garden. Father had already been deported, and mother and the kids were waiting for a transport. A telegram had come about me, and the Village Soviet were already after me. We put out the light and sat trembling up against the wall under the window, because activists were going round the village peering in at the windows. I left again the same night and took my kid brother with me. . . .'[45]

The state-sponsored break-up of farms and families has led to a steady decline in the rural economy and culture, to such an extent that Shukhov, who left it all ten years ago for war and then captivity, can no longer understand letters from home:

The thing Shukhov didn't get at all was what his wife wrote about how not a single new member had come to the kolkhoz since the war. All the youngsters were getting out as best they could – to factories in the towns or to the peat fields. Half the kolkhozniks had not come back after the war, and those who had wouldn't have anything to do with the kolkhoz – they lived there but earned their money somewhere outside. The only men in the kolkhoz were the brigade leader, Zakhar Vasilyevich, and the carpenter, Tikhon, who was eighty-four, had married not long ago, and even had children already. The real work in the kolkhoz was done by the same women who'd been there since the start, in 1930.[46]

What has Shukhov salvaged from the external collapse of the community to sustain him through the trials of the camp? A few rules of personal etiquette, some his own, others shared by his fellows, intended to preserve self-respect: taking off his cap before eating, no matter how cold the weather, not spitting fishbones directly on to the floor, not eating fish eyes unless they are still attached to the skeleton.

Eating is the thrice daily ritual that sustains his body and nourishes his spirit:

Pavlo sat down to his double helping, and so did Shukhov. They didn't say another word to each other. These minutes were holy. . . .

[Shukhov] began to eat. He started with the watery stuff on the top and drank it right down. The warmth went through his body and his insides were sort of quivering waiting for that gruel to come down. It was great! This was what a prisoner lived for, this one little moment.[47]

This is one of the passages the reader remembers most vividly after finishing the book. It helps to set the tone for the whole work. Another is the passage in which Ivan Denisovich exercises his skill as a bricklayer, working with a team that, thanks to the brigade leader, is for the moment passably coordinated. These are the moments that give his life some meaning. They are moments of complete absorption in the present. The satisfaction with which he lines up the breeze blocks and judges the exact amount of mortar has nothing to do with the construction of the future: it is simply pride at doing a job properly. The Purpose has been completely replaced by the Immediate.

Of course Shukhov's rules of personal conduct are not universally valid. Everyone in the camp lives by his own standards, which he has to work out for himself, and each man must seek physical and spiritual survival in his own way. Some are more successful than others. Fetyukov, the 'jackal', who has lost his self-respect and transgresses the understood rule that one does not *ask* for a draw on a cigarette, is doomed to an early death, like those who lick the used bowls of gruel. At the opposite end of the scale, Buinovsky, the forthright, outspoken naval captain, still has notions of dignity altogether too unyielding for the camp. 'You've no right to strip people in the cold! You don't know Article Nine of the Criminal Code!' he protests when subjected to a bodily search after roll-call. 'They had the right and they knew the article', comments either the narrator or Shukhov (it might be either in this passage) to himself. 'You've still got a lot to learn, brother.'[48] But Buinovsky at least *is* learning: after the midday meal he has learnt to sit quietly awhile in the warmth and relative satiety, doing and thinking nothing.

It was moments like this (though he didn't know it) that were very important for him. This was the sort of thing that was changing him from a bossy, loudmouth naval officer into a slow-moving and cagey zek. He'd have to be like this if he wanted to get through his twenty-five years in camp.[49]

The two Estonians, who only met by chance in the camp, survive by sharing everything and forming their own little nationally identified sub-family. Alësha the Baptist survives by prayer and faith. He even rejoices in his ordeal, seeing freedom as a condition where faith is 'choked by thorns'. He is capable of childlike joy at the rising of the sun. He is a humble, conscientious worker who fits into the team wherever the brigade leader wants to put him. His morality, rather different from that by which most zeks feel they have to live, is expressed in one of his readings from the Gospel:

'But let none of you suffer as a murderer, or as a thief or as an evildoer, or as a busybody in other men's matters. Yet if any man suffer as a Christian, let him not be ashamed; but let him glorify God on this behalf.'

His comrades respect him, and he clearly contributes to the cohesion of the brigade. But his faith has a hermetic quality that makes it inapplicable to most people. Shukhov's reaction is:

'I'm not against God, understand. I believe in God, all right. But what I don't believe in is Heaven and Hell. Who d'you think we are, giving us all that stuff about Heaven and Hell? That's the thing I can't take.'[50]

Coming as it does at the end of the work, this remark of Shukhov's cannot but make the reader reflect that hell is present in ample measure in this world. Perhaps, then, at least the potentialities for heaven exist here too? At any rate, the whole thrust of the story is to draw our attention away from the other world – whether the Communists' Purpose or Alësha's Heaven – to this world, to the immediate good and evil, beauty and ugliness that exist here. That is really the importance of the novella. No specific ideology emerges: the work as a whole has a certain positive agnosticism about it. Every individual has his own, more or less primitive, system of beliefs and values to counterpose to the system, and more than one of them is moderately effective in ensuring survival, at least for the time being. None of them can entirely guarantee it. Solzhenitsyn sketches sympathetically a number of responses to the ordeal, which share as their highest common factor a certain humanism and self-discipline, a mixture of self-reliance and wary solidarity with colleagues.

When *Ivan Denisovich* first appeared, Roman Gul' wrote that it 'cancels out the whole of Socialist Realism'.[51] George Lukacs, on the other hand, could call it (along with Solzhenitsyn's other novellas) 'a significant step in the renewal of the great traditions of the Socialist Realism of the 1920s'.[52] The curious thing is that both, in their own terms, were right. Lukacs believed that the golden age of Socialist Realism had preceded the bureaucratic sponsorship of the doctrine in 1932, and in his view *Ivan Denisovich* marked a return to the aesthetic principles of which official Socialist Realism was a distortion: a return to genuine *narodnost'*, to real concern with social values, to meticulous and honest realism in the reporting of social life. On the other hand, the work rendered official Socialist Realism obsolete by describing the actual suffering behind the façade of purposefulness and heroism – in fact by pointing to real meaning and genuine reality where previously the Purpose had overshadowed everything.

In the following chapters we shall see how other recent Soviet novelists have broken away from the teleological view of man in the direction indicated by Pasternak and Solzhenitsyn, towards a more sober and honest depiction of reality, towards greater attention to immediately surrounding things and people, and towards a concern with meaning rather than purpose.

3

Village Prose: Vasily Belov, Valentin Rasputin

Of all the fictional subjects which have attracted Soviet writers between the mid-fifties and the present, the village and the life of the peasants has been the dominant one, certainly in quantity and arguably in quality too. Almost every major writer of the period has written somewhere at length about peasants, and most of them have composed long works devoted to the life of the village. Until recently, of course, peasants formed a large majority of the Soviet population, and agricultural problems have been a constant preoccupation of the political leadership. Even so, it takes some explaining just why this theme has fascinated writers over the last generation to such an extent. In the Stalinist years peasants appeared in most Soviet novels, but they were usually depicted as survivals from the past, picturesque perhaps, *narodnyi* certainly, but as people whose way of life was still backward, degrading and needed to be modernized through the collectivization and mechanization of agriculture, through education, culture and party organization. Nowadays the approach is quite otherwise: the peasant and his way of life are seen as having an autonomous value of their own, worth studying and even preserving for what they have to teach us. The peasant has become, in fact, in his own unheroic way, a 'positive hero', though one of a type very different from the confident, activist figures of Stalinist fiction.

Why has this happened? Some of the reasons are to be found in the history of Soviet society during and after the Stalin years. These have been Russia's great years of industrialization and urbanization, when tens of millions of people left the countryside and moved into the towns to live permanently. In the process much that was characteristic of peasant life has been destroyed. The manner in which the

50

collectivization of agriculture was carried out certainly made this breakdown of the peasant way of life sharper and more bitter than it has been in almost any other country. At the same time, the collectivization – together with the war and the general political oppression – actually *preserved* certain aspects of peasant life more than they would perhaps have been preserved under a gentler evolution. The shattering social and political upheavals which it was Russia's misfortune to undergo affected the young, educated and male inhabitants more than it did the old, uneducated and female. It was on the whole the former who went into the towns and the army (and probably suffered more from arrests and purges), the latter who stayed on the land to eke out what living they could. Furthermore, the very pace of modernization in the towns and the armed forces usually meant that few resources were left for the countryside, so that there cultivation continued with methods that in most European countries had been abandoned by the First World War. Finally, the peasants' passive resistance to the statization of agriculture compelled the government to compromise with them by allowing them to keep the old household plot of land, in drastically truncated but still viable form; and these plots in fact provide vitally needed supplies for the towns and armed forces to this very day.

The Soviet government has thus first of all destroyed the bulk of the peasant way of life, then put what remained in cold storage in order to concentrate on other aspects of society and the economy. This policy, which was supposed to be aimed at the precise opposite, actually *deepened* the already existing sharp division in Soviet society between the town and the village.[1] This is true even though an unusually high proportion of the population have lived both in the village and the town at some time during their lives, usually transferring from the former to the latter. Life in the towns is more secure, more comfortable and more prosperous, access to education, culture and human company is far better; and on top of all this, the rural inhabitants were until very recently effectively fixed to their workplace and made second-class citizens by being denied the internal passport required for more than the briefest journey from one part of the country to another. Those who could get away from the village – young men going into the armed forces, or young people generally who had qualified for specialized or higher education – did so, and then tried their best not to return. Their parents and their less capable, ambitious or forceful contemporaries stayed behind.

The split between town and country was therefore also a split in the personalities of numerous Soviet individuals. In the confused circumstances of the thaw this split occupied writers considerably. A well known example is Yury Kazakov's story *The Smell of Bread* (*Zapakh khleba*, 1961) in which a townswoman returns briefly to her native village, which she has not seen for fifteen years, to dispose of the property of her recently dead mother. At first the countryside is merely a pleasant diversion for her, but then the smell of bread in her mother's old house, and most of all the sight of her grave, affect her violently and she breaks out in uncontrollable wailing and sobbing, rubbing her face in the earth she has so long neglected. The return of long forgotten – half-suppressed – memories reminds her of the fullness of her personality in a way which overwhelms her.[2]

In a similar story, *The Return Home* (*Poezdka na rodinu*, 1956) by Nikolai Zhdanov, a secure and well-appointed party official, Varygin, also returns to his native village, for the funeral of his mother whom he never saw in the years before her death. He rediscovers in the crosses of the cemetery, in the smell of incense, in the rough wooden furniture of his former home hut a world which 'according to his conceptions, had long ago ceased to exist.' His mother's fellow villagers, sensing a rare opportunity to get the ear of someone influential, begin to mumble to him tales of bureaucratic ignorance, arbitrariness and corruption, but he cuts them short and rushes back to the town and to his comfortable carpeted office. However, even when safely re-ensconced there, he cannot shake off the memory of what he has seen, and the timid question of an old peasant woman: 'Have they done right by us or not?' The village leaves in fact in his mind an enduring deposit of bewilderment and guilt about himself and about the society in which he lives.[3]

This theme of the social, cultural and psychological split between town and country was to prove a very fruitful one in fiction, for what it revealed both about the Soviet Union's social structure and about Soviet man's image of himself. Given earlier fictional tradition, one might have expected it would be the rural innovators, tractor drivers, electricians, agronomists, and so on, who would be the heroes of modern 'village prose'. But in fact almost without exception the principal figures have been ordinary peasants, and very often the oldest and most backward of them. It is as though the present recently urbanized generations wanted to retrieve, before it finally disappears, the memory of a past which has been slighted too long, and thereby to restore a sense of tradition and psychological wholeness, a spiritual integrity which modern urban civilization does not seem to them to offer. As Sergei Zalygin has said:

Our generation is probably the last to see with its own eyes a thousand year old way of life out of which nearly all of us have grown. If we cannot describe it and the decisive changes that have transformed it in a very short time, then who can?[4]

Just as in England George Ewart Evans and others have been collecting oral testimony to a past which would otherwise be irretrievably lost, so the writers of 'village prose' in Russia – where the task is both more difficult and more important – have tried to rescue the social history of their country. It is an expression of what Boris Shragin has called the 'nostalgia for history': a tribute to their parents and grandparents, and yet at the same time a guarantee of the future, in the sense that a nation which has lost its past cannot conceive of a meaningful future.[5]

The changes of the post-Stalin period have made this problem of recapturing the past more pressing in that the state and party, having left the kolkhozes to devise their own survival for a generation, have finally devoted a much larger share of the nation's resources to agriculture, and have even seriously debated reforming its internal structure, in order to overcome the conspicuous backwardness of the rural sector. It was Khrushchev who by his personal style and his projected reform programme moved the peasant to the forefront of Soviet politics. He mobilized journalists and writers, notably Valentin Ovechkin, to give a frank picture of the atrocious conditions of rural life, and arouse the awareness of intellectuals and of the bulk of the party bureaucracy, still lulled by ritual evocations of a flourishing collective agriculture. Khrushchev did not dissent from the generally accepted view that peasants had to be changed, but he believed it could not be done by continual exhortation from the centre, especially if unaccompanied by the investment of material resources. He gave agriculture greater priority, a larger budget and a new dynamic image (even if in some ways misplaced) in his Virgin Lands programme, and he tried to grant more initiative to the men on the spot, the kolkhoz chairmen and the local party secretaries, who knew the soil and the climate and the men with whom they had to work. He tried to get the most talented administrators out of their armchairs and into the fields, close to the peasants. He invested more in the village so that better facilities would be available there, and so that peasants would have material incentives for working on the collective fields rather than devoting their time to their own little private plots.[6]

Most of Khrushchev's agricultural reforms did not work out as intended. Some of them were impractical, some were blunted by conservative opponents, and some were vitiated by Khrushchev's own view of himself as the nation's No. 1 kolkhoz chairman, competent to solve all problems for all farms in all areas. But once he had set in motion a relatively frank debate about the Soviet countryside, he had unleashed something which was difficult for both him and his successors to control. Disappointed with his reforms, writers began to look further than administrative solutions and tried to understand more about the peasant way of life and peasant agriculture *from the inside.* Valentin Ovechkin, who in his famous series of sketches *District Routine* (*Raionnye budni,* 1952–56) had staked much on finding the right administrators to run the kolkhozes and rural party units, seemed towards the end of his life no longer to believe that organization was the vital factor. Martynov, his 'good' *raion* party secretary, notes in his scrapbook: 'Sometimes in our attitude to the people we are like an oversensitive and anxious Mama, who simply cannot accept the fact that her son has long been a grown man.'[7] And Ovechkin himself is said in 1962 to have submitted a memorandum to the CPSU Central Committee recommending that the kolkhozes be reformed 'on the Yugoslav model' – which implies largely private farming coordinated by a network of state cooperatives. The only result of his proposal was that he was confined for a time to a mental hospital, where he tried to commit suicide.[8] But what he recommended directly has been implicit in much subsequent writing, in sketches and journalistic reporting as well as in works of fiction: that agriculture should be left in large measure to the peasants themselves, who understand it best and whose livelihood depends on it.

Efim Dorosh's rambling *Rural Diary* (*Derevenskii dnevnik*) started in 1956 as reportage not far from the early Ovechkin outlook. But as instalments were published over the years up to 1970, the traditional peasant way of life became more and more the main object of concern. Changing and modernizing agriculture came to seem far less important than actually preserving peasant customs from those who would thoughtlessly destroy them. The villages, the fields, woods and lakes of the Rostov region, north of Moscow, the local linguistic usages, the private cows and garden plots, the onion domes of the churches, the fretwork friezes of the peasant huts – all these things

Dorosh sees as a single ecological and human organism which bureaucrats and planners disturb at their peril. Kolkhoz chairmen and party secretaries play a positive role only in so far as they understand this. Much of Dorosh's criticism was directed at Khrushchev's ill-conceived campaigns, particularly at the universal sowing of maize, and at his failure to understand the economic and cultural importance of the private plot; but from the final pages of his diary, published in 1970, it is clear that he was also worried by post-Khrushchev schemes like the amalgamation of small hamlets into larger semi-urban settlements, and the building of multistorey apartment blocks in the village.[9]

As so often, the writer who expressed most forcefully and unambiguously what others had adumbrated was Solzhenitsyn. In *Matrëna's Home* (*Matrënin dvor*, 1963) he painted a portrait and stated a set of moral values that were to serve as a paradigm for much subsequent rural fiction. In the neglected hamlet of Tal'novo, demoralized and exploited for the needs of a neighbouring industrial settlement, he shows an old peasant woman as having maintained a humility and selflessness such as is vital in binding communities together:

Misunderstood and rejected by her husband, a stranger to her own family despite her happy, amiable temperament, comical, so foolish that she worked for others for no reward, this woman, who had buried all her six children, had stored up no earthly goods. Nothing but a dirty white goat, a lame cat and a row of fig-plants.
None of us who lived close to her perceived that she was that one righteous person without whom, as the saying goes, no village can stand.
Nor any city. Nor the world itself.[10]

A pre-Soviet concept of the 'positive hero' re-emerged with Matrëna: the passive, tolerant, unintelligent, self-sacrificing person, open to others and their needs, incapable of struggle and achievement, but offering a society, torn by more than a generation of war, oppression, industrialization and strident political rhetoric, an image in which to seek self-renewal. She is a *nec plus ultra* in this respect: none of the other principal figures in rural prose reaches her degree of meekness and altruism – apart from anything else most of them have families to provide for – but her moral qualities remain a counterpole for those who would abandon the Socialist Realist hero. As though to confirm this, the Soviet critic A. Dymshits commented sourly: 'The Soviet village, the Soviet land, stands not upon righteous sufferers, but upon active, creative people, capable of tilling the soil and transforming the world.'[11] One might reply to this 'tilling the soil, yes; transforming the world, no.' Even the more active rural 'positive heroes' have remained appreciative of the quiet virtues of Matrëna.

The problems raised by Ovechkin, Dorosh and Solzhenitsyn have been explored by a number of writers. Prominent among the older generation were Fëdor Abramov (born 1920) and Sergei Zalygin (born 1913). Abramov, himself a native of a village in Arkhangel'sk province, became a literary scholar in Leningrad, and first attracted attention with an article written in 1954, in which he attacked the 'varnishing of reality' practised by most rural writers of the late forties and early fifties.[12] Not content to preach on the subject, he launched into a long series of novels (only recently completed) about the northern village of Pekashino during and after the Second World War. This is a sober and painstaking chronicle, immensely detailed, evoking the everyday activities of village life, sweeping huts, milking cows, mowing hay, ploughing, sowing and reaping. Both the slow movement of his novels and the narrative language capture the rhythms of peasant life, and one has the impression of a generalized peasant voice speaking through the author, in the laconic syntax, the dialect words, the simple and direct imagery drawn from natural processes. The cycle goes through two main stages. In the first, during and immediately after the war, Abramov shows how peasant traditions, already badly shaken by mass collectivization in the thirties, are further threatened by the conscription of all the able-bodied men and by the inhuman demands placed on the remaining women, old men and children. In the fatherless Pryaslin family he summarizes the solidarity which binds the poverty-stricken peasants, even when individual members rebel against the privations and the authoritarian rule of party and state in the village. After the war, and especially in the last novel, as well as in shorter works like *Pelageya* and *Al'ka,* Abramov portrays a more prosperous village life, but one in which much of this solidarity has been lost with mechanization and the incursion of accompanying urban customs, like 'clocking in' and 'out' of work. Prosperity seems to pose problems almost as serious as poverty.[13]

Zalygin takes us back to the origins of the problems treated by Abramov, though the geographical setting of his novels is Siberia, where he shows us peasant communities of the early Soviet period, in revolution, civil war and collectivization. These are communities in crisis, at turning points in their evolution, when far-reaching questions of their identity, their conception of themselves, arise. What is a peasant? What should be his relationship to his home, his family, his village, and to the land and its fruits? Should the village have its own self-government, and if so, of what kind? Should peasants involve themselves in wider political movements, and if so (during the civil war at least), on which side? What should be the peasants' relationship to the outside world, especially to the towns and to urban political authority? These questions are thrashed out in packed meetings, in the open air or in smoke-filled huts; the dialogue is full of the peasants' new sense of responsibility for reshaping their own destiny, and of the threat posed by new forms of external authority, which do not really understand the peasant way of life. All around them is Siberia, a land only fairly recently mastered and brought under the plough, so that its assimilation is closely linked to the creation of a new communal destiny, while its open spaces are an almost metaphysical challenge to its inhabitants. As Zalygin himself has said:

Probably if Russia reached in the east only as far as the Urals, then Russians would have a rather different national character. . . . In our modern sense of space isn't there a kind of surmise, a premonition of another world, in which 'things aren't like that', and above all 'time is quite different', and the limits of human life are not simply birth and the grave.[14]

This reflective, philosophical streak is much stronger in Zalygin than in Abramov, and it is especially noticeable in his best novel, *The Commission* (*Komissiya*, 1975), where the author draws extensively upon chronicle and legend, and also gives sympathetic attention to peasants' religious beliefs.[15]

*   *

This side of Zalygin is deepened by the two leading village novelists of the younger generation, Vasily Belov (born 1932) and Valentin Rasputin (born 1937). They share the concern of their elders to portray meticulously a fading peasant culture and way of life, but more consistently they allow their depiction of rural transformation to raise broader questions about the whole nature of man's endeavour to create a perfect society on earth. They also enlist folklore and legend as a source of insights different from, and perhaps superior to, those available to the more literal-minded rural chronicler.

Among Vasily Belov's *Random Sketches* (*Sluchainye etyudy*, 1968) is one, *'There Was No Fire'* (*'Ne garyvali'*), in which the author, overtaken by a snowstorm as he is approaching a village, seeks shelter with an old peasant woman in her hut. He is puzzled by the layout of the village as he stumbles through it in the blizzard: the huts straggle out in four directions as though on the arms of a cross, but where the centre should be there is nothing but wasteland. Perhaps, he asks the old woman, there was once a fire which destroyed the centre? No, she replies, 'the people all left. Some were "dekulakized", some were killed in the war. And some went into the town. . . . Those were good, stout houses – and they were stout folk as lived there, in the centre. No, there was no fire, my dear, no fire at all.'[16]

This is the experience which might be said to haunt all of Belov's fiction: the tearing of the heart from the Russian village by collectivization, war and urbanization. His whole literary output is connected with the peasantry of the Vologda region, in the far north of European Russia, an area which occupies a special and important place in Russian culture (and Abramov writes about the neighbouring region of Arkhangel'sk). It was spared the worst effects of serfdom in the seventeenth to nineteenth centuries, being an area too bleak and remote to be attractive to the diplomats, army officers and civil servants to whom the Tsars were in the habit of donating land and peasants. For this reason, independent peasant agriculture and crafts flourished here as nowhere else in Russia. It also became one of the major centres for the settlement of Old Believers and other sectarians who wished to elude the authorities. Oral folk literature was probably more strongly developed here than elsewhere, and certainly it survived longer. In the Soviet period, the isolation of many of the farmsteads hampered collectivization, so that individual agriculture held out longer here than elsewhere. In the literary world, Konstantin Konichev, Mikhail Prishvin and Alexander Yashin kept the heritage of this northern culture alive during the Stalin period. It is no accident, then, that the far north has been the home par excellence of 'village prose'.

Like so many writers coming into their own during and immediately after the thaw period, Belov was very concerned with problems of language, and particularly of the narrator's language. He wanted to clear away the weary bureaucratic patina which had accumulated over so many words and phrases, obscuring and dulling their meaning, yet he felt that mere originality, the invention of new words and phrases, or the use of old ones in strange combinations, would not accomplish this.

Usually important concepts are weakened by frequent use of the words that express them. And then we are ashamed to employ those words, or we seek new ones, not yet mauled by idle tongues and pens. But as a rule no good comes of that. For the important concepts will have no truck with our verbal frenzy, they live beyond our ken, returning again and again to nourish with primeval meaning the words which express them.[17]

Belov's method is to employ the oldest and simplest words, but to illuminate them from within, as it were, by putting them together in a manner which suggests the speech of his characters, the northern peasants. This method was evidently reached as a result of experience and reflection:

The problem of the stylistic coordination of direct speech and narrative is very interesting. Indeed, I would say that for me it has been a rather painful one. The trouble is that either the character strings along behind the author and uses his language, or the author strings along behind his character and starts to speak with his words. But in fact I think that there does exist in its own right a certain subtle and indefinable zone of contact between an author's language and that of his characters.[18]

In essence, what he worked his way towards is much the same as what Solzhenitsyn achieved in *Ivan Denisovich*: a language close to that of the main character, but somewhat more generalized, somewhat more capable of reflection and interpretation. Not only that, but, again like Solzhenitsyn, Belov developed the capacity to switch narrative viewpoints smoothly and sometimes quite rapidly, achieving what one might call 'multiple subjectivity'.

This is especially well seen in the first work that really brought him national attention, *That's How Things Are* (*Privychnoe delo*), published in 1966 to the general acclamation of critics of all persuasions, from the liberal *Novyi Mir* to the highly conservative *Oktyabr'*. Quite apart from the work's intrinsic qualities, it came perhaps at a time when the reading public had already been sensitized to the rural theme by Kazakov, Solzhenitsyn, Dorosh and others, but still found it fresh and unusual. The action is very simple and reflects the usual concerns of 'village prose'. Ivan Afrikanovich Drynov and his wife Katerina have nine children and cannot earn enough on the kolkhoz to feed and clothe them all. Katerina's brother, Mit'ka, comes from the town and urges Ivan to return with him, to earn some proper money and perhaps eventually resettle the whole family there. Ivan is persuaded against his better judgement and tears himself away from the village. He gets only a few stations down the line, however, loses his ticket, is taken off the train for travelling without one, and returns home. In the short time he is away, Katerina, broken by their parting and by the labour of supporting nine children so soon after a recent childbirth, has a heart attack and dies. Ivan returns home only in time to grieve at her graveside.

Throughout the story, humans and animals are seen on the same level, as part of the same picture. It opens with Ivan's drunken monologue to the village gelding, Parmen, as they return home with stores. He is a gentle, affectionate, easy-going man, on good terms with everyone, including the horse, who is in fact the more rational of the two: he finds the way home in spite of Ivan's fuddled efforts to take him the wrong way. Ivan's rambling chatter adumbrates the main theme of the work, that of mortality. He remarks affectionately and mockingly to Parmen:

'I remember you when you were so high, frisking about, your hooves bucking away. You didn't have a care in the world in those days. And now what? Well, you get plenty of vodka to haul, and you get fed and watered, but what'll happen to you after that's over, eh? Why, they'll cut you up for sausages like your dad – they could come for you at any moment – and what are you going to do about it? Not a thing. You'll just trot along as though nothing were going to happen!' [19]

Children fit naturally into this world where men and animals reminisce and philosophize together. One chapter consists entirely of a brief presentation of the needs and the imaginative world of each of Ivan's nine children, including the new-born baby, in a third person narration which might be that of a father's affectionate observation: the language is basically the author's, but with an admixture of colloquialism which brings it close to Ivan's, and with a concreteness and simplicity which reflect the nature of the children's pre-occupations. Ivan's world is fundamentally the same as his children's, in their need for love, and in their growing curiosity and delight in the natural world around them. The parallel is directly drawn when Ivan walks over the frozen snow in the early morning:

Ivan Afrikanovich walked on for a long time over the fields covered with frozen snow. His legs bore him of their own accord, and he ceased to be aware of himself, he merged with the snow and the sun, with the blue, hopelessly distant sky, with all the smells and sounds of eternal spring.

Everything was ice-cold, stretching broadly away. Smoke was rising peacefully from the distant village chimneys, the cocks were crowing, the grouse were grumbling away, and the snow sparkled white, fast-bound by the frost. Ivan Afrikanovich walked on and on over the crunching snowcrust, and for him time ceased to exist. He was thinking of nothing at all, just like his little child lying smiling in the cradle, for whom there was no difference between sleeping and waking.

And for both of them at that moment there was no end, and no beginning.

The parallel is supported by Katerina's half-joking observation: 'Nine kids we've got, and the tenth is Ivan Afrikanovich – often just like a little child himself, he is.'[20]

In a later chapter Belov extends this technique to the family cow, Rogulya, writing for her a mixture of biography and autobiography, as it were. Again the parallel with Ivan is drawn: at the moment of Rogulya's most intense feeling of life, in mating, the same image is used, the sun in the bright blue sky, as during Ivan's early morning walks.

The author depicts Ivan's emotional world in close association with the seasons. The early events of the work, including the birth and the walk in the snow, take place in early spring, Ivan's departure and Katerina's death are in high summer, during the haymaking, while the period of grief and mourning coincide with the autumn. The work closes with the first frosts of winter.

Ivan's tragedy is his attempt to break out of the natural unity of men, children and animals. The attempt itself is an indication of the demoralized state of the village, the devaluation of the traditional peasant way of life. Ivan is a born peasant, who can lose himself in the rhythms of agricultural work. But the authorities interfere in the peasant way of life, preventing Ivan, for example, from mowing enough hay to keep Rogulya alive. For this reason Ivan is very vulnerable to Mit'ka's jeers at his unrewarded labours:

Whichever way you turned, everything seemed to show that Mit'ka was right. Ivan started to ponder morosely on things. It was as if he had a debt he had not paid off. As if something essential, without which life was impossible, had become superfluous, stupid, worthless, even treacherous.[21]

Mit'ka's most successful insinuation is that Ivan's children will not thank him for staying in the village. This is decisive in inducing Ivan to leave. His character immediately changes: he becomes tight-lipped, stubborn, and even violent, raising his hand to Katerina for the first time in their marriage and threatening the kolkhoz chairman with a poker in order to get his passport. Significantly, the document which gives him the right to travel anywhere does not bring him any real feeling of relief: such freedom is alien to his strongly rooted nature. Nor can he stand it in practice. He becomes helpless as soon as he leaves the village, becomes separated from Mit'ka, and loses his railway ticket. Although he subsequently recovers both, he can by then only gasp: 'I don't want anything, just let me get back home.'

Katerina's death challenges the naïve pantheistic mysticism by which Ivan has hitherto lived. He has never been a Christian: indeed, he swapped the old Drynov family Bible for an accordion, in accordance with his own instinctive concept of the divine. Katerina's death brings about a genuine break in the unity in which he has lived. He cannot comprehend how it is that she has gone, but everything else has stayed put. Walking confusedly through the forest one day in his grief, Ivan loses his way, stumbles helplessly among unfamiliar trees, spends a night in the open, and begins to fear that he too will die, from hunger and exhaustion:

Ivan Afrikanovich had never before been afraid of death. He had always thought: it's impossible that nothing should remain of a man. The soul, or whatever it may be, *that* must remain, that couldn't just disappear altogether. And God or not-God, there must be something on the other side. . . .

But now he suddenly felt frightened in the face of death, and in his despair hard, fleeting thoughts went through his mind.

'No, of course, there's nothing there. Nothing. Everything will disappear, everything will come to an end. And I will disappear, that's how things are. . . . Well, Katerina has disappeared, hasn't she? Where is she now? Nothing remains of her, and nothing will remain of you. You used to be, and now of a sudden you're not any more. Vanished into thin air. . . . But then who thought it all up, and why? Life, this forest, things like, well, mosses, boots, berries? How did it all start, how will it end, what is it all about?'[22]

Ivan gropes his way towards a new understanding of himself as a finite being among other finite beings, part of the life of nature, which continually renews itself. This is as far as he can get in coming to terms with death.

In some ways Ivan Afrikanovich is a kind of peasant Yuri Zhivago. He shows the same childlike sensitivity, the same preoccupation with ultimate questions, especially that of immortality, and the same irresponsibility towards a loved family (he leaves Katerina soon after childbirth, at the height of the haymaking). Belov's novel, furthermore, has some of the characteristics of Pasternak's: the sense of the deep inter-relatedness of men, animals and things, of individuality as rooted in some super-individual personal being, as well as the indifference, indeed distaste, towards politics and the people who act through politics.

In his later works, Belov maintains this outlook but broadens his approach by bringing to bear on his rural material a fuller awareness of history and peasant folklore. In *A Carpenter's Tales* (*Plotnitskie rasskazy*, 1968), the framework is the lifelong feud of two old villagers, Olesha[23] Smolin and Aviner Kozonkov. The narrator, a townsman returned to his native village for the vacation – and in the process of rediscovering his roots – hears from both of them the story of their lives. He also tries misguidedly to reconcile them, not realizing either the depth of their enmity or the paradoxical need they have for each other as butts for the accumulated resentments of unsatisfactory lives.

The conflict is in the past, but the shadow remains over them. Aviner comes from a family of poor peasants: his father was perpetually borrowing money and having his property confiscated for tax arrears. He himself grew up lazy and crafty, adept at getting out of work and at shifting the blame for his misdeeds onto others. These qualities well fitted him to become a founding member of the local poor peasants' group (*gruppa bednoty*) after the Revolution, and later a secretary of the village soviet. He took a leading role in the anti-religious campaign (urinating from the church tower before hurling down the bells) and in the expropriation of the better-off peasants during collectivization. In fact, though, like many early party activists, he did not do well out of his tenure of office, and remains in his old age an impecunious and eccentric villager. He is portrayed as a thoroughly unpeasant-like personality, tottering uncertainly through the snow on a stick, with long white hands, smart and quick in his motions. He has no instinct for family life. His house, guarded by a huge and noisy wolf-hound, is unwelcoming, and the narrator feels embarrassed when visiting him. His wife plays no real part in his life, his daughter is a discontented and affected townswoman, and his little grandson, neglected all day, lies on the stove and wails importunately. Aviner creates around himself an atmosphere of cold and avarice.

Olesha is a complete contrast to Aviner. He comes of a sturdy peasant family. His father cleared a cutting in the forest, grew flax there, earned the money for a horse, and achieved a modest level of prosperity which survived NEP but was dissipated by the kolkhoz. Olesha is a man skilled both as a farmer and as a carpenter. His hut is cosy, samovar always on the boil, and his wife is a cheerful companion. He loves to tell stories of his past, not, as does Aviner, in the hope of wheedling a personal pension, but for the sheer pleasure of it.[24]

This contrast has a moral dimension. Olesha is a man who has worked out his own morality. His initial model was his father, who taught him to plough almost before he was strong enough – 'His whole life was open for everyone to see. He worked all his life to his dying hour, and he who works has nothing to hide.'[25] But the circumstances of Olesha's own life, as shaped by church and state, have brought him 'confusion', as he terms it. He dates his first moral dilemma from the time his mother instructed him to tell the priest 'I am a sinner.' He was unable to recall committing any sins, for which the priest called him a liar and his mother gave him a hiding. From then on he used to smoke in order to have a sin to confess – a prerevolutionary example of the *mauvaise foi* induced by an externally imposed ideology. He carried from this experience the later mature reflection, reminiscent of the peasant sectarians, that 'if you repent, then do so to yourself. No priest can stand against your own conscience. . . . To live without conscience is no life at all. We would all slit one another's throats.'[26]

In the outlook which the narrator learns through his conversations with Olesha, conscience, regular work, creativity and immortality all belong together. A man who works creates something to which he has a right during his life, and which gives service to himself, his family and to others. He helps to create the prosperity of the community. At one stage Olesha reproaches Aviner:

'For you . . . everything in the village was very simple: on the one side poor peasants, and on the other kulaks. And between them the middle peasants – neither one thing nor the other. Three categories. In actual fact there were more like thirty-three. Why, even the cobblers and charcoal-burners got it in the neck. "Private enterprise" you used to chant, "they're running their own business."'
'Well, and wasn't it their own?'
'Of course it was. Whose else should it have been? Without that private business everyone for miles around went barefoot the next autumn, when Misha the cobbler was cleaned out.'[27]

In Olesha's view, a man who by his own labour creates wealth for himself and for the community is not a kulak. But a man who sells what he has *bought,* or who hires others to do his work for him, is an exploiter. When Aviner calls Fedulënok an exploiter because he hired labour for the haymaking and harvesting, Olesha corrects him: 'That wasn't hiring, that was pomochi. . . .'[28] *Pomochi* is the term for the traditional mutual help given by villagers to one another during periods of intense work, such as haymaking and harvesting, when no family can cope single-handed with the demands of its own plot of land. In comparison with this inherited system, the collective labour of the kolkhoz is shown to function badly. It is organized by officials who do not understand the land, and the proceeds are not for the benefit of the community but go to maintain an army of officials. 'And the kolkhozniks get what's left over. Sometimes damn all.'[29] This poverty and lack of independence is what has demoralized the village, so that all the able-bodied men have pushed off elsewhere, and the only person left to mind the horses is an old woman with a hernia.

Like Ivan Afrikanovich, Olesha is troubled by the problem of death and the ending of personal identity. The author gives him an improvised answer, reminiscent of that offered by Yury Zhivago to Tonya's mother. Schubert's song-cycle *Die schöne Müllerin* is being played on the transistor radio, and the narrator remarks that in some form Schubert has survived in his songs. Similarly:

'You've made me a bath-house. . . . When you die, I shall come on vacation and take my baths. I shall be thinking about the same things as you are now, and I shall remember you. So you see, in fact you'll still be inside me, even though you've been dead many years.'[30]

The idea is put forward only tentatively, and Olesha is not convinced by it, but it fits the tone and structure of the work, with its strictly delineated contrast between the men of good conscience who work and those of bad conscience who neither want to nor know how to. This is the fundamental contrast between Olesha and Aviner.

In *Vologda Whimsies* (*Bukhtiny vologodskie*, 1969), Belov's form is the traditional Russian *skazka* (fairy tale), with a considerable dose of primitive pagan animism and a dash of zany humour thrown in. The work consists of a series of short fantastic tales told by an old *skazitel'* (folk narrator), Kuz'ma Ivanovich. He is the resourceful, resilient peasant of the *skazka,* with an endless fund of bright ideas and convenient wizardry for all occasions. He lives on easy terms with men and animals, and indeed with the supernatural – he has a life before birth and one after death. In this brightly-coloured world, the activities of the Soviet state appear as yet another pagan force, capricious and sometimes threatening, but similar in nature to the other difficulties the peasant has to face.

The implications of the genre Belov has chosen here are intriguing and ambiguous. The word *bukhtina,* as we are given to understand from Dal's definition at the head of the work, denotes a mixture of joke, nonsense and legend. The *bukhtina,* Kuz'ma Ivanovich asserts, is 'essential to life – a bukhtina cheers you up without wine, takes years off you.'[31] In that way it contains some core of spiritual truth. At the same time, there *is* a distinction between it and truth as we normally understand it, and even as it is normally presented in a work of fiction. This distinction is underlined in Kuz'ma Ivanovich's remark: 'I don't know what folk have come to nowadays. When you tell them fairy tales [*bukhtiny*] they drink it in. But if you start telling the truth, nobody listens.'[32] The implication is that here Belov is talking of the gullible modern audience of mass communications. He feels the need to redress the balance by telling *bukhtiny* of the more traditional kind.

Clearly the work represents an attempt to understand fifty years of Soviet rule in the village from the viewpoint of traditional Russian peasant culture, though transmitted in a self-consciously literary way. Sometimes Kuz'ma Ivanovich acts out figures of speech: thus, when he is hungry, he literally 'puts his teeth on the shelf'. Or he highlights concepts in comic manner. When he is in danger of being elected brigade leader after the war, he dramatizes the bureaucratization of agriculture as 'an infectious disease, brought back from Germany after the war ... passed on through pencils and paper.' When, in spite of his best efforts, he *is* in fact elected brigade leader, he solves the dilemmas of that post by the simple expedient of appointing every member of his brigade to an official position of some sort – their income rises steeply, and they no longer have to do any work. He decides that the only way to get maize to grow in the unpromising soil is to stop the sun going behind the clouds, which he does by fastening it to a piece of string like a kite.[33] These and other devices, as in Saltykov-Shchedrin's fables, satirize contemporary reality by a mixture of irony, exaggeration, literary conceit and earthy common sense.

Again as in the fable, animals sometimes represent human types. The ruff (*ërsh*) is a sly, vicious fish and a perpetual troublemaker whom Kuz'ma Ivanovich calls a *khunveibin,* the usual Russian name for the Red Guards of the Chinese Cultural Revolution. There is the good natured bear who drinks all winter in his lair and, having drunk, becomes so generous that he will do all sorts of work for people without payment. Eventually he has to beg in order to survive, and in the end he is hunted down and slaughtered by state trappers as a 'creature of prey'. It is the ruffs who flourish in this society, while the bears are eliminated.

Perhaps the most intriguing part of the work is Kuz'ma's visit to the underworld, which, like that of Tvardovsky's Vasily Terkin, is used to illuminate the modern Soviet world. First of all, Kuz'ma learns from the infernal gatekeeper that heaven and hell have been combined in an 'amalgamation of departments':

'Is that better or worse?'
'Depends how you look at it. Now everyone is equal, all sinners have had their rights restored.'
'So it's all right to sin now?'
'That's your affair. It doesn't concern us.'

In this amoral world, men do not act – they spend their time thinking – not about anything in particular, but about the process of thinking. Nor is it possible to do any normal work: when Kuz'ma wants to cut some firewood (any peasant's hands would itch to do the same), his old friend Andrei, partner of many an earthly prank but now a denizen of the underworld, tells him he must have a 'number' from the authorities. Nobody will speak to him further. Kuz'ma soon decides, with the insouciant contempt for the authorities permitted to the hero of a *skazka,* that he will quit this amoral, solipsistic, impersonal and bureaucratic world, return to life before the grave, and achieve immortality in his own individual way by sticking days *on* the calendar instead of tearing them off.[34]

Since 1972 Belov has been publishing what is apparently intended to be a cycle of novels dealing with the far northern village during the last period when it lived more or less by its own laws and traditions – on the eve of mass collectivization at the end of the twenties. Hence the title of his novel *The Eve* (*Kanuny,* 1972–76). It expands the historical themes of *A Carpenter's Tales* into a more or less explicit apology for the ideas of Bukharin and the Right Opposition of 1928–29.[35] Instead of Aviner Kozonkov we now have Ignakha Sopronov, another outcast of the peasant community, poacher and barge-hauler in his time, despised and beaten by the village lads and girls alike. Significantly, he is surrounded by demonic imagery, which Belov did not use for Aviner. He makes his first appearance dramatically and unexpectedly to young Petya Girin when the latter, playing a prank, is wrapped in a sheet, disguised as a corpse. Later, he materializes at the altar in the middle of a wedding service, which he disrupts with political speeches.[36]

Like Aviner, Sopronov makes it his business to set up a group of poor peasants and to enforce a crude threefold classification of the rural population as 'poor peasants, middle peasants and kulaks'. At the public meeting he calls for this purpose there is much opposition to both ideas. Afrikan Drynov (father of Ivan, who is thus retrospectively given ancestry) protests that giving credits to poor peasants is like giving medicines to a dead man. Daniil Pachin, a kulak in Sopronov's eyes, has three cows, but is defended by numerous onlookers, in the spirit of Olesha, as a man who does not engage in commerce for profit or hire labour; and he is in fact saved at the last moment by a letter from none other than Kalinin, the president of the Soviet Union. For the moment Sopronov is defeated and dismissed from his post as secretary of the local party cell. But he goes out shouting 'It's not you who appointed me; it's not for you to dismiss me!'[37]

At the centre of the community which Sopronov is trying to destroy are two well-established families, newly united by marriage between Pashka Pachin and Vera Rogova. We see much of the traditional, busy way of life of both families. The wedding is described in loving detail, both the lament in the bride's house, according to old custom, and the ceremony in the church (interrupted by Sopronov). Pashka is a true son of his family: two days of peaceful married bliss are enough for him, and he already itches to start ensuring his new family's prosperity by felling a huge fir tree and building a windmill. In a long set-piece, complete with *chastushki* (ditties) and ribald couplets, the author describes the *pomochi,* the villagers coming together to fell and transport the tree in return for the hospitality of the Pachin family.

As soon as the mill is nearly complete, however, Ignakha Sopronov announces that, on the strength of it, Pashka's taxes are being trebled: so that, even before the mill can be of use to its owner, it is a burden to him. This is the product of the party's new policy from the Fifteenth Congress of December 1927, when the Bukharin wing suffered its first serious reverse. The party decided then to strengthen the organization of poor peasants and to squeeze the 'kulak' by taxing him ruinously. Sopronov brings to these tasks a strong element of personal malice, especially against Pashka (whom he tries to shoot at the end of the novel).[38]

What is going on is clearly shown to be the destruction not only of peasant prosperity but in a very real sense of the village community itself. When news of the tax rise reaches the village, many families are found to be threatened with destitution:

That night half the village got no sleep. In many homes lamps and tapers burned till dawn. In the morning the womenfolk let out the animals and started to rush from house to house: in many homesteads women could be heard crying or men swearing and shouting. Cows, calves and sheep wandered restlessly round the back alleys; all the animals could feel the tension, and bleated, mooed and snorted in bewilderment and alarm. Children and little sleepy toddlers got under their elders' feet, and were cuffed or had their ears boxed for nothing. Some tried crying, but soon gave up, because nobody took any notice of them.[39]

This is not simply a political novel, however. It has a philosophical underpinning which goes further than that outlined in *A Carpenter's Tales.* Father Irinei, the aged rural dean, sees the basic cause of the growing destruction in the fact that Bolsheviks 'are taking away from man his immortality . . . without which life is meaningless', and by depriving the people of their faith are driving them back to primitive paganism.[40] As for intellectuals, reason without faith, he warns, 'is doomed to sterility and ends by denying even reason itself.'[41] This reproach is addressed to Prozorov, a former landowner, once a member of the Social Democratic Party, and an atheist, but now nevertheless very critical of the Bolsheviks. Prozorov is the nineteenth-century *intelligent* (significantly his surname recalls Chekhov's *Three Sisters*), tormented by the absence of God and by the meaninglessness of life in the face of inevitable death. 'Why has nature, in my person, become conscious of itself?' he asks. His inner emptiness seems part of the silence and of the eery, 'unnatural' midnight light of the northern summer night, and he is haunted by the perfect mirror image of the empty sky in a completely calm pond:

As a child, at his aunt's, he used to stand on the river bank and stare at that bottomless inverted sky. It had seemed to him then that where the grass under him gave out there was a bottomless abyss. He had been terrified of jumping into that gulf of sky, and it was so pleasant afterwards to return to reality, to feel the sandy bed under his feet, and to break with his elbows the infinity reflected in the water. That, however, was in the pond: up above in the sky that same infinity never disappeared, it was always there, and there was no way of escaping from it. . . .[42]

As so often in Belov, the natural image here becomes an expression of Prozorov's state of mind, and of the metaphysical terror which drives him close to suicide. What returns him to life is a dream he has, in which he imagines that he is dead and that he perceives his own non-existence. He wakes on the thought that he cannot be dead because he is still able to think, and this reassertion of his own existence is a great relief to him. (This experience is remarkably similar, psychologically and philosophically, to Descartes's description of the night in a 'stove' when he discovered his basic principle, 'I think, therefore I am.')

Pashka Pachin, when he thinks Ignakha Sopronov is about to kill him, experiences the same splitting of the personality into observer and lifeless observed matter. In both cases the narrator interprets this as showing the soul to be separate from the body, and coming from higher or deeper origins, which, if man denies them, become threatening emptinesses.

Most of the villagers still have contact with their 'soul' in this sense, through their communal experience (from which Prozorov is excluded by education and the remnants of his social rank), in the songs they sing at festivals and during *pomochi,* in dancing and games, in fairy tales, and in the daily and annual rhythm of agricultural work which makes up the texture of the novel. Sopronov, who has broken away from these roots, now wants to destroy them, and thus to 'take away man's immortality', as Father Irinei observes. By implication, one may say that this applies to the whole of what we know the Bolsheviks are about to do in the villages.

So Belov, the lyrical and reflective ruralist, has become a political writer, whose implicit message is that the party should re-examine the whole basis of its approach to agriculture and the village. But, as we have seen, this political stance reflects a firmly founded philosophical position.

*   *

The individual psychology of the peasant, already more developed in Belov than in Abramov or Zalygin, is analysed yet more meticulously in the work of the Siberian writer Valentin Rasputin. Comparatively speaking, he is less interested in the external and collective aspects of village life, nor does he attempt to mould his language to the peasant way of thinking. His language is more classical, more obviously authorial, though still containing a sprinkling of dialect words and phrases. His contribution has been to translate the familiar themes of 'village prose' into a network of closely observed individual emotional relationships, which he does usually by portraying some crisis as it affects the villagers, in *The Final Stage* (*Poslednii srok*, 1970) the death of an old woman, in *Mark You This* (*Zhivi i pomni*, 1974) the clandestine arrival of a deserter just before the end of the war, in *Farewell to Matëra* (*Proshchanie s Matëroi*, 1976) the impending flooding of an island village for a hydroelectric scheme.

In *The Final Stage* death becomes the prism through which the changing village is seen. However, as we shall come to expect with Rasputin, death also raises metaphysical concerns. How does an eighty-year-old woman look back on her own life in the light of imminent death? How do her children regard her death, and how do they evaluate what they have imbibed from their mother and from the village of which she is a part?

The four children reunited by her expected death are very different from one another. Indeed, as they gather on the first evening round the wooden table their father put together fifty years ago, little seems to unite them. Varvara, the eldest daughter, who has stayed in the countryside, is heavily middle-aged, exhausted by years of child-rearing, gauche and sentimental, resentful of the greater sophistication of the townsfolk of the family. Lyusya, now a townswoman herself, is more straightforward, neat and efficient, spiritually very distant from her mother and from the village which she left years ago. Il'ya, small and balding, nervous from years of living with a dominating wife in the town, tends to agree with whoever is speaking. Mikhail, the youngest, who has stayed in the village to look after mother, is alternately dashing and morose, forthcoming and retiring. There are two boundary lines which are conspicuous as potential flashpoints of hostility among them, that which divides town from country, and that which divides men from women. Varvara and Mikhail feel a certain inferiority in the face of their urban siblings; and the other boundary is no less important since, while the men can drink and behave irresponsibly, the women (including Mikhail's wife, Nadya) must remain sober and cope with the practical problems raised by illness and death. As it happens, these two boundary lines intersect, so that no one of the children understands any of the others fully. Varvara and Mikhail are united in their resentment at the fact that Il'ya and Lyusya rarely visit their mother, but Varvara is shocked and repelled at Mikhail's drinking.

Each of the children differs also in his or her attitude to death. Mikhail welcomes its imminence as a release, and does not trouble to hide the fact. Varvara, gauche and uncertain of herself, surrounds it with exaggerated respect and drama, breaking out into sporadic wailings, and admonishing her insufficiently awestruck confreres to show more concern. Lyusya, by contrast, deals with it by brisk denials, by abrupt assertions that mother will live another ten years, and that everyone must get on and live their lives. Il'ya, not certain what he feels, alternately supports Mikhail and Lyusya. None of them makes real contact with their mother, or tries to understand what death, or her past life, mean to her. In fact the author presents their various evasions as a kind of foreground chatter, against the more sombre background sections where he tells of Anna's own reactions, using his own authorial language.

Anna views death calmly, as a friend with whom she is intimate as with none of her children, as the natural culmination of and release from a life which was hard, monotonous and often far from rewarding, but which has meaning for her because it was the only one she had and because she had produced offspring as its continuation. She thinks of death as a time of revelation and perhaps of consolation:

She believed that when she died she would learn ... many secrets which it is not given to us to know in life and which would reveal to her the ultimate mystery: what her life had been, and what it would be in the future. She was afraid of trying to look ahead, but all the same in recent years she had thought more and more often about the sun, the earth, the grass, the birds, the trees, the rain and the snow, and about everything that exists alongside man, giving him joy, and preparing him for the end by promising him succour and comfort.[43]

This withdrawal from people and activities, the involuntary meditation upon nature is a preparation for her renunciation of individual human status.

She has always lived in the same village, 'like a tree in the woods, carrying out the same human tasks as her mother had done'. Her children have all seen something of other places, but she does not envy them. The extent of her alienation from the urban world is shown in her reaction to the letters she receives from her youngest daughter, Tanya (who never arrives to see her on her deathbed). She trembles before them as before hieroglyphic tablets containing secret and sacred messages. Nor can she really understand most of them: her picture of town life is so dim that she does not see how people lacking a plot of land and a cow can avoid starvation.[44]

She has remained the same person, but the village has changed greatly and irreversibly. Quite apart from the collectivization, a timber works has been set up not far away, and attracts the able-bodied young people by offering them twice the wage they can earn in the village. Furthermore, after the war, during the amalgamation of collective farms, theirs was subordinated to one fifty kilometres away, from where it is unprofitable to send machinery to cultivate the village's infertile fields. So the village is gradually dying out, its ploughed land running to weed. Anna is aware of this change, and tells her crony, Mironikha, the only person with whom she maintains a relationship based on mutual understanding: 'After we're gone there'll be a different kind of old woman around: literate, up to date, understanding what's going on in the world. You and I are in the wrong neck of the woods. We've strayed into other people's lifetime.'[45]

To see her family again before her death does not in any real sense renew relationships, but does enable Anna to look back on her life as a whole. Her children are the product and meaning of that life, and it is her vision of that fact which dictates her parting exhortation to them: 'Make sure you visit one another often, and don't forget one another.

And come back here as well: your whole kith and kin is here. And I shall be here, I'll not be leaving anywhere.[46] That is her vision of the integration of family and village. But, of course, her children do not share it.

The village is Mikhail's fate now, one to which he has been condemned by his mother's longevity. His way of life means continual anxiety and self-denial, from which he seeks refuge in drink. As he explains to Il'ya while they sit in the bath-house in splendid masculine seclusion sharing a bottle of vodka intended for the funeral: 'We're bound hand and foot at home and at work. You just have to gasp how much you were supposed to do and haven't done. All the time, you ought to do this, you ought to do that. . . . But once you've had a drink, there's no problem about that: you've done everything you had to do'.[47] He finds release for his worries and his pent-up aggression towards his mother in a horrifying scene when, before her face, he invites anyone who will to take her off his hands.

For Lyusya the significance of the home village is quite different. Her professional life and its cares have taken her over completely, and memories of her rural childhood lie 'shoved into a distant and dusty corner, like a grab-bag of old rubbish which had served its time'. Walking one day, however, in the hills above the village, she comes upon abandoned fields, and realizes with a pang of guilt that she had once harrowed that field with an old exhausted horse. Momentarily she is overcome by remorse at having abandoned and forgotten this part of her own and others' heritage. But it is not suggested that this experience changes her life in any way, except perhaps in hastening her determination to get away and return to the town where she will not be disturbed by such memories.

None of the children stays long enough to see the event they have come to witness and mark. Their arrival gives Anna unexpected strength, and she revives for a few more days, long enough for them to feel that there is no point in hanging about in the village waiting for what may still be months ahead. Then, as soon as they go, their mother dies. The author offers no further comment, but all the earlier material would lead us to expect that her children will never meet together again. A family has broken up, and a rural community has moved one step closer to final dissolution.

In *Mark You This* Rasputin shifts even more to individual psychological analysis, but in doing so continues to throw light on the forces that hold families and communities together. The plot is a simple one: in the last winter of the war a deserter, Andrei Gus'kov, returns to his native Siberian village, on the banks of the Angara. Knowing he would certainly be shot if he showed himself, he settles in an old hut across the river and makes his presence known only to his wife, Nastëna. They re-establish a clandestine married life and Nastëna becomes pregnant, but in the end, torn by the double life she has to lead, the secrecy she must maintain and the disgrace to which the birth of an apparently illegitimate child would expose her, she commits suicide.

The focus of the work is on the development of Andrei and Nastëna and their relations with each other. Nastëna (like Shukshin's Egor Prokudin[48]) is an orphan of the social upheavals of the early thirties: her father was killed 'by a stray shot' in the collectivization, her mother died of starvation in the famine of 1933.[49] When Andrei married her and brought her to his parents' home in the little village of Atamanovka, it was a great and joyful change in her life, even though her mother-in-law turned out to be lazy and ready to exploit the new worker in the house. The first four years of her marriage with Andrei (until he was drafted into the army) were mixed, the chief problem being that she did not bear any children. Andrei at times would overwhelm her with reproaches and even beat her – though, of course, there was absolutely no evidence that she rather than he was infertile.

This brings us to the question of why Andrei deserted. The reason was partly an external one: he had fought for more than three years and then been invalided with a serious injury to a hospital in western Siberia, and he took it for granted that he would be given leave to see his family before having to report back to the front. Instead he received the unexpected order to return to his unit straight away. No less important, however, was Andrei's feeling of guilt towards his wife, of an incomplete relationship with her, something which he wanted to repair before his possible death. This feeling expresses itself in a haunting dream, in which Nastëna appears to him in the form of a ragged small girl, complaining of having a horde of children to look after, and reproaching him for staying away from home and not helping her with them.

There are a number of points of interest about this dream. First, that Nastëna also dreams, from the other side, as it were, that she had gone to Andrei on the battlefield to beg for help with her children. Excluding telepathy for the moment, that suggests some strong common and unacknowledged feeling in their married relationship.

Secondly, the dream situation is, in one obvious sense, the *reverse* of their actual marital problem. Yet in another sense it represents the truth of their relationship: Nastëna had remained the ragged orphan, taken for granted by Andrei, as well as by his mother, seen as a beast of burden, and forced in addition to take the *emotional* weight of blame for perceived marital failure. Matured by the hardships and deprivations of war, Andrei comes to realize the importance of his marriage to him and how he had under-valued it and almost disrupted it by his behaviour. This new awareness is what stimulates the disastrous journey home which drags out and transforms itself into desertion before he even reaches his goal.

However, Andrei is more complicated than that. There is about him a strong streak of irresponsibility, and of inability to accept and respond to other people's feelings. On his way home he strikes up a strong (and apparently adulterous) relationship with a mute woman. She is a kind of super-(or sub-)Nastëna, who accepts him with a ready but rather expressionless smile, shows no strong feelings and demands nothing of him. In the end he can stand it no longer, but for a time it fulfils his nature. This episode illuminates his relations with Nastëna when he returns. He imposes himself on her, demands that she keeps his existence a secret and succeeds, ironically at this stage, in getting her with child, whilst at times seeing quite clearly what he is doing and being consumed by contrition. Absolutely characteristic is his first reaction to the news of Nastëna's pregnancy: without a thought for her embarrassing situation, he is simply overjoyed at the prospect of leaving progeny in the world, and feels he has not lived in vain. And this remains his dominant feeling, even though he is aware of the strains he is putting on Nastëna. The resultant discord undermines their relationship and drives Nastëna further towards her end.

The artificiality of their situation gradually destroys both of them as personalities. One day Andrei crosses the river secretly and goes to look at Atamanovka, but his strongest emotion is one of destructiveness: he is strongly tempted to set fire to the windmill where he loved to work as a boy, and he captures and kills a calf in front of its mother, not so much for meat as out of the sheer will to destroy. Significantly, at this moment he remembers and longs for the mute woman, Tanya:

He would have liked to take her away with him to the ends of the earth, where there were no people, and there lose the power of speech and, as an act of vengeance, enjoy having his will of her, then take pity on her and again have his will of her – she would tolerate it all and be happy with the least trifle.[50]

Later on, as physical and emotional exhaustion take their toll, Andrei becomes suspicious of Nastëna, takes her slightest reluctance as proof that she wants to abandon him, and in this way gradually destroys the intimacy they still manage to recapture at first.

The effect on Nastëna is no less strong. We are shown her life against the background of the last months of the war and the victory celebrations. But she can no longer be part of it, alienated as she is by the secret she carries within her. When the first menfolk return from the front and the women gather,

She could neither talk, nor cry, nor sing along with everybody else. As never before, Nastëna realized that she hadn't the right to do anything like that. It would all be a pretence and a deception – so she just had to listen and watch what the others were doing and saying, being careful not to give herself away or attract attention.[51]

She has to learn to lie and to steal – a gun, some potatoes, whatever Andrei needs. She has to practise deception to get away to see him. And in the end she has to allow herself to be driven out of the house when her mother-in-law finds out she is pregnant and naturally assumes that she has been unfaithful to Andrei. At the same time the police are looking for Andrei, and the villagers begin to suspect that Nastëna knows where he is, so that people take to following her and watching her movements. In this way she ceases, both subjectively and objectively, to be a member of the community. She becomes an orphan yet again, in a new and as yet unfamiliar way, and in the end these strains destroy her completely.

The village community plays a major part in Nastëna's fate. It represents the only security she has known since early childhood. She shares, and is content to share, the hardships of rural female labour during the war, haymaking, reaping and even logging. She tries to share also in their celebrations at the long-awaited victory. But the community is not a tolerant one. When her pregnancy becomes obvious, her old friend Nadya takes her in, but no one else offers her anything but ridicule and condemnation. The kolkhoz chairman follows her to discover Andrei's hiding place, and his pursuit is the last straw that drives her to suicide.

Mark You This provides a counterpoint to Rasputin's other major novels, for it suggests that the forces which bind a community together – loyalty, patriotism, puritan morality – can also lead to the rejection of individual members of that community. Villages are not only idyllic and harmonious societies which may be undermined by external forces: they carry within themselves some of the seeds of their own destruction.

In *Farewell to Matëra* death is writ large, for what is now imminent is the death of a whole community, the island village of Matëra on the Angara, due to be flooded by the completion of a hydroelectric scheme. This village is everything that Soviet economic growth has consigned to the past. Wandering by the river, Dar'ya, the old woman who is the focal character of the novel, reflects that 'there is nothing more unjust than when everything, whether a tree or a man, lives long enough to become useless and turns into a burden; of the countless sins sent into this world to be redeemed and expiated, that one alone is held to be unpardonable.'[52]

Dar'ya has lived on the island all her life and has never seen any other place. Her identity is with the meadows she has scythed, the fields she has ploughed, the cows she has milked, and above all with the hut where she and her forbears have lived and the graves where they lie. She knows her ancestry going back a century and a half, and she sees the meaning of her life in continuing her ancestors' traditions, guarding and extending their achievements for her descendants. This meaning of course is abruptly nullified by the island's impending destruction. Hers is a particularly dramatic and painful example of the general fate of old people in rapidly modernizing societies.

Sometimes Dar'ya is depressed by this fate, but often she fights vigorously against it to reassert the values she has lived by, in reaction against, for example, her grandson Andrei, who has no time for the ramshackle old village and leaves it for the last time without a backward glance. He is going off to work on the hydroelectric dam which will destroy it, because he believes that mankind is advancing, building a great future, and he wants to be 'on the front line'. Pavel, his father (and Dar'ya's son), demurs at the military imagery, but understands the sentiment, and can sympathize with it. Dar'ya, however, regards the whole idea of a great man-made future as dangerous folly:

'I've taken a good look at people in my life, and I can tell you, they're like children. Whatever they may think of themselves, they're all like children really. To be pitied. And if you don't pity yourself, that's only because you're young. While your juices are fresh, you think that you're strong, that you can do anything. No, my lad. I don't know anybody who isn't to be pitied. Even if he has seven-league boots.... You can't leap out of your human skin, Andrei, you just can't do it. No one ever has. If you try, you'll only bark your shins and rupture yourself to no purpose. You won't achieve anything. And while you're straining every nerve to quit your own skin, death will come for you, and won't let you go. People have forgotten their God-given place, that's what I say. We're no better than those who have lived before us. And we've no right to take so much upon ourselves.'[53]

People used to live according to their conscience – or at least would know what conscience was when they transgressed its commands – before they took on themselves overweening projects beyond their power to fulfil. Dar'ya sees man's attempt to master nature as worse than self-defeating:

'Man thinks he's master of life, but he lost that mastery lo-o-ong ago. . . . Life has got the better of him, has climbed onto his back and demands what she wants of him. He ought to take the time to turn around, hold her back, slow down a bit and take stock of what's still there and what's been carried away by the winds. But no, no, he makes it worse, he tries to drive her on and on! That way he'll overstrain himself, he can't last out. In fact he's overstrained himself already. . . .'[54]

This is not just a grandmotherly comment on modernity. It is a reflection on the Promethean Soviet experiment supported by the plot, structure and narrative stance of the whole work.

The new sovkhoz settlement, to which the inhabitants of Matëra are to be moved, consists of multi-storey apartment blocks surrounded by tiny garden plots, all in a forest clearing on the northern slope of a hill. Because of incompetent building, there is water in the cellars, and hence nowhere to keep food. There is no meadow land for grass, which makes it impossible to keep cattle, and the ground is so rocky that topsoil has to be brought in from elsewhere for the gardens. 'It's all topsy-turvy, bringing the earth to the gardens, instead of the gardens to the earth.'[55] Pavel, as a member of the intermediate generation, accepts the need for progress, but does not see why it has to be accomplished in such an ill-considered manner. 'I must be getting old,' he thinks, 'if I don't understand it. The young people understand. It doesn't even occur to them to question it. If things are done that way they think it must be right. . . . Everything that happens is for the best, so that life shall be happier and more interesting.'[56]

As this excerpt suggests, Pavel begins by doubting himself and ends by doubting what is going on around him. He is appalled by the dependence to which the younger generation is forced, not only in their outlook, but in their very physical needs:

If the earth won't grow bread, then bread will be brought to you, ready threshed, baked, in black, white and grey loaves – take what you want! If you no longer have a cow to milk, then milk will be brought, so that you don't have to bother with cows and scrub around the bushes gathering hay.[57]

Above all, Pavel cannot see Dar'ya adapting to this way of life. He finds it physically impossible to imagine her in this 'settlement of urban type', because he knows she will find nothing to do there: her long-established skills will be useless, and her habits meaningless. So powerful is this feeling that Pavel puts off ferrying Dar'ya across from the doomed island till the last possible moment. Eventually Vorontsov, chairman of the village soviet, comes to him in fury because the state commission is due to take over the reservoir basin the next day. He and Pavel go out in a motor boat in the middle of the night to take off the last remaining old women, now cowering in a barrack-hut built by Kolchak's men in the civil war, because all the other buildings have been burnt down.

At this point, near the end of the work, another world, pre-communist, pre-industrial, pre-scientific, even pre-Christian, reasserts itself. From the beginning there have been scattered intimations of this world. There is a strange little animal on the island, little bigger than a cat, and it is the Master (or perhaps one should say the Spirit) of the island. It knows every plant and every living creature on the island, it knows their *feelings* and their *future*, it knows how human beings dream at night, and how they reach out in those dreams to their dead loved ones:

Only at night do the living cast off from the firm shore and make contact with the dead: the dead come to them in the flesh and ask for the truth, so that they may pass it still further on, to those whom *they* remember. And there is much that the living say in a state of unconsciousness and release but which on waking they cannot remember, as they grope to explain to themselves the last few fleeting visions.[58]

It is this rich interior life that the old women are still in contact with; and by ignoring or denying it the young have converted it into a negative power, so that it rides them and destroys them. Dar'ya harnesses this power of the unconscious and ancestral by meditation, ritual and prayer. When she feels lost and wants to know how to order the final parting from the old family hut, she goes to the cemetery to spend time among the family graves (now with their crosses and nameplates removed) and to confess to them her bewilderment and her feeling of guilt at not having protected them better. It seems to her that she hears them replying and telling her to tidy up and decorate the hut as for a festival. Her self-assurance recovered, she spends the last couple of days whitewashing the hut and embellishing it with fir branches. On the last day she is 'filled with a blessed and tranquil feeling that she was doing everything aright', and spends the last night in prayer. The whole of the next day, while the hut is being burned, she wanders around the island, away from the village, and afterwards remembers only that she had 'walked on and on, as far as her strength would take her, without stumbling, and that all the time some small animal which she had never seen before seemed to be running along at her side and trying to look into her eyes.'[59]

The indomitable spirit of the island is symbolized by the huge old larch tree near the cemetery 'rising above everything else as a shepherd towers over his sheep'.[60] Each year the islanders used to bring it Easter and Whitsun gifts to placate its regal spirit. Some said that it alone riveted the island to the river bed, and that as long as it stood the island would remain. The lumbermen come along to fell it with a confidence which, significantly, they express in arithmetical form ('She'll not get away from us – five fives are twenty-five with us.'); but, though they try axes, mechanical saws and fire, nothing will pierce or consume the tree's ancient, tough bark.[61]

The ending picks up these intimations of another world. The motor boat on which Pavel and Vorontsov go out to the island gets lost in the fog and drifts helplessly about in the broad river, unable to get any bearings. On the island itself the old women cower in the hut occupied by Bogodul (himself a strong pagan figure, described in terms not unlike the larch tree, with tough, blackened skin so hard that no snake bite can pierce it).[62] In the mysterious light they hear the intermittent noise of a motor boat, which fades away before the howling of the Master.

Thus the past and present of Matëra fade out in fog which makes the world of clairvoyant animals, communication with the dead and immortal trees seem just as real as that of sovkhozes and hydroelectric power stations. What has seemed imminent and inevitable throughout the work now suddenly seems doubtful and unreal. For a moment – but it *is* the end of the novel – the ancestors have taken over again.

It is striking that both Belov and Rasputin should have come to this vision of man as ruled by subconscious collective and ancestral spirits – ruled by them because he tries to deny them and has thereby lost his conscious, moderating and creative contact with them. Man in his pride has in effect tried to deny the roots of his own being, and has thereby released destructive forces within himself, over which he has no control: this is the grim warning that emerges from the work of these two writers.

*   *

The works of the rural novelists have played a paradoxical role in the development of Soviet fiction. On the one hand, they constitute a vindication of some of the features of Socialist Realism, in that they depict society realistically and they present positive heroes, of a kind, with their roots in the *narod*. On the other hand, the reality they describe is of the village in the grip of an alien bureaucracy and losing its values and culture in the face of the encroachments of urban and industrial civilization. The heroes are no longer active, struggling and optimistic, but passive, easy-going and on the whole gloomy about the future. Worst of all, perhaps, the sense of community which gives them their strength derives not from any vision of the future but from common suffering lived through in the *past*, and from memories of a communal life which is now largely destroyed. The residual morality is Christian or even pre Christian rather than communist.

These features of 'village prose' have aroused considerable official misgivings. Today, as in the Tsarist past, literary criticism in Russia often seems to be a substitute for free discussion about serious social and political issues. To some extent 'village prose' has replaced the organized political advocacy of a looser collective farm structure and of greater autonomy for the individual peasant household. More generally, it has been a touchstone for the whole progress of Soviet society and the place of moral values within it. In 1967–68 *Literaturnaya Gazeta* brought together some conflicting views on 'village prose' in a way which raised these general issues. Opening the attack on the genre, V. Kamyanov contended that the humble 'people of good conscience' who are its heroes are static as personalities and wholly inadequate as models for Soviet man in a complex and fast changing world. He dismissed their outlook and language as 'thinking in sighs'.[63] V. Kozhinov, his most consistent opponent, asserted that, on the contrary, it is precisely in the modern urban world that men have most need of positive moral guidance. The peasant, he affirmed, has an 'integrity of being and consciousness which is lost by people from other walks of life, a unity of practical, reflective, moral and aesthetic activity.' 'The peasantry,' he added, 'is not the "ideal" or "highest" part of the people, but it is an indispensable basis for the perpetual "renewal of the vital forces of nations"'.[64]

F. Levin agreed with Kamyanov that an urban, educated man

cannot turn to his semi-literate grandmother as the source of all wisdom, but argued that nevertheless 'village prose' had a positive role to play in the evolution of Soviet culture and society: 'We all know,' he admitted, 'that at history's harshest junctures our high moral principles have on occasions suffered. These principles have been violated, and as a result we have been morally debased. Callousness, indifference, selfishness, duplicity and cowardice have all been more or less widespread. . . . And so now we see some writers drawn to their "roots", to people who live a simple working life and are not trying to get anywhere.'[65]

Another aspect of 'village prose' which delighted some critics and alarmed others was its potential espousal of the cause of old Russia. A whole school of writers in the journal *Molodaya Gvardiya*, headed by V. Chalmaev, took the opportunity to rehabilitate the 'Russian soul' and to glorify a variety of aspects of prerevolutionary Russian history and culture. In *Novyi Mir*, I. Dedkov and A. Dement'ev replied by taking up the defence of Soviet internationalism, Dedkov maintaining that the ideals of 'village prose' were universal human ones, and not specifically Russian.[66]

The critic who took furthest his interpretation of 'village prose' was Lev Anninsky, who identified it not so much with Russian values as with the reassertion of *personal* values in general against a technology and a society which was threatening to become impersonal. In some of his writing Anninsky takes up a more or less openly neo-Kantian position, rejecting the whole post-Chernyshevskian positivist tradition (which, of course, though he does not say so, includes Lenin). For example, in an article contrasting Belov with the urban writer Andrei Bitov he asserts:

The world of personality presupposes the existence in man of a special sphere, to which philosophers have given various names – from Kant with his moral law to contemporary investigators who connect this second nature of man with the concept of culture in its broadest sense. But this sphere cannot simply be deduced from the natural, phenomenal qualities of the individual person. It presupposes from the outset a collectivity of people – and not the kind of quantitative collectivity which leads to the hypertrophy of the unspiritualized natural qualities of the individual . . . but a collectivity of the spirit, of the ideal, which alone can bestow meaning on the existence and dignity of the personality.[67]

Here, cumbersomely expressed (perhaps deliberately so), is a rehabilitation of the neo-Kantian notion of an autonomous, non-phenomenal sphere of 'freedom' or 'spirit' in man, as indeed of the

Slavophile idea of *sobornost'* (spiritual community), which was a general feature of early twentieth-century Russian religious thought and then of émigré Christian personalism.

Interestingly enough, since Anninsky wrote those lines, Belov and Rasputin have both moved nearer to his position, as one can see from examining their latest works, quoted above. What Anninsky says may not hold true for all writers of rural fiction, but he has well captured the dynamic which moves its most serious and reflective practitioners.

4

Vladimir Tendryakov

Vladimir Tendryakov (born 1923) was one of the 'thaw' novelists who attracted greatest attention, both in his own country and in the west. His relative frankness, the sharpness of the conflicts he portrayed, the forthrightness of his characters, the bluntness of his language – all this was in welcome contrast to the insipid monumentalism and 'conflictlessness' of Stalin's last years. His article on the 'positive hero', which was quoted in Chapter 1, helped to set the tone for much of the fiction of the mid- and late-fifties, in which positive heroes once again had something to be heroic about, negative characters put up a real fight, and reality was presented in its authentic imperfection, no longer entirely bathed in the glow of future 'magnificent prospects'.

Of the major figures of that early 'thaw' period, Tendryakov is almost the only one who has gone on writing and publishing in the Soviet Union ever since. Yet the western public has lost interest in him. Whereas many of his early works were translated into English, nothing he has written since the mid-sixties has become available. This is not because he has deteriorated as a writer: in fact, his most interesting works have been written since the mid-sixties. All the same, there is no doubt that this neglect of him is in a way justified. He is important because he is symptomatic rather than because he is a good writer. He has little capacity to create living characters, or to present ideas in the roundness and complexity which the western reader has always expected and the Soviet reader now expects to find in a novel. Tendryakov remains, at heart, a polemicist and a disappointed myth-maker.

Nevertheless, it is important to investigate him, because he presents the spiritual issues confronting Soviet man almost more clearly than any other writer, and his failure – if that is what it is – is also highly symptomatic. He has written an enormous number of novels (*povesti*, admittedly, rather than *romany*) – perhaps too many – dealing with most of the important problems of modern Soviet society: peasant life and agricultural administration, industrialization and urban government, the arts, religion and education. The last is a particular hobby-horse of his, and has made him from time to time the focus of heated pedagogical debates.

If one had, nevertheless, to select a single preoccupation as dominant in Tendryakov's work, it would be that of the 'positive hero', and indeed the 'negative hero' as well, the inner evolution of the two figures and their relationship to the rest of society. This was as true in the late seventies as it was in the early fifties. Tendryakov is a good deal more sceptical, not to say gloomy, than in his first youth, but he is recognizably the same author. What distinguished him from his Stalinist predecessors was that from the beginning he strove for a better subjective understanding of both heroes and villains. Originally he did this in order to renew the Myth by making its characters more credible and interesting, but in practice he helped to prepare the breakdown of that Myth by introducing, through his detailed and relatively individualized analyses of subjective experience, concerns more appropriate to the novel than to the epic.

His first published fictional work, *The Fall of Ivan Chuprov* (*Padenie Ivana Chuprova*, 1953) illustrates many of his typical traits. In its external features the action resembles the sketches of Ovechkin being published at the time (1953, the year of Stalin's death): the old-fashioned, 'bad', authoritarian kolkhoz chairman is defeated and replaced by a new-style, 'good' Khrushchevian one. Where this work differs markedly is in that it is the *negative* character, the old chairman, Ivan Chuprov, who is presented in the greatest detail and from the inside, quite unlike Ovechkin's Borzov. Chuprov is more than just authoritarian: he has a positively Balzacian feeling for power and wealth. Identifying himself totally with his farm, he succeeds by high-handedness, intrigue, ruthless exploitation of his men, and, where necessary, corruption, in making it the wealthiest and most successful in the district. He falls, furthermore, not (as in Ovechkin) because of the virtue and greater popularity of his opponents, but also because of inner weakness. The very pride which fuelled his success makes him feel humiliated when times change and he is subjected to criticism which he knows to be justified. He never really mobilizes for his own self-defence the resources and connections that have enabled him to be successful.

In other respects the structure of the Myth still holds in this work. The ultimate victor, the secretary of the kolkhoz party organization, is presented purely from the outside, and his victory, not actually depicted but clearly foreshadowed at the end, points towards the more democratic and humane society of the future. The novel was written, like many others of the time, in the confidence that openness and criticism would show the mistakes of the immediate past to have been merely a deviation, and would enable party and people to resume together their march towards the future. The heightened subjectivity, the dramatic dualities in which Tendryakov couched his plot and framed his characters were intended to show how greater honesty and greater attention to personal and human factors could contribute towards this progress. The implication was that such factors had, at least in the recent past, been undervalued in the falsely conceived interests of the state and economic development, and that it was necessary now to correct this bias, so that the building of a truly human community could be resumed on firmer foundations. We have already seen similar lessons expounded in Ehrenburg's *The Thaw* at about the same time.

What has never ceased to preoccupy Tendryakov ever since has been the persistence of evil and of 'negative' characters even in developed Soviet society. He has found the relative optimism of *The Fall of Ivan Chuprov* difficult to sustain. His vision of a close community united by the common drive towards the Purpose and led by 'good' party secretaries began to fade during the late fifties and early sixties, giving way to a concern with evil as an abstract, even metaphysical entity, and as a constituent and ineradicable part of society (Soviet as much as any other). More and more a common pattern appeared in his plots: the stability of a functioning and reasonably happy community is shattered by the sudden intrusion of evil – evil, moreover, not obviously explicable in terms of the standard Myth. In *Three, Seven, Ace* (*Troika, semërka, tuz*, 1960), for example, an isolated, almost innocent working team of loggers is jolted out of its peaceful existence by the arrival of a former convict, whom, ironically, they rescue from drowning and try to incorporate in their collective. In return he brings them gambling, corruption, uncontrollable passions and finally murder. The Pushkinian overtones of the title, the undetermined, classless nature of the tragedy, the irony of the plot –

all this suggests that morality and tragedy are unrelated to stages of social development, and that class struggle is irrelevant, a suggestion that contemporary critics were not slow to pick up. (The important thing is, though, that Tendryakov was allowed to go on publishing.) In *Ruts* (*Ukhaby*, 1956), the Soviet system is actually seen as involved in evil of a kind: the director of a machine tractor station who has helped to carry a wounded boy miles through the forest cannot, once back at his official desk, bring himself to provide a tractor to continue the rescue operation, for fear of what his superiors will say about the unauthorized use of productive machinery. Schizophrenia of the political and the personal is shown to lie deep in the consciousness of both officials and people.[1]

In *The Short Circuit* (*Korotkoe zamykanie*, 1962), one of the fundamental Soviet myths, that of electrification, becomes a symbol functioning in a highly ambiguous way. A power failure plunges a modern city into 'medieval gloom' and causes the death of a worker in a chemical works whose ventilation depends on electricity. At several points the author draws the parallel between the electric power network and the bonds which join together a society. At times it is hinted that some of the spiritual energy which should bind men to other men has in fact been diverted to machinery. The grid manager, Sokovin, entertains, we are told, a 'fatherly feeling' towards the electric generator and is fascinated by the 'mystery' of its functioning, but has lost the habit of valuing human beings or reacting to the 'mystery' of their existence until he is jerked out of his attitudes by the news (false, as it turns out) that his son is dead. Progress is shown to be by its nature ambiguous, with potentialities for evil as much as for good, for restricting or endangering as much as for developing men's lives. Everything depends on the working of the human 'spiritual network', in which everyone is 'part of a world consisting of opposite poles tightly bound to one another,'[2] but some are incapable of recognizing this, and opt out, weakening or overloading the system for others.

Tendryakov's complex use of the twin Soviet myths of electrification and progress indicates his desire to penetrate beyond the façade to the spiritual realities underlying it, in the hope perhaps ultimately of renewing those myths and discovering the real, temporarily lost, road to the Purpose. In fact, even as his work has become more pessimistic, he has still seemed haunted by this ultimate goal in which he finds it more and more difficult to believe. The distance which he has moved since his early kolkhoz novels is shown by comparing *The Fall of Ivan Chuprov* with *The Death of the Boss* (*Konchina*, 1968). The latter is a much longer and more ambitious work, more searching and wide-ranging in its implications: indeed, it might be regarded in some ways as an allegory of the history of the Soviet people, especially the peasantry, up to Stalin's death. The central event, to which the title refers, is the death, apparently in March 1953, of Evlampy Lykov, a kind of super-Chuprov, chairman of a kolkhoz in the northern village of Pozhary since 1930 (like many of Tendryakov's rural novels, this one is set in Vologda region, where the author himself, in common with Vasily Belov, was brought up). The author uses Lykov's death structurally to bring the villagers together as he presents their individual fates and the history of the collective farm that unites them. Lykov recalls Stalin not only in the timing of his death: one also notes the stocky build, the steely, unfriendly eyes with the cunning sparkle. Surprisingly elected over two more prominent rivals in 1930, Lykov soon revealed an unexpected talent for leadership, or at least for giving orders, along with a total capacity to regard the farm as an extension of his own personality. The *ideas*, however, and the agricultural knowledge for the collective came from the former private farmer and village intellectual, Ivan Slegov. In Slegov we find, in concentrated form, traits of both the peasantry and the intelligentsia of early twentieth-century Russia: he actually attended a *gimnaziya* before the Revolution, but returned to the village full of enthusiasm for improving the level of peasant agriculture. Tendryakov presents his evolution through a long flashback to his youth in the twenties, when he was deeply impressed by Lenin's *State and Revolution*. He believed that people 'will gradually become accustomed to observe the elementary norms of community life . . . *without the special apparatus* of coercion known as the state.' Yet there was an insecure and anxious quality to this faith of his: 'One must believe it, otherwise life is meaningless.'[3] The great obstacle to this vision, as he saw it, was private property, and he dreamt of the time when the longing for it would be overcome among his fellow villagers:

At the moment you are all destitute, you hide your few miserable kopecks from each other in stockings, in money boxes, at the bottom of trunks under grandmother's skirts. But just think, if you were to take those kopecks out and put them all in one pocket, what riches there would be! Not for the tavern, not for drinking – no, we will buy machines and set them to work . . . Then there will be electricity, to turn night into day . . . A land flowing with milk and honey is no fairy tale! . . .

And the time will come, not immediately, not even soon, perhaps, but it will come eventually, when everyone will look round and realize – all this began with Vanya Slegov![4]

To fulfil this mixture of idealism and personal ambition, Ivan takes a lead in setting up a collective farm, and contributes to it his own pedigree horses and expertly fattened pigs, gritting his teeth and conscientiously overcoming his own 'private property instincts'. Disillusionment follows swiftly and sharply. He soon finds his horses neglected and emaciated, his pigs herded together with the scabby, diseased animals of the poor peasants. Any attempt he makes to save the worthwhile specimens reinforces the suspicion that he is a kulak. In the end, driven to despair, Slegov tries to set fire to the stable in which his unfortunate animals are quartered. He is forestalled by Lykov himself, who fells him with a heavy wooden stake and breaks his back. Instead of delivering him up to the police, however, Lykov offers to employ him as chief accountant and agronomist for the kolkhoz. This unlikely partnership – the stocky, grey, power-loving chairman and the embittered, unwilling but broken-backed intellectual – proves remarkably successful. In its outlines it recalls the way in which Stalin broke the spirit of the Russian intelligentsia and then offered them a limited cooperation, backed by terror and the absence of any alternative. Slegov's outlook, moreover, has much in common with that of the Left Opposition of the twenties whose ideas Stalin caricatured in the first Five Year Plans and in the collectivization and dekulakization programmes. By a mixture of skilful agriculture, ruthless exploitation of the kolkhozniks and adroit business dealing, Lykov and Slegov are able to make their farm an oasis of relative prosperity during the terrible famine of 1933, whose horrors Tendryakov does not shirk:

Next door, in Petrakovskaya, the cattle were dying of starvation, and people were eating little loaves of bread made of nettles, hemp and steamed angelica gruel. And not only in Petrakovskaya. The country was going through the famine year – 1933.

In Vokhrovo, the district town, in the station square, Ukrainian kulaks, expropriated and exiled from their homeland, lay down and died. One got used to seeing the dead there in the morning, and the hospital groom, Abram, would come along with his cart and pile the corpses in.

Not everyone died. Many wandered along the dusty, sordid alleyways, dragging dropsied legs, elephantine and bloodlessly blue, and plucked at every passer-by, begging with dog-like eyes. In Vokhrovo they had no luck: the inhabitants themselves, to receive their ration, had to stand in the bread queues all night.[5]

Thereafter, Lykov acts like the prior of a rich monastery, handing out work and alms to those whom he judges worthy, and turning away the rest. He surrounds himself with a court: Lëkha Shablov, the surly but servile chauffeur, Valerka Chistykh, the receptionist, who sits in an anteroom and carries out the preliminary filtering of the numerous petitioners, and Al'ka Studënkina, his secretary and mistress, who, when her own charms fade, arranges later liaisons for her master, like some female Potëmkin. Impressed with these regal arrangements, all the kolkhozniks, and increasingly even the local party authorities, go in superstitious awe of Lykov.

However, as in *The Fall of Ivan Chuprov* (and it is to be noticed that the focal event of this novel falls in the watershed year of 1953, in which the former was published), young forces are growing up in the village, with new ideals – or rather taking the old ones seriously. Ironically, they are encouraged by Lykov himself, in the interests of his private empire. He appoints his nephew, Sergei, to run a new agronomic experimental station which he has established to the greater glory of Pozhary. For Sergei, agronomy is not just an abstract science, and the poverty of the neighbouring villages is not just an opportunity for exploitation: they are a direct challenge to his conscience. Walking through Petrakovskaya and seeing its destitution in person, he realizes with horror that hitherto he has allowed others to do his thinking and perceiving for him and has never accepted genuine responsibility for anything. He determines to do something *himself* about the poverty. He gets the opportunity when the amalgamation of kolkhozes takes place in 1947: Petrakovskaya joins the Lykov farm, and Sergei offers to become the brigade leader responsible for the village. He discharges his responsibilities in a totally different way from the elder Lykov, not by leadership and command, but by gaining the *trust* of his peasants. He allows them to guard the grain stores themselves, instead of locking the supplies away from them; he mobilizes the old women to work as a team shifting manure, instead of calling in expensive outside services to fertilize the fields. To Slegov, incredulous at the improvement in morale and productivity in Petrakovskaya, he retorts: 'Even in your old age you're still looking for a hero. A hero, a great leader, who can present a plump helping of happiness to you on a plate.'[6]

So far, the work has evolved rather like *The Fall of Ivan Chuprov*, though with a much richer range of suggestiveness. But the ending is altogether more ominous. Lykov, confronted for the first time in

Sergei by a force which he cannot tame, moves towards a frustrated and blustery old age. He talks more and more of death, seeing it as an absolutely annihilating force. 'A dead prince is worth less than a live cockroach,' he likes to repeat, with singular lack of perception, as it turns out: his own immortality is the one source of power Lykov is quite incapable of appreciating. The chairman's dead body is a potent force: it draws his former associates and underlings from miles around to pay their last respects, and their coming is the structural pretext for the author to expatiate on their fates. Even more important, the habits of mind he has inculcated remain to dominate the villagers' attitudes after his death. The dead prince is in fact worth far more than the live cockroach:

Do not malign yourself, Evlampy Nikitich! The dead often live on among the living. Evlampy Nikitich has died, Evlampy Nikitich is still alive. Alive in the women who have just mourned him as their 'breadwinner', alive in Pashka Zhorov [one of the most poverty-stricken kolkhozniks], warm yet in the accountant Slegov. . . . Lykov has become a habit. People do not part quickly or easily with their habits – only in pain and struggle.[7]

This valedictory comment by the narrator sounds like a tract for the times. The omens are gloomy. Lykov's sons, like wild dogs released from the leash, spend a night of drinking and debauchery, at the end of which they murder Lëkha Shablov with an axe (an echo, perhaps, of the fate of Beria?). The members of Lykov's 'court' flee the village. The way is open for Slegov to take over, with Sergei as assistant and heir apparent. In 1953 Tendryakov would have chosen that ending without hesitation. But by 1968 things were different. Slegov feels too weighed down by his long partnership with Lykov: he has acquired too many habits that he does not feel resilient enough to break. Lykov is indeed both dead and still alive, and the soil of Pozhary 'still awaits its spring . . .'.[8] The Purpose still wavers uncertainly on the horizon, but it is receding rather than drawing nearer. The idealism of the early Bolshevik experiment has been exploited, degraded and perhaps destroyed altogether by Stalin.

If *The Death of the Boss* is a kind of allegory for the socio-spiritual development of Soviet society, then *On Apostolic Business* (*Apostol'skaya komandirovka*, 1969) is a presentation of its metaphysical malaise. Tendryakov solves neither the artistic nor the philosophical problems of his subject-matter, but the novel is important for the clarity with which he states the problem.

That problem, as foreseen by the writers of *Problems of Idealism*, is the failure of positivist and materialist philosophies, whether in their original form or translated into political and economic programmes, to satisfy men's aspirations. This is clearly not only a Soviet problem, though it is one posed with peculiar sharpness by Soviet society. The central character of *On Apostolic Business* exemplifies it very aptly, for he is a scientist in his mid-thirties, successful in his career working for a popular scientific journal, living in a well-appointed Moscow flat, and happily married with a small daughter. He is a product of the Soviet system, but has his counterparts in every developed society. Outside the upper reaches of party and state, it is difficult to imagine a Soviet life with more prospects and greater affluence and stability. Yet gradually Yury Ryl'nikov, seized by what he himself as narrator calls an 'illness', comes to find his existence meaningless and painful, and eventually leaves his family, job and flat and goes off to the countryside to seek God by joining a rural church congregation and doing manual work on a collective farm.

His crisis has a number of aspects. First is the discovery, soon after moving out of the old communal apartment, that material well-being is not an end in itself, or even a joy, once the immediate novelty has worn off. 'We are no happier,' he confesses,

'but we have many more worries, for now we have our own daily growing fastidiousness to service. . . . Beware of superfluous pleasures in life, for the stronger they are, the more you are vulnerable to trivia, and little things turn into problems. Successful people are a burden above all to themselves. The ephemerality of the world is most apparent in its joys: as Ecclesiastes said, "Vanity of vanities, all is vanity."'[9]

This is reminiscent of the discovery Innokenty Volodin makes on his first night in prison in Solzhenitsyn's *The First Circle*.[10]

Even more important, perhaps, is Yury's loss of faith in the capacity of science to reveal the ultimate truth about the world. Preparing an article on the origins of the universe, he comes to feel that none of the various hypotheses advanced can, in the nature of things, ever be fully substantiated, and that, therefore, in ultimate matters, science has no better claim to our confidence than religion:

What are the merits of the Zel'dovich-Smorodinsky hypothesis compared with another, according to which a mysterious god created the world out of chaos in six days? . . . At least that's simple and clear, and at least one can imagine it, without any of those confusing neutrons and anti-neutrons. Neither hypothesis is the truth [*istina*], but in the last analysis they are equally valid. So in fact science has nothing over naïve legend.[11]

He is haunted by the words of a scientist: 'Our knowledge is an island in the infinite ocean of the unknown, and the larger the island becomes, the greater grows the extent of its boundaries with the unknown.'[12] The narrator does not name the scientist, but the thought is very close to Bulgakov's remark in *Problems of Idealism*:

No matter how much positive knowledge develops, it will always remain limited in its subject-matter: it studies only fragments of a reality which is constantly growing before the eyes of the scientist. The aim of complete and perfect knowledge of the empirical world is unattainable and misconceived.[13]

If these experiences are to be taken seriously, then two purposes current in Soviet (and not only in Soviet) society, the building of material abundance and the pursuit of scientific knowledge, lose their ultimate justification. Modern man's habit, again not only Soviet, of seeing his own identity in terms of such justification becomes tenable only at a short-term and instrumental level. And indeed Yury begins to doubt whether he has a meaningful self, seeing that the only 'goal' of his life which no one can possibly deny is death. One senses here the influence of Tolstoy; yet, compared with, say, Levin in *Anna Karenina*, Yury's experience is, if anything, intensified by the loss of the generally accepted Purpose by which he, in common with many other Soviet citizens, has lived. He is confronted with the grave as a stark travesty of that Purpose: 'My ultimate goal is the grave! In the whole boundless universe there is nothing more meaningless than me.'[14]

But if there is no purpose outside individual physical existence, then is there any ground for supposing that moral obligations exist? Yury is suddenly confronted with the Kantian prerequisites of practical reason:

We are told to live for others, to sacrifice our lives for the common good. But why should I give up my one and only life for others, unless I can be convinced that those others will live meaningfully? Why should I sacrifice myself just so that someone else can live an aimless and superfluous life? In what way is he better than me? No, if that is how things are, then let me live out my meaningless days for my own pleasure.

Live in order to live! Once I accept that, then nothing will stop me acting basely, killing, stealing, anything as long as it's for my pleasure.[15]

Faced with the modern Soviet equivalent of the 'death of God', and haunted by the Dostoevskian fear that 'everything is permitted', Yury casts around for any kind of firm rock on which he can anchor. What he is reacting against is summed up for him in a passage of Montaigne – though in fact the thought is more characteristic of the eighteenth-century French materialists or the nineteenth-century British utilitarians. What Montaigne asserts is that pleasure is the self-evident aim of men's lives, that it is obviously 'desirable' since men do in fact 'desire' it. This philosophy, Yury believes, can be refuted even by the experience of scientists: 'Did Giordano Bruno choose suffering at the stake for his pleasure?'[16] Bulgakov made the same point in his article in *Problems of Idealism*:

Happiness is a natural aspiration of man, but it is in accordance with morality only when it is a fortuitous, not an intended accompaniment of moral activity, of service to good. Such happiness can, it seems, not be made an aim in itself, since it does not consist of anything autonomous. If on the other hand one equates 'good' and 'pleasure', then that principle will justify the most monstrous vice, the most animal egoism, the total inundation of all spiritual needs in sensuality.[17]

What can be saved from Yury's apparently total loss of values? Reflecting on the emptiness of his pleasures, the limits of his reason, and the shakiness of his morality, Yury nevertheless discovers a ground for asserting man's dignity:

The world is infinitely large, and 'I' am triflingly small, lost in space beside the Earth. 'I' am small, yet who else gave a measure to six billion light years of unending space? It was 'I', thanks to the experience of counting the years and the miles on this planet. 'I' am the point of departure for everything. If it were not for 'me', with my reason, it would be impossible to say that the world exists. 'I' am necessary for the very concept of existence.[18]

Here behind Yury there hovers the ghost of Pascal, a thinker who was very important to Dostoevsky, Tolstoy and the Christian existentialists:

For after all, what is man in nature? A nothing compared to the infinite, a whole compared to the nothing, a middle point between all and nothing, infinitely remote from an understanding of the extremes. . . .
Man is only a reed, the weakest in nature, but he is a thinking reed. There is no need for the whole universe to take up arms to crush him: a vapour, a drop of water is enough to kill him. But even if the universe were to crush him, man would still be nobler than his slayer, because he knows that he is dying, whereas the universe knows nothing of the advantage it has over him.[19]

A personal tragedy brings home this recognition of the fundamental importance of personality for human values. Rita, a hysterical woman from a flat upstairs, appeals one day for his help and sympathy after the departure of her latest 'husband', but her appeal strikes Yury as so false that he excuses himself and hurries on his way. The next day Rita commits suicide, and Yury, stricken by remorse, reflects: 'Every flash of reason is a flash illuminating the whole of creation. To kill a human life is to kill a whole infinite world. How simple it would have been to save Rita.'[20]

Yury recognizes the value of the personal, but at the same time is tormented by the inadequacy of purely human purposes and faculties. That is the experience that leads him to feel that he needs some kind of religious belief:

If I recognize god, that he is, that he exists, that he is the creator of the world and its rational principle, then does it really matter whether I know when the world began and when it will end? Is it my business to worry about such questions? It is enough for me to believe that someone knows, someone inconceivably more important than me, someone to whom I owe my existence. Then my incapacity to answer these questions is perfectly right and proper: they are not my questions, they are not for me to answer.... I do not know what His meaning consists of . . . but it is sufficient for me that *that meaning exists*, that I, as I am, am needed by someone, am not useless. *I am not meaningless!*[21]

This is a key passage for what it tells us about the 'faith' which Yury tests out in the course of the novel. It is essentially a negative faith – indeed, not really a faith at all, but rather a yearning: 'Whether he exists or not, one thing is certain – I need that god.'[22] The god in whom he claims to believe is an intellectual convenience, a mere receptacle for man's inadequacies, not at all the God of Pascal or Dostoevsky. Yury's faith implies the actual abdication of human faculties, not merely a recognition of their inadequacy. This would certainly not have been accepted by any of the major writers of *Problems of Idealism*, and to that extent Tendryakov is distorting the ideology he wishes to refute. In effect, what he has done is to substitute a 'god' for the Purpose in which Yury, as a sophisticated Soviet intellectual, can no longer believe.

Yury thus departs for the village to fill an emptiness in himself, not because he really believes in God. He goes to find release from the duplicity of his professional and personal life through simple manual labour and the support of a community of believers. His actual experience in the countryside is disappointing in almost every respect. The old woman with whom he lodges in apostolic poverty cannot read the Bible, takes literally the gloomiest predictions of the Revelation of St John, and treats religion as a refuge from an unhappy life. Anna, the village's most outspoken believer, already imprisoned for her evangelical activities, is forbidding and narrow-minded. The priest is a mere youth, newly ordained, thirsty for serious conversation with an intelligent man, but he has retained his childish faith intact, accepts every word of the Bible, and is shocked by Yury's critical approach to the sacred texts. Yury's workmates simply laugh at him, while the local party secretary is suspicious of him, and almost has him arrested.

Of all the villagers, only the kolkhoz chairman, Gusterin, a lonely eccentric who spends his scanty spare time reading history books, has any real sympathy with Yury's spiritual search, or remotely the understanding required to criticize it seriously. He sees that Yury's formulation of faith implies the subordination of man's faculties to a God-given purpose which men do not even comprehend, and hence reduces God to an inhuman scarecrow. He correctly sees this faith as the projection on a cosmic scale of the relationship which, to his regret, exists in the Soviet countryside, where the average kolkhoznik, through laziness and the habit of being dominated, does not take part in the running of the collective, but simply picks up his pay and leaves the worries to the bosses. This is why, in his view, young people leave the villages, in search of a fuller life in the towns – the very pilgrimage which, ironically, Yury has just made in reverse. We might go further than Gusterin and say that Yury's God reflects the whole relationship between Soviet society and the authorities, in which the entire burden of seeking meaning and purpose is assumed by the latter, and with it the prerogative of deciding men's fates.

Yury is shaken by Gusterin's criticism, as also by the unsympathetic attitudes of the other rural believers. Besides, he receives a bitter letter from his wife, Inga, reproaching him with a lack of frankness and openness. This confirms on the level of personal relationships what Gusterin has already told him: that he is not really acting in a humane and adult way, but more like a deprived child. In the end he decides to return and at least try to resume his conjugal and paternal responsibilities. He does not know whether he will prove capable of this – and neither, it must be added, do we, the readers, since the presentation of his family life has been rather thin.

What he takes with him from his period of self-imposed exile is a new humanist and secular understanding of the immortality of the soul. Even when he ceases to feel the need to believe in a god, Yury still retains the Kantian sense that men neither love nor create if they think their lives will end with the grave. The key to his new understanding he finds in an essay by the scientist Bekhterev, 'The immortality of the human personality from the scientific point of view,' which he expounds freely himself:

The famous scientist asserts that the spiritual side of man never disappears without trace, but lives on in his descendants. And so, more than a hundred and fifty years ago, a certain man, Gavriil Romanovich Derzhavin, used his spiritual energy to write a poem. He himself died, but his spiritual side, a part of his soul, continues to live even today among us. In this case I can identify whose soul it is, but in most cases the spiritual continues its life anonymously. For example, you . . . are sitting at a table. Someone once used his spiritual energy on the problem of how to put a table-top on four legs. We don't know how many thousands of years ago that man died, his name is forgotten, his bones have decayed, but his spirit, and a definite part of his soul lives among people in the form of material tables at which they eat, drink, work and hold meetings.[23]

This is the same concept which Vasily Belov puts in the mouth of the narrator in *A Carpenter's Tales*, and similar to that of Pasternak's Yury Zhivago. Yury Ryl'nikov returns to Moscow on a train consisting of 'combinations of metal, wood and the undying soul of Stephenson', to an uncertain fate. The ending is not merely open, it is genuinely ambiguous, and must reflect the author's real doubts about his principal personage and his ideological evolution.

Of all the works Tendryakov has published since 1969, only *Spring Somersaults* (*Vesennie perevërtyshi*, 1973) shows any possible way forward out of the socio-spiritual dilemmas exhibited in *The Death of the Boss* and *On Apostolic Business*. Here, as in so many works of ten to twenty years earlier, springtime and adolescence coincide. But the emphasis has shifted a long way since then, in Tendryakov's works as in those of others. In the 'youth prose' of the fifties and early sixties adolescence was interesting because of where it was leading; but in this particular story Tendryakov is concerned rather with what the youthful perception can uniquely tell us about the world – with youth, in other words, not as a stage in development, but as an unrepeatable and valuable moment in the human understanding of things.

The main characters are schoolchildren in their early teens, facing their first independent encounters with good and evil, beauty and ugliness. Dyushka Tyagunov, on whom the story focusses, comes to these encounters equipped with the simple and self-sufficient moral concepts of childhood:

Dyushka knew what was good and what was evil because he had already lived in this world for thirteen years. Good was getting high marks at school, good was obeying one's elders, good was doing exercises every morning. . . . His marks at school were not all that high, he did not always obey his elders, he did not do exercises – after all, no one is perfect – but he was not ashamed of himself, and the world seemed clear and comprehensible. But then something odd happened. Quite suddenly, just like that. And that clear, stable world started to play tricks with Dyushka.[24]

What sets it all off is the sudden realization that a schoolgirl from the same class, Rimka, bears a remarkable resemblance to a picture he has seen of Pushkin's wife, Natal'ya Goncharova. Dyushka has left Rimka only a quarter of an hour earlier, in the street, and he rushes out to see if she is still there:

In the street something had happened in those fifteen minutes. The sky, the sun, the sparrows, the schoolgirls – everything was the same, and yet it was not the same. The sky was not simply blue, it beckoned and drew one on as if it were possible to rise on tiptoe and stay that way for ever. The sun was suddenly shaggy, unkempt, roguishly cheerful.[25]

There is a Pasternakian touch here in the way that external objects change their appearance and nature in accord with the mood of the beholder. It is not only sense impressions that change their character as Dyushka falls in love: intellectual concepts do so as well. Mathematics has hitherto been simply an imposed task, in which one did or did not score high marks. Now, partly under the inspiration of his comrade Levka, it becomes a potential tool for understanding the universe. Dyushka is particularly haunted by the notion of infinity, of the endless spaces beyond the stars, feels himself 'face to face with it – a maturing, fragile intelligence and the inexhaustible enigma of existence.' The main point of his speculation is that, if Levka's ideas about infinity are correct, then the chance combination of atoms of which an individual is composed must eventually repeat itself. This is an eccentric way of regarding immortality, or even metempsychosis, but the point is that for the moment it convinces Dyushka, even holds him spellbound, for he is only too willing to regard Rimka as a reincarnation of Natal'ya Goncharova. The combination of female beauty and mathematical reasoning has changed his whole view of the world. Furthermore, though he may be drunk with meditations on the nature of the universe, he has also won a new power to sympathize with his fellow men, as when his frail schoolfriend, Min'ka, weeps over family troubles:

At Min'ka's words, the universe, which had blazed up yesterday, shrank and fizzled out. What did it matter that the sun is a mere speck of dust, that the earth is unintelligible, that you yourself are nothing, what did it matter why people live? What mattered was Min'ka and his tears. He wanted to love and pity everything in the world – the brownish springtime street, the crane towering above the roofs, and the trampled boards of the sidewalk which Rimka's nimble feet had just touched.[26]

If the world suddenly becomes rich with the possibility of compassion and understanding, it becomes, for the same reason, laden with potentialities for evil. 'How should the lad know', comments the narrator, 'that together with love comes hate, together with the urgent desire for brotherhood the bitter feeling of loneliness. Often even adults don't understand that.'[27]

Evil presents itself brutally and unambiguously in the form of San'ka Erakhov, the school bully, who kills frogs by tying them on a piece of string and hurling them against a wall: and what he especially enjoys is forcing small boys against their will to participate in his sport. Dyushka, with his newly heightened appreciation of the world, stands up to San'ka, not as a class enemy, and not from any kind of principle, but 'simply because he is what he is.'[28]

The parents' generation, by and large, does not present an inspiring example to the children. Adults are all businesslike and brisk, totally absorbed by their own professional and civil life. Dyushka's father is a timber engineer, who once, fifteen years ago, gave his wife some daffodils, but has since forgotten the meaning of the word 'spring'. He tries to persuade Dyushka that killing frogs is a trivial matter, not worth getting excited over, while in Dyushka's mind it is by now the very incarnation of evil. The mother, a doctor, still remembers and vaguely hankers after lost beauty and love, but finds that her patients demand all her energy and devotion. The only adult who stands out, and who fires Dyushka's imagination, is Min'ka's father, Nikita Bogatov. He is quite unlike the kind of adult on which Soviet children are usually invited to model themselves. He is an eccentric, a man without a permanent job and incapable of holding one, a dreamer longing to be a poet, 'a Dante from the village of Kudelino celebrating his Beatrice.'[29] He loves his wife and family deeply, but causes them endless suffering by his fecklessness and unpracticality. Min'ka faces the strange paradox that 'Mama is good and Papa is good, but life at home is bad.'[30] That is one of the mysteries that Dyushka has to try to accommodate in his new, more complex awareness of the world. Significantly, when Nikita quotes poetry that he loves and would like to emulate, his choice falls on Pasternak:[31] there is something of Yury Zhivago in his nature, irresponsible but imaginative. Unexpectedly, it is Nikita who rescues Dyushka in his hour of greatest need, ambushed one day by San'ka, who wishes to exact revenge for his defiance. It is noteworthy, too, that the frail Min'ka is the only boy who stands up for Dyushka at the ensuing school investigation of his fight with San'ka. He pays for his courage, as San'ka later attacks him and stabs him with a knife. Both Min'ka and his father are wholly unexpected 'positive heroes', a new twist to Tendryakov's untiring search.

Spring Somersaults shows, in fact, how far its author has evolved since his 'defence of the positive hero' nearly twenty years earlier. Now it is the weaklings and the dreamers who are the 'heroes', if that word is still appropriate, and their heroism derives not from belief in the future, but from strong, often impulsive feelings about the present moment. Good and evil are fluctuating entities: sometimes they are paradoxically intertwined, sometimes one predominates and crushes the other. Time no longer moves in linear fashion towards the future, but is cyclical or seen as subsumed in eternity: 'yesterday there was no haze on the birch tree, the buds had not yet opened, but today they have.' 'Time flows, trees are born and die, people are born and die. From deep antiquity, from the faceless distances to this moment it flows, carrying Dyushka with it, even further on into awesome infinity.'[32] Time is defined no longer by the Purpose, but by the Infinite, with all the implications that surround that concept. The characters, similarly, find the absolute, if they find it at all, in eternity as reflected through the present moment.

Tendryakov is a contradictory writer who has reproduced with extraordinary faithfulness the contradictions of his age. Gripped by the hope that human beings could live an ideal life in a community united by the common determination to build a great future, he has found himself less and less able to sustain that hope. Groping, as a result, towards a new, less teleological conception of man, he has had the greatest difficulty in freeing himself from the tense, dualistic approach to action and personality with which he began his literary career. Even his gentle or uncertain characters often express themselves in confident and uncompromising language; their inner doubts are neatly sorted out into clear dichotomies, and the rhetoric of struggle still characterizes their very thoughts. Tendryakov has absorbed and reflected the profound intellectual and spiritual change going on around him in the Soviet Union, but he often seems incapable of penetrating to its inner meaning. This is especially evident in his studies of religion: even *On Apostolic Business* (which is the most searching of them) draws back from a genuine confrontation with religious faith, though Tendryakov obviously understands very well the crisis which has driven so many Soviet intellectuals to seek it. Only in *Spring Somersaults* does he show signs of having moved beyond the spiritual heritage of his youth, and perhaps therewith he enters a new stage.[33]

5

Alexander Solzhenitsyn

The name of Alexander Solzhenitsyn is much better known than those of most of the writers discussed in this book. Nevertheless, I hope enough has already been said to show that he is by no means a lone figure, and that quite a number even of officially published Soviet writers share his approach to the novel as a kind of moral chronicle or 'literary investigation', uncovering the truth about the history of Soviet society and using the material thus brought forth to illuminate man's moral and spiritual nature. In this trend, Solzhenitsyn (born 1918) stands out as the pathfinder, the first to probe in an existential manner the major problem of Soviet society, namely the extremely harsh, brutal and arbitrary nature of its penal system. For that reason it seems appropriate to consider here his two longest works on this subject, *The First Circle* and *The Gulag Archipelago*.

We have already seen from *One Day in the Life of Ivan Denisovich* that Solzhenitsyn likes to conduct his narrative from a vantage point very close to his main character or characters, in order to achieve the vividness, intimacy and authenticity lacking in so much earlier Soviet fiction, and that he likes to allow environment and objects to absorb by association as much personal meaning as possible (what L. Rzhevsky calls 'indicative' or 'significant' realism – *znamenatel'nyi realizm*).[1] Yet he also aspires to large structures and a comprehensive vision, in which appearance, pretension, ideology and false consciousness are revealed for what they are, and a kind of rock-bottom reality emerges beneath the turmoil. The scale and inclusiveness, indeed the ultimate objectivity, of this vision are difficult to reconcile with the rather private and subjective narrative stance. Solzhenitsyn's solution to this dilemma has been what he himself calls the 'polyphonic novel', in which 'each character becomes the central one while he is in the field of action'.[2] The juxtaposition of different viewpoints and different private worlds then creates an effect which might be termed either 'ironic' or 'three-dimensional'.

The First Circle (*V kruge pervom*, 1968) is just such a polyphonic novel. It is a panorama of Stalinist society – or at least of its two upper 'circles' – at the turn of the forties and fifties, focussed on the system of prisons and labour camps. Through the feelings and perceptions of a multitude of characters, it constructs a whole moral cosmos. For all the variety of viewpoints presented, the work is informed by a basic duality, that of imprisonment and freedom – but not only in the obvious sense. Spiritual freedom by no means corresponds to freedom in the juridical sense: indeed, such spiritual freedom as exists in the novel is found among those who are under physical constraint. The irony of this mismatch is a fundamental structural feature of the novel, and is also the means by which the author, without recourse to Olympian judgements, leads us to his conception of the truth.

The duality actually goes far beyond questions of freedom and constraint, even in the wider sense. In its fullness, it can perhaps be set out as follows:

Power	Love, friendship
Exploiting people and things	Appreciating people and things
Violence	Creativity
Dominance and subordination	Mutuality
Ethic of well-being and success	Ethic of conscience and genuine humanity .
Fear of suffering	Acceptance of suffering
Emptiness of self	Rich interior life
Words as barrier or façade	Words as communication
Ultimate goal posited (History, Progress, etc.)	Renunciation of ultimate goals; instead the eternal moment

All the major characters and many of the minor ones are presented in the light of these categories. Some lie on one side of the divide, some on the other, some are in transition between one and the other. Nerzhin has nearly reached the love/friendship pole; Stalin is anchored firmly in the power pole; Volodin is half way between the two, but has cast off from the shore of power and violence; Rubin firmly and infuriatingly straddles the two.

The focus of the novel is the *sharashka* of Mavrino, the privileged special prison where highly qualified prisoners carry out work of special importance to the state. This is a setting like that of Mann's *The Magic Mountain* or Camus's *The Plague*, cut off from common humanity for the intense interaction of those confined within it.

> ... the entire outside world – the universe with all its stars, this planet with all its continents, the capitals of the world with all their glitter and pomp – had all vanished into oblivion, transformed into a black ocean, virtually invisible beyond the barred windows and the dim yellow glow of the lights round the perimeter.
>
> Brightly lit within by the MGB's inexhaustible supply of electric current, the two-storeyed building of what had once been the estate chapel, its walls the thickness of four and a half bricks, sailed aimlessly and serenely through that black ocean of human destinies and human folly, casting faint streaks of light from its portholes in its wake. . . .
>
> The men floating in this ark were detached and their thoughts could wander unfettered. They were not hungry and not full. They were not happy and therefore not disturbed by the prospect of forfeiting happiness. Their heads were not full of trivial worries about their jobs, office intrigues, or anxieties about promotion, their shoulders unbowed by cares about housing, fuel, food and clothing for their children. . . . Men of outstanding intellect, education and experience, who were normally too devoted to their families to have enough of themselves to spare for friendship, were here wholly given over to their friends.[3]

The image of the ark suggests the role of its inmates: they are the few survivors from an era of more humane culture and values, carrying its seeds through the darkness of the great flood towards – they know not what. They are bearers, too, of a 'weightless' pure humanity in an era when men seem overwhelmed by their own inhumanity. The ark is not the only literary or mythological reference point Solzhenitsyn enlists. The situation he is depicting, the gravity of the moral dilemmas it presents, are more or less without precedent in world history, and for that reason Solzhenitsyn feels the need for literary traditions by means of which to gain a footing, a basic orientation. The most important of these landmarks are, it seems to me, Dante, Goethe and nineteenth-century Russian Populism.

The legacy of Dante is structurally the most fundamental. Dante was attempting, in the uncertainties of the late Middle Ages, to find an adequate way to present man's moral nature, indeed to construct a whole cosmology on the basis of moral categories. The *sharashka* is The First Circle, as Rubin tells new arrivals, where the Christian God puts the sages of antiquity whom he cannot admit to Paradise but does not like to consign to hell. That is Rubin's view, but then he still believes in Stalin. The more cynical Valentin Pryanchikov retorts: 'I could find a much simpler way to explain to the comrade what a special prison is. You know what they're always telling us in the newspapers: "It has been shown that the better sheep are fed and looked after, the higher their yield of wool." '[4]

He is right, of course. Yet it is also true that the prisoners can use the relatively healthy and humane conditions of their confinement to rest a little from the torments of the nether circles and undertake the kind of self-examination and interaction with other intelligent and cultured men which they would not bother to pursue in freedom and would have no strength to endure in more normal prisons. The 'circles' of the novel have, in other words, a Stalinist and a humanist significance, which intersect and impart dynamism to the structure. Here it *is* possible to move from one circle to another, not only because the MGB, the Ministry of State Security, may so decree, but also because spiritual ennoblement – and debasement – is possible.

The fundamental dualities of the novel, and their relationship to the 'circles', are raised in the seventh and eighth chapters, in the argument between Rubin and Nerzhin. What sparks it off is Nerzhin's antiheroic quotation from Tao philosophy: 'Weapons are the instruments of misfortune, not of honour. The wise man conquers unwillingly.' This is an affront to Rubin's whole Marxist-Leninist view of history and human nature. He believes that struggle is the essence of history – class struggle of course – and that the victors will normally be the more progressive. His own imprisonment he sees as an unusual and tragic mistake, to be borne (under regularly repeated protest) because the factors which have caused it are part of a grandiose and *necessary* historical process. 'Doesn't the law of life mean anything to you?' he exclaims exultantly to Nerzhin. 'Don't you realize that everything is conditioned by immutable laws and goes exactly the way it should? So it's useless to root around and come up with this sort of corrupting scepticism.'[5] He appends to this assertion a little couplet which is highly significant in view of the novel's images:

> A moth's life lasts but a moment,
> An oak tree grows a hundred years.

This is the traditional Socialist Realist hero's disdain for individual, 'fortuitous' phenomena, his trust in the majestic sweep of history, in which the vanquished are perhaps to be pitied, but certainly have nothing to teach the victors. Nerzhin's understanding is quite different:

'The happiness that comes from easy victories, from the total fulfilment of desire, from success, from feeling completely gorged – *that* is suffering! That is a spiritual death, a kind of unending moral indigestion.'[6]

It is the victims, on the contrary, who really learn the nature of happiness:

'Thank God for prison! It has given me the chance to think things out. To understand the nature of happiness we first have to know what it means to eat one's fill. Remember how it was in the Lubyanka and when the security people were grilling us? Remember that thin barley or oatmeal porridge without a single drop of milk? Can you say you *ate* it? No. It was like Holy Communion, you took it like the Sacraments, like the *prana* of the yogis. You ate it slowly, from the tip of a wooden spoon, entirely absorbed in the process of eating, in thinking about eating — and it spread through your body like nectar.'[7]

This is the revelation of Ivan Denisovich raised to a more conscious and intellectual level. At its highest level it is the 'eternal moment', in which the moth outlasts the oak tree, the moment of perfect happiness when Goethe's Faust can say 'Oh moment, stay – thou art so fair!' Again, however, as with Dante's circles, Goethe's 'eternal moment' can be interpreted in a number of ways. In the Faust pact it was originally to be a sign that Faust's eternal striving had ceased and that the Devil had won his soul; in the event Mephistopheles only wins the exclamation from him by deceiving him into thinking that he has initiated a programme of public works, draining a swamp to bring prosperity to thousands, whereas actually the sounds he hears are Mephistopheles' minions digging his, Faust's, grave. God intervenes and Faust's soul is saved after all. With typical inconsistency Rubin doubts the orthodox Soviet interpretation of this ending – that Faust is saved because he has discovered supreme happiness in serving mankind:

'on the basis of this fragment from *Faust* I developed a theory in one of my lectures before the war – my lectures were very bold for those days. My theory was that there is no such thing as human happiness – either it's unattainable or it's illusory. Well, after I'd finished, I was handed a note from a student – a scrap of paper torn from an exercise book: "I'm in love and I *am* happy. What do you say to that?"'
    'And what did you say?'
    'What could I say?'[8]

Rubin's tireless intellectual energy and insight has led him to sense what duller Marxist-Leninists cannot, that there is no place for human happiness in his philosophy. This happiness is immediately restored by his student – in a most un-Marxist (or at least a-Marxist) way. And indeed Rubin himself experiences such a moment – most unexpectedly during a night of illness and bitter argument – when he crosses a courtyard in the snow:

feeling the innocent, child-like touch of the cold snowflakes on his beard and flushed face, Rubin stopped in his tracks and shut his eyes. He was enveloped by a delicious sense of peace. This powerful sense of being was all the keener for being so short-lived. What happiness it would be if he didn't have to go anywhere and beg for things, if he had no desires at all but could just stand here like this the whole night, as blissfully as the trees, catching the snowflakes as they came down.[9]

Rubin is a living bundle of contradictions. In his theories he belongs to the world of Stalin and his Minister of State Security, Abakumov, in his personality to the honest zeks. 'All his life he had never lacked friends, but in prison it seemed to be his fate that his friends did not share his outlook, while those who did were not his friends.'[10] He loves German culture and the company of Germans, but at the same time is ideologically suspicious of the entire German nation, feeling that they did not do enough to stop Hitler. He is a man of humane and cosmopolitan literary taste at a time when, by theories that he agrees with, 'humanitarianism' is considered weak and 'cosmopolitanism' is a term of abuse. He works with scientific and political zeal at the task of reducing voice characteristics to machine-readable form – and then finds that he likes the actual voice of the man whom he is supposed to be tracing for the MGB. In his brilliant parody of the trial of Prince Igor, he devastatingly probes the mentality of the police and judicial officials whose ideology he shares. He remembers his part in the dekulakization and his political denunciation of his own brother with shame. His contradictions are summed up and synthesized in his project for the establishment of Civic Temples. Despite all his disdain for the 'medieval mumbo-jumbo' of his mystically inclined fellow zek, Sologdin, Rubin realizes that something is badly missing in the society whose political foundations he so warmly applauds:

It was true, for instance, that moral standards had declined, particularly among the younger generation, and that people were losing their sense of values.
    In the old days people had leaned on the Church and the priests for moral guidance. And even nowadays, what Polish peasant woman would take any serious step in life without consulting her priest?
    It could be that the country now needed firm moral foundations, even more urgently than the Volga-Don Canal or the great new dam on the Angara River.[11]

To achieve this Rubin would restore – in a new form, of course –

some of the old festivals and rituals, and erect suitable buildings for their practice, with stained glass, murals and even priests – or, as he would call them, 'servants of the cult'.

Rubin ends, as he begins, in a contradictory position. He 'cannot help liking on purely human grounds' the voice of 'this man who had been brave enough to telephone a flat under surveillance', yet knows that '*objectively*, although this man imagined he was doing good, he was in fact working against the forces of progress.' He is fascinated by the new science of 'phonoscopy', which enables him to identify someone's telephone voice and to play the investigator's role with conviction and success, yet at the same time is appalled by the blunt brutality of the MGB official Oskolupov, whose peremptory order reflects interest neither in science nor in justice: 'arrest both of the swine.'[12]

At the apex of the zone of internal unfreedom, where Rubin has one foot, stands Stalin, the source of the compulsions which chill and bind all those in the official hierarchy, hollowing out their personalities, and filling them with practices and habits of his own:

Sitting up behind his dozen fortress walls, one man suffered from insomnia – and he had trained the whole of Moscow's officialdom to watch with him into the early hours. Knowing the habits of their sovereign, all three-score ministers sat like schoolboys, waiting for his summons. To keep themselves awake they summoned their deputies, the deputies harried their section heads, research assistants climbed step-ladders and looked up card indexes, clerks dashed up and down corridors and typists broke pencils.[13]

Before him the most dreaded figures in the land are powerless. Abakumov trembles before the lightest glance of his tiger-like eyes and the quiver of his lower lip. He vents his frustration and fear on his own deputy, Sevast'yanov, who passes it on down the line. That is the sole source of solidarity in the hierarchy: fear and consciousness of rank. When Abakumov's subordinates enter his office, they advance silently in single file down the centre stripe of his carpet in correct order of precedence. When Stalin wants something done, he has only to raise his finger and everyone scrambles to action, for fear of losing their comfort, their prestige, their privileges, and worse, if they fail.

. . . it was more than flesh and blood could bear to be hopelessly caught up in impossible, grotesque, crippling schedules. You were trapped and held in a deadly grip. The system crushed you, driving you harder and faster all the time, demanding more and more, setting inhuman [deadlines]. This was why buildings and bridges collapsed, why crops rotted in the fields or never came up at all.[14]

When Yakonov, head of the Mavrino 'institute' is ordered to

complete the scrambler device in double quick time, he knows he cannot do it, but can see no way of ducking out of his responsibility. He can see himself being sent back to prison, where he spent six years once before, a period which, unlike Nerzhin, he regards as simply 'a ghastly lapse, something obscene and sickening, the greatest catastrophe of his life'. Since his ethic is success, he can regard it in no other way. But in his present extremity, he does remember his former fiancée, Agniya, a girl of otherworldly sensitivity and fastidiousness, who used to reproach him 'for doing what seemed the most ordinary things – things which to his astonishment she regarded as base and despicable. Yet strangely enough the more she found fault with him, the fonder he became of her.'[15] Once, outside the church of St John the Baptist, overlooking central Moscow, she had said to him sadly: 'I'm sure you're going to be famous, successful and have all the things you want. . . . But will you be happy, Anton? . . . You must beware, too. If we get too interested in what's going on around us, we lose . . . we lose . . . how can I put it? . . . When a bell stops ringing and the chimes fade away, you can't bring them back – and the music is gone forever. Do you see what I mean?'[16] Later, when he debased himself by publishing an article required of him on 'the rottenness of Western society, morals and culture', she returned his ring to him marked 'To the Metropolitan Kirill' (the first Russian to pay homage to the Tatar Khan, begging guarantees for the safety of the clergy).

Now the walls of Stalin's version of the Tatar yoke have closed down completely on Yakonov and all like him. Solzhenitsyn's portrait of Stalin shows the old tyrant suffering from all the ills, in hyperbolic form, that cluster to his pole of the moral universe. The ruling passions of his life are fear (space makes him feel weak; the short distance from his chauffeur-driven car to the foyer of the Hall of Columns is a nightmare; a picture of Alexander II's assassins makes him splutter in wordless panic); vanity (he laps up the endless printed panegyrics to him, admires his portrait in everything from oils to flowers, and even then wonders if his people really appreciate him fully – an ironic question with double meaning); ambition (ultimately, perhaps, he should become Emperor of the Planet, why not?). He is desperately lonely: the growth of his power has certainly meant growing personal isolation. But the values by which he has lived his life have always prevented friendship, for they have always excluded trust.

He had not trusted his own mother; neither had he trusted God, before whom as a young man he had bowed down in His temple. He had not trusted his fellow Party members, especially those with the gift of eloquence. He had not trusted his comrades in exile. He did not trust the peasants to sow their grain and harvest the wheat unless he forced them to do it and watched over them. He did not trust the workers to work unless he laid down their production targets. He did not trust the intellectuals to help the cause rather than to harm it. He did not trust the soldiers and the generals to fight without penal battalions and field security squads. He had never trusted his relatives, his wives or his mistresses. He had not even trusted his children. And how right he had been![17]

That sums up Stalin's view of social and family cohesion. (And the only exception, of course, was Hitler, whose subsequent betrayal only confirmed his universal distrust.)

In the midst of this spiritual emptiness, Stalin feels a persistent attraction towards the symbols of Russia's past authority, the Church and the Imperial state. He feels drawn again to the religion of his seminary youth – a faith consisting largely of repetition, ritual, obedience and dogma. The habits it nurtured break out in the strangest places. Puzzling out his pathfinding article on linguistics, Stalin writes 'Language is created in order to . . .', 'The superstructure is created by the base in order to . . .' – and here the narrator breaks off to comment: 'poring low over the paper, he did not see the angel of medieval teleology smiling over his shoulder.'[18] This is an important interjection, for the narrator mostly prefers, in the Stalin chapters, to work through reported internal monologue: this is one of the very few places where he allows himself a direct comment. Stalin may be an unbeliever, but his outlook on life is fundamentally a religious one, and of a primitive sort. His communism is not like that of Lenin and his cosmopolitan colleagues, 'wagging their little beards, wringing their hands, spitting, wheezing and shouting at him from the bookshelves: "We told you so! This wasn't the way to do it!"'[19] It is a hierarchical, rigidly ordered world-view equipped with a none too certain Heaven and an all too vividly apparent Hell, and topped by a primitive, unknowable and vengeful God (Stalin's only successful rival). Stalinism is, in fact, the latest version of the official ecclesiastical medieval cosmology, and one in which the sense of hierarchy and the realm of the devil are hypertrophied in the form of Necessity. This has profound implications for Stalin's personality and for the whole of the society over which he rules. He has in effect tried to force society into this mould by creating a secularized hell whose first circle the novel's characters – imprisoned and 'free' – inhabit, in their different ways. Their Limbo is part of a perverted cosmos, based on a perverted moral order, in which voice codes are invented and perfected for purely inquisitorial purposes. Genuine science, on the other hand, is the product of the few lone minds Sologdin celebrates and of the genuine believers mentioned by Nerzhin: Pascal, Newton, Einstein.[20] The spiritually 'free' characters are engaged on the search not for voice codes but for a genuine morality, in conditions which pose moral dilemmas very sharply; and the narrator, like Dante in late medieval Italy, is trying to construct a meaningful cosmos out of corrupt materials.

It is instructive to observe the point at which Stalin's Marxism breaks down, impotent, and reveals the medieval cosmology behind it. He has been trying to describe *language* in Marxist categories, and finds it impossible to do so. It is not part of the superstructure, not part of the base, not a mode of production – so what is it? It fits into none of the categories of his scholastic pseudo-science. But language is a constant concern of those who are searching seriously for their own moral nature. In their seminal dispute, Rubin and Nerzhin disagree over the origin of the word *schast'e*, which means 'happiness': whatever their disagreement, however, they both concur that to understand a concept properly it is useful to know something about its derivation, in other words that language has a historical dimension which can alert us to double-think, and to distorted or restricted uses passing for genuine concepts. The same point is made in a different way by the eccentric, unscrupulous but often perspicacious Sologdin, who refuses to use the modern westernisms characteristic of pseudo-science (and especially of Marxism), and seeks instead the 'ultimate clarity' of old Russianisms: thus 'moneybaggery' (*tolstosumstvo*) in place of 'capitalism'.

These characters are trying to take language back to its roots, reacting against a society in which language often seems to mean nothing at all because it is entirely divorced from reality. The society's means of communication are clogged by lies: the fawning lies of Stalin's *Short Biography*, the vicious lies of the pamphlet on Tito, the camouflage lies of the dressed-up prison cell shown to Eleanor Roosevelt, the elaborate, institutionalized lies of a literature which can barely conserve '1/32 of the truth' and has to be taught to schoolchildren by a kind of forced feeding. Just as Stalin, in his 'armour-plated study' feels safe from 'objective reality', so also literature averts its gaze from such things as the horrifying sights of the Tashkent flea-market and builds up its own world, 'made up of everything except what you could see around you with your own two eyes.'[21] The necessity of continually constructing pre-packaged universes makes it very difficult for writers to write at all – they find they have nothing to say.

What depressed Galakhov was that he couldn't think what to write about – with every page it seemed to get more difficult. He tried to work to a timetable, to fight his boredom, his fatigue, his distractions, the temptation to listen for the postman and slip out to have a look at the paper. . . .
   Every time he started a new book, he felt hopeful, he swore to himself and his friends that this time nothing and no one would prevent him, he would write a genuine book. He set about it with enthusiasm. But very soon he noticed that he was not alone. Swimming in front of him was the ever clearer image of the one he was writing for and through whose eyes he re-read every paragraph he had just written. And this was not the Reader – brother, friend and contemporary, it was not even the reviewer as such, it was always for some reason one particular, famous reviewer, the reviewer-in-chief – Zhabov.'[22]

The erection and propagation of false worlds is a full-time process, occupying thousands of the most talented people, draining from words their real meaning, making human communication more difficult, producing a society in which people distrust each other and keep their real feelings, their real selves hidden for so long that they no longer even feel certain who they are. Their selves become in effect reduced to the surface satisfactions, discomforts, worries and ambitions that obsess all the officials and their families.

In contrast to the clogged, spurious communication afforded by the floods of officially approved propaganda stands the vibrantly allusive use of language between two people who know and love each other well: Gleb and Nadya Nerzhin in their mere half-hour of conversation, obstructed as it is by the silent, rock-like presence of the guard standing over them. Similarly, the magnificent verbal improvizations of Rubin, Nerzhin and Potapov add an extra dimension to the inmates' experience. Real literature – Esenin's poetry, Goethe's *Faust*, or even Dumas's *Count of Monte Cristo* – instructs, diverts or provides matter for reflection in a way which deepens the prisoners' perceptions. Even Galakhov finds it easy to use words when he gets on to exchanging wartime reminiscences with Shchagov: for after all, at the front the language of struggles and campaigns has real meaning.

The implication of all this is that language is not merely a tool of communication but carries something basic within it that affects the content of communication. Perhaps language reflects the underlying structure of the human mind and heart, like the 'existential acts' that are the *real* decisions in the novel, perhaps it bears the marks of generations of inherited experience. What is certain is that when it is torn away from its task of faithfully naming, ordering and explaining reality for human beings, then it becomes a potent weapon of non-communication and atomization, and therefore of deception and tyranny, which in the end enslaves not only those whom it deceives, but also those who misuse it. Stalin has literally no way any more of discovering when his subordinates are lying to him. How can real conspiracies be distinguished any more from invented ones? How can Abakumov discover whether work he has ordered is really being done? It is no accident that the action of the novel revolves around the attempt to eliminate everything human from language by encoding the voice and using it for inhuman purposes.[23]

The duality on which the novel rests naturally provokes the question: is it possible to move from the sphere of power and unfreedom to that of love and freedom? Can one regain conscience and humanity once they have been lost? We have seen that Yakonov at any rate has troubling memories of what he has lost. But the social and career life of the Makarygins is calculated to obliterate any such memories under the weight of everyday well-being and the fear of losing it. The elder Makarygin elevates life's little pleasures into a religion with his 'tobacco altar', and his mock-philosophical maxim 'Fumo, ergo sum'. It is literally the case that life without pleasure seems to him no life at all. Momentary doubts about the suffering of innocent people are brushed aside by justifications such as that of Alexei Lanskoi: 'Nobody can do just what they want. Only history does what it wants. That sometimes seems appalling to people like you and me, but, Klara, you have to face the fact that there is a law of big numbers. The bigger the scope of some historical development, the greater the probability of particular errors . . .'.[24] Necessity rules, in short.

Innokenty Volodin, the young diplomat married into the Makarygin family, lives by the same code, which indeed he tries to formulate as a philosophy, using the maxims of Epicurus: 'The highest criteria of good and evil are our own subjective feelings of pleasure and displeasure.' 'A belief in immortality arises from the insatiability of men's appetites. To the wise man the term of our life is quite sufficient to encompass the whole gamut of pleasures to which he may aspire and, when death comes, he rises, sated, from the banquet of life and makes room for others. One lifetime is long enough for the philosopher; a fool would not know what to do with eternity.'[25] In fact, however, his spiritual evolution away from this position has already begun before the novel opens. He has been looking through his dead mother's notebooks (we know from an extra chapter written later that she was a young lady of St Petersburg seduced by one of the sailors who dispersed the Constituent Assembly in January 1918 – so Innokenty might be said to be a direct child of the Russian Revolution at the very phase when it was passing from democracy to authoritarianism[26]), and they turn out to contain reflections of a kind very different from those he is used to:

'Compassion is the spontaneous movement of the virtuous heart.'
    Compassion? Innokenty frowned. He had been taught at school that pity is as shameful and degrading for the one who pities as for the one who is pitied.
    'Never be sure that you are more right than other people. Respect their opinions even if they are opposed to yours.'
    This was pretty old-fashioned! If my view of the world is right, how can I respect those who disagree with me? . . .
    Yes, his mother had been a weak woman, he couldn't see her putting up a fight, the very idea of it was absurd.[27]

What is remarkable nevertheless is that these weak and at first sight unconvincing sentiments remain in his mind as a kind of potential antidote to the insipidity and weariness of which he has become conscious in his social and married life. 'If we are always cautious, do we remain human beings?' His decision to warn his mother's old doctor of the danger of arrest, the act with which the novel opens, is the turning point of his life, and, as we realize when his character is more fully laid before us, it is a decision which he has reached because of his doubts and his reading of the old notebooks. The morality of another generation, though repudiated and indeed crushed, retains odd traces of its power even to the present.

Some of the other characters live through similar moments of decision, when they assert their own identity. Bobynin, for example, refuses to help Abakumov speed up the work on the scrambler. From the position of dual superiority afforded by his specialist knowledge and (paradoxically) by his prisoner status, he tells the all-powerful Minister of State Security: 'You took away my freedom a long time ago and you can't give it back to me because you haven't got it yourself. I'm forty-two years old. You gave me twenty-five years. I've done hard labour, I know what it is to have a number instead of a name, to be handcuffed, to be guarded by dogs, to work in a punitive brigade – what more can you do to me? Take me off this special project? You'd be the loser.'[28]

Similarly Gerasimovich, offered an assignment perfecting tiny cameras to photograph people without their knowledge, refuses with an ironic disavowal of apostolic status, even though he could gain early release by accepting, and save his wife from untold humiliation: 'No, it's not in my line! . . . Putting people in prison is not my line! I'm not a fisher of men.'[29]

These moments of individual decision are what stand against and discredit Necessity, the Law of Large Numbers which the apologists of Stalinist statehood cite, and the science which treats human beings as objects.[30]

With Innokenty's arrest and induction into the strange anti-world of the Lubyanka, he sees the reverse side of the privileged life he has enjoyed hitherto. The guardians of the Lubyanka, true to their ideology, turn Innokenty into an object by studiedly impersonal treatment of him, in order to eliminate his sense of personal worth and convert him into malleable material. After a night of this treatment, in spite of – or rather, because of – his suffering, he sees many things more clearly:

. . . according to Epicurus, only what I like is good, and what I do not like is evil. This was the philosophy of a savage. Because Stalin liked killing people, did this mean that he regarded killing as good? And if someone found displeasure in being imprisoned for having tried to save another man, was his action therefore evil? No – for Innokenty good and evil were now absolute and distinct, and visibly separated by the pale-grey door in front of him, by those whitewashed walls, by the experience of his first night in prison. Seen from the pinnacle of struggle and pain to which he was now ascending, the wisdom of Epicurus seemed no more than the babbling of a child.[31]

This, of course, is the first stage of the path Gleb Nerzhin has already been traversing, from being a promising and reliable young army officer (though, like Volodin, with a muffled awareness of the falsity of public life) to being a deprived, incarcerated, but self-reliant and more mature zek. Prison and labour camp have given him much:

'Think how fortunate we are to be sitting here round this table, able to exchange ideas without fear or concealment. We couldn't have done that when we were free, could we? . . . I swear I will never forget the real human greatness that I have come to know only in prison!'[32]

He has also discovered genuine criteria for distinguishing good and evil, which he lacked in the 'thriving and superficial world': 'the lower I sank in that inhumanly ruthless world, in some strange way the more I listened to those few who, even there, spoke to my conscience.'[33] The camps force him to do what so many nineteenth-century intellectuals dreamed of doing – Going to the People: this too he finds deeply instructive, but in an unexpected way:

If Nerzhin had now learnt to drive a nail home without bending it, or to plane two wooden boards to exactly the same thickness, it was not to prove himself in the eyes of the ordinary people, but to earn his soggy hunk of daily bread. The brutal education of camp life had destroyed yet another of his illusions: he understood that he had reached rock bottom – beyond this there was nothing and nobody – and that the People possessed no advantage, no great, homespun wisdom. . . . They did not stand up to hunger and thirst any better than he, and they were not less daunted by the grim prospect of ten years in prison. They were no more resourceful in the face of such crises as transfers to another prison or inspections – though they were, if anything, more apt to be taken in by informers. They were also more liable to fall for the blatant lies told by the authorities. . . . Few of them had the sort of beliefs for which they would willingly have sacrificed their lives.

The only solution left, Nerzhin now felt, was simply to be oneself.[34]

This is a lesson, moreover, in which he is confirmed by the one peasant for whom he has real respect, Spiridon. He is at first bewildered by the latter's insouciant account of how he gave up dekulakizing, how he tried to avoid fighting for either the Reds or the Whites, the Soviets or the Germans, regarding them all as a plague. But later he comes to understand this as a sign that for Spiridon the supreme value is the family. Besides, Spiridon's ultimate criterion for morality is 'the wolfhounds are right and the cannibals wrong',[35] an assertion which Gleb interprets to mean that men must act in accordance with their own natures – but only after making the utmost efforts to determine what that is, for which purpose the labour camp, with its extremes, is better equipped than he had expected. So his encounter with the people has given him certain rock-bottom standards of right and wrong, of which he was not sure before, as well as confidence in his *own* judgement.

Nerzhin's path should not be interpreted as a straightforward model for imitation. For one thing it leads him to no definite conclusions. He recognizes that his scepticism is but 'a roadside shelter where I can sit out the bad weather', though it is also 'a way of ridding the mind of dogma'.[36] However, he has already reached the stage where he is no longer prepared to compromise with the authorities, and for that reason is hurled out of the 'first circle' into the nether regions where (for all we know and he knows) death may await him. A certain minimal something has been asserted by his act, a certain humanity rescued, even though the van in which he is carted off is marked

'MEAT'. Nerzhin is not the positive hero – for the very form of the polyphonic novel excludes such a figure. However, he is the person who has been most genuinely open to a variety of views and personalities – who in short has exemplified the polyphonic principle, not in art, but in real life – and has proved able thus to discover and act in accordance with his own nature.[37]

In *The Gulag Archipelago* (*Arkhipelag Gulag*, 1973–76), Solzhenitsyn enormously extends the scope of his presentation of the Soviet penitentiary system, but this work is infused with the same duality and the same existential concern. Notice first of all the genre in which he has couched his testimony: 'an experiment in artistic investigation'. That may seem a self-contradiction, but it should alert us from the start to the fact that this is a work which in some ways challenges our habitual epistemology. As Alexander Shmeman says, talking of western social science and modern art:

The failure of *investigation*, the failure of *art* . . . Solzhenitsyn shows that they are but two expressions, two aspects of one and the same failure. In the last analysis, this is the failure of the very world view shaping our modern civilization. What ultimately makes investigation fail is precisely its divorce from art, from the power to transform information into life, data into experience, truth into the *whole truth*. And what ultimately makes art fail is its rejection of investigation, and thus also of any obedience to truth and of a genuine encounter with reality. It is this double divorce, the source in our world of lies and of ineffable tragedies that Solzhenitsyn denounces and challenges in the subtitle of his *Gulag Archipelago* and tries to overcome in his 'artistic investigation'.[38]

And indeed, what existing genre could do justice to the theme? The historian proceeds from documents, artefacts and recollections, not from personal suffering. Memoirs and autobiography focus on a single man's life, not on the fate of millions. Anthropology is concerned with men's customs, their outward forms of community life, rather than with the theodicy of the individual. Solzhenitsyn is concerned with all these things, and therefore *The Gulag Archipelago* has about it something of each of these genres, but behind it all is the controlling intelligence and sensibility of the novelist, integrating the sprawling material vision, and asking the vital question 'How was this possible?' The novelist, that is, in the Russian sense, where the categories of social commentator, theologian and prophet are also implied. It is almost as though Calvin had devoted his genius for classification, theological and legal-psychological analysis to the study of the Institutes of the Anti-Christian Religion, or as if Marx had used the recollections of long-lost zeks instead of Blue Books to produce a massive Anti-Capital. Indeed, Anti-Christ and Anti-Capital are two presences that might be said to hover over the whole book: the perverted economic system that needs slave labour to carry out a process of primitive capital accumulation far harsher than anything Marx ever dreamt of.

Solzhenitsyn has no doubt where to locate the main explanation of the hyperbolic evil which characterizes the Gulag and raises it above the mundane and timid evil of the past:

To do evil a human being must first of all believe that what he's doing is good, or else that it's a well-considered act in conformity with natural law. Fortunately, it is in the nature of the human being to seek a *justification* for his actions.

Macbeth's self-justifications were feeble – and his conscience devoured him. Yes, even Iago was a little lamb too. The imagination and the spiritual strength of Shakespeare's evildoers stopped short at a dozen corpses. Because they had no *ideology*.

Ideology – *that* is what gives evildoing its long-sought justification and gives the evildoer the necessary steadfastness and determination. *That* is the social theory which helps to make his acts seem good instead of bad in his own and others' eyes, so that he won't hear reproaches and curses but will receive praise and honours. That was how the agents of the Inquisition fortified their wills: by invoking Christianity; the conquerors of foreign lands, by extolling the grandeur of their Motherland; the colonizers, by civilization; the Nazis, by race; and the Jacobins (early and late), by equality, brotherhood, and the happiness of future generations.

Thanks to *ideology*, the twentieth century was fated to experience evildoing on a scale calculated in the millions.[39]

There have, then, been previous ideologies that justified mass murder. What is it that has made Bolshevism exceed the achievements of all its predecessors (even Hitler Solzhenitsyn sees, by and large, as an apprentice of Lenin and Stalin)? Above all its denial of man's spiritual nature, its drive to reduce men to mere matter and self-interest, to objects in an ineluctable causal process, what Solzhenitsyn calls in his *Letter to the Soviet Leaders* 'the economic and mechanistic crudity of its attempts to explain that most subtle of creatures, the human being, and that even more complex synthesis of millions of people, society. . . .'[40] This was what enabled Lenin to call for the 'purging of the Russian land from all kinds of harmful insects', to pervert the whole judicial machinery in the name of 'revolutionary legality', to establish 'exterminatory-labour camps', where the undesirable could be first isolated from society as a prophylactic measure, then forced to work for the benefit of that society, and finally liquidated. That also was the justification for giving certain people unlimited power, so that they could manipulate base untrustworthy human beings for their own good. These are the Blue Caps, the members of the Soviet security services:

Excluded by the nature of their work and by deliberate choice from the *higher* sphere of human existence, the servitors of the Blue Institution lived in their lower sphere with all the greater intensity and avidity. And there they were possessed and directed by the two strongest instincts of the lower sphere, other than hunger and sex: greed for *power* and greed for *gain*. (Particularly for power. In recent decades it has turned out to be more important than money.)

Power is a poison well known for thousands of years. If only no one were ever able to acquire material power over others! But to the human being who has faith in some force that holds dominion over all of us, and who is therefore conscious of his own limitations, power is not necessarily fatal. For those, however, who are unaware of any higher sphere, it is a deadly poison. For them there is no antidote.[41]

This is not merely an Olympian historical judgement. When he speaks of 'their career choice', Solzhenitsyn is referring to his own memories of the autumn of 1938 when 'we young men of the Komsomol were summoned before the District Komsomol Committee not once but twice', and invited to enter the NKVD training school, 'for the Motherland'. This was the moment of existential choice of the kind that faces many of the characters of *The First Circle*. Every rational argument, every consideration of self-interest seemed to urge the young men to accept the offer, and yet very few did so:

It was not our minds that resisted but something inside our breasts. People can shout at you from all sides: 'You must!' And your own head can be saying also: 'You must!' But inside your breast there is a sense of revulsion, repudiation. I don't want to. *It makes me feel sick*. Do what you want without me, I want no part of it.

This came from very far back, quite likely as far back as Lermontov, from those decades of Russian life when [everyone agreed] frankly and openly [that] there was no worse and no more vile branch of the service for a decent person than that of the gendarmerie. No, it went back even further. Without even knowing it ourselves, we were ransomed by the small change in copper that was left from the golden coins our great-grandfathers had expended, at a time when morality was not considered relative and when the distinction between good and evil was very simply perceived by the heart.[42]

The implication is that the currency reserves of morality are being swiftly consumed by the corrosive ideological teachings that the Soviet authorities impose on the population. Solzhenitsyn is often accused nowadays – not only by Sakharov – of exaggerating the importance of ideology; but it is important always to remember how he conceives of ideology. He sees it not simply as an external imposition, as mere propaganda, but as a spiritual force (albeit of a base sort) which remoulds men's conceptions of themselves and of those around them, and which therefore affects every single action they perform. A man who conceives himself to be a creature of selfish, material and acquisitive instincts, the prisoner of biological and social laws, will not respect himself and, given the opportunity, will tyrannize and exploit others. For why should he not do so if only his self-interest is at stake? This is the fateful chain of argument which Tendryakov explored in the person of Yury Ryl'nikov.

At any rate, the Solzhenitsyn of 1938 was a staunch Marxist-Leninist, his refusal to enter the security services was illogical, and he admits that, given a little more pressure, the remaining small change would probably have proved insufficient. Indeed, in Book 3 he tells how, in his first camp, he allowed himself to be enrolled for the security service, in effect as a *stukach* (informer), but was transferred before he had the opportunity to denounce anyone. The inherited morality of a literary intelligentsia could not have stood up against the enticements of rank, status and participation in the collective:

I remember very well that right after officer candidate school I experienced the *happiness of simplification*, of being a military man and *not having to think things through; the happiness of being immersed* in the life *everyone else lived*, that was *accepted* in our military milieu; the happiness of forgetting some of the spiritual subtleties inculcated since childhood.[43]

He recalls in a personal confession how easy it was in the army (how much more, then, in the *Organs*?) to be convinced of one's own superiority:

I issued commands. I addressed fathers and grandfathers with the familiar, downgrading form of address - while they, of course, addressed me formally. I sent them out to repair wires under shellfire so that my superiors should not reproach me. (Andreyashin died that way.) . . . I forced my soldiers to put their backs into it and dig me a special dugout at every bivouac and to haul the heaviest beams to support it so that I should be as comfortable and safe as possible. . . .

That's what shoulder boards do to a human being. And where have all the exhortations of grandmother, standing before an ikon, gone! And where the young Pioneer's daydreams of future sacred Equality![44]

What converted Solzhenitsyn from his self-assured Marxist-Leninist elitism to the scepticism and then Christianity of his later years? In one sense the question does not need to be asked. The experience of the camps, the revelation of their systematic inhumanity, were quite enough. Yet, as Solzhenitsyn's whole testimony shows us, external reasons are never sufficient by themselves to change a man's heart; an internal stimulus is needed too. In his case it seems to have been the conversation in the camp hospital with Boris Kornfel'd, the doctor who had been converted from Judaism to Christianity. The part which Solzhenitsyn remembers as decisive is highly significant. Kornfel'd said to him:

'I have become convinced that there is no punishment that comes to us in this life on earth which is undeserved. Superficially, it can have nothing to do with what we are guilty of in actual fact, but if you go over your life with a fine-tooth comb and ponder it deeply, you will always be able to hunt down that transgression of yours for which you have now received this blow.'[45]

It was this call to a sense of sin which remained in Solzhenitsyn's mind. It was in fact a Puritan conversion, appealing perhaps to the Puritan element which is strong in Bolshevism, especially among the earlier generations of idealistic, ascetic and self-sacrificing Bolsheviks, to which essentially Solzhenitsyn – somewhat belatedly – belonged. It was this insight which, together with the sufferings and experience of the labour camp, brought Solzhenitsyn to his confession and statement of faith:

It was granted me to carry away from my prison years on my bent back, which nearly broke beneath its load, this essential experience: *how* a human being becomes evil and *how* good. In the intoxication of youthful successes I had felt myself to be infallible, and I was therefore cruel. In the surfeit of power I was a murderer, and an oppressor. In my most evil moments I was convinced that I was doing good, and I was well supplied with systematic arguments. And it was only when I lay there on rotting prison straw that I sensed within myself the first stirrings of good. Gradually it was disclosed to me that the line separating good and evil passes not through states, not between classes, nor between political parties either – but right through every human heart – and through all human hearts. . . .

Since then I have come to understand the truth of all the religions of the world: They struggle with *the evil inside a human being* (inside every human being). It is impossible to expel evil from the world in its entirety, but it is possible to constrict it within each person.

And since that time I have come to understand the falsehood of all the revolutions in history: They destroy only *those carriers* of evil contemporary with them (and also fail, out of haste, to discriminate the carriers of good as well). And they then take to themselves as their heritage the actual evil itself, magnified still more.[46]

The experience of arrest is equivalent to the Day of Judgement: it is the moment when worldly riches, rank and status suddenly cease to have any meaning, it is the great leveller. From that moment on a man must depend on his inner resources alone. Arguing against Shalamov's expressed view that labour camp is invariably degrading and reduces the prisoner to a sub-human level, Solzhenitsyn rejoins:

wouldn't it be more correct to say that no camp can corrupt those who have a stable nucleus, who do not accept that pitiful ideology which holds that 'human beings are created for happiness', an ideology which is done in by the first blow of the work assigner's cudgel?

Those people became corrupted in camp who before camp had not been enriched by any morality at all or by any spiritual upbringing. (This is not at all a theoretical matter – since during our glorious half-century millions of them grew up.)

Those people became corrupted in camp who had already been corrupted out in freedom or who were ready for it.[47]

Arrest, prison and labour camp are thus the great proving grounds in which the worth of a man's soul is determined. Some were able to come through, like the old woman in Butyrki prison in 1937, who was interrogated every night to reveal the means by which the Metropolitan had escaped from her house to Finland:

At first the interrogators took turns, and then they went after her in groups. They shook their fists in the little old woman's face, and she replied: 'There is nothing you can do with me even if you cut me into pieces. After all, you are afraid of your bosses, and you are afraid of each other, and you are even afraid of killing me.' (They would lose contact with the underground railroad.) 'But I am not afraid of anything. I would be glad to be judged by God right this minute.'[48]

This is the duality which runs right through *The Gulag Archipelago*, as it does *The First Circle*. It can be traced back to the moment of choice which faced the author himself. Unlike the relatively cool tone of *The First Circle*, in *The Gulag Archipelago* the writer is constantly engaged in heated repartee with antagonists, specified and unspecified. He answers questions, anticipates objections, unmasks hypocrisy, ridicules orthodoxy, parodies official language, and pours withering scorn on the comfortable illusions of those who imagine that 'the party has revealed and dealt with the past'. The vehemence of the language is that of a man who is exorcizing his own inner demons – which of course is literally the case. The most persistent of his interlocutors is in effect the former Solzhenitsyn, the staunch Marxist-Leninist, the arrogant young army officer, the aspiring novelist who wanted to write a cycle of laudatory novels about the Revolution. It is against him that the contemporary Solzhenitsyn, taught by bitter experience, hurls his deadliest thunderbolts.

The anguished and acrimonious tone of these polemical passages alternates with the more collected and magisterial tone of the chronicler, the folklorist, the anthropologist arranging and expounding his strange material. The collective and objective are constantly interwoven with the personal, subjective and confessional. This is what gives the work its existential quality, what makes it (in the Russian sense) a novel as well as a history.

It is not my purpose here to examine Solzhenitsyn's later works, but what we so far have of his cycle of novels on the revolution and civil war suggests a major shift in his writing. If *The First Circle* and *The Gulag Archipelago* were polyphonic works, then *August 1914* and *Lenin in Zurich* are definitely 'monophonic'. There is no encounter of open minds, of people facing existential decisions and uncertain of the outcome. *August 1914* is a celebration of the Russian people, of their endurance, simplicity, piety and capacity for self-sacrifice, qualities which Solzhenitsyn shows in individuals of every estate, but especially in peasants, junior army officers and engineers. The action is military, and the moral underpinnings are natural and religious. Two scenes in particular are emblematic: the suicide of Samsonov and the burial of Colonel Kabanov, both of which take place in the forest. The novel is also a portrayal of the beginning of Russia's fatal decline, crushed between a corrupt and snobbish court above and uprooted, intolerant revolutionaries below. Georges Nivat has aptly called *August 1914* 'a modern Russian *bylina*',[49] and the word captures well the sense of epic certainty which, in spite of tragedy, animates the work. The narrator's position is monolithic and quite clear throughout, and a number of authorial spokesmen can be easily discerned: Vorotyntsev, Varsonof'ev, Andozerzkaya, Arkhangorodsky. His outlook is, however, also frequently expressed in the form of popular sayings, so that his stance is more that, perhaps, of the Greek chorus than of the Olympian observer. Nevertheless, some of the single-mindedness, externality and finality of traditional Socialist Realism has returned to this novel. Perhaps what we are now seeing taking shape is an inverted version of Solzhenitsyn's project of the thirties, to write an epic cycle of novels about the Revolution – only now the aim is denunciation, not glorification. Such a transition towards 'anti-Socialist Realism' would impoverish his writing, for at his best Solzhenitsyn is an existential novelist, not a political one.

6

Vladimir Maximov

No less than Solzhenitsyn, Maximov (born 1932) is a novelist of the 'extreme situation'. The heroes of his early works are explorers in the *taiga*, escapees, criminals, wanderers without passports or residence permits, living on the edge of Soviet society – where the life of the man without documents or official standing is not only precarious but degrading. These extremities confront men inescapably with themselves: they have no way of evading their deepest nature, when face to face with deprivation, horror and death. In his first work that caught public attention, *We are Taming the Earth* (*My obzhivaem zemlyu*, 1961),[1] Maximov shows us the members of an expedition in the Far North, faced with sickness and death. What they learn about themselves is that the fashionable cynicism and disillusionment that pass for a philosophy of life in less testing circumstances have no meaning here; and that extraordinary danger brings out both the best and worst in men. Also that no one, not even he who has been through similar situations himself, has the right to judge the behaviour of others. In *Man is Alive* (*Zhiv chelovek*, 1962),[2] Maximov shows us men on the run from justice, living a kind of twilight life in which they often murder and betray each other simply in order to achieve personal survival, yet at the same time can endanger themselves by acts of apparently gratuitous generosity and devotion.

In his larger novels Maximov's vision expands to take in the whole Soviet working class: he becomes, one might say, the spokesman for a whole society in an 'extreme situation'. Soviet workers have had to cope with the breakneck work pace, the appalling housing shortage, the seething human turmoil of the first Five Year Plans, then with the sacrifices demanded by the Second World War, while permanently

123

under threat from a harsh and indiscriminate political tyranny. His first full-scale novel, *The Seven Days of Creation* (*Sem'dnei tvoreniya*, 1971) aims, through the panoramic presentation of a working-class dynasty in a period of profound social upheaval, to speak for this entire society *in extremis*, learning about its own nature, its past, its historical mission, and the road to its redemption. It is the story of the ordeal of a family and of a nation. The hero, collectively, is the Lashkov family, working-class inhabitants of the railway junction city of Uzlovsk, and especially the patriarch of the family, Pëtr Vasil'evich, an old Bolshevik of Civil War vintage ending his life in disillusionment. A commissar and a trusted and respected party worker in the twenties, he lacked the cynical careerism to take him to the top (and probably ultimate disaster) in the thirties. He stayed in his modest home, doing his job as a guard on passenger trains right up to the time of the novel's action, apparently in the early sixties, when he is nearing retirement. He is, or has been, a harsh and narrow-minded father, accustomed to be obeyed rather than loved by his children:

The commonest word in his vocabulary was 'mustn't'. You mustn't do this, you mustn't do that. You mustn't do anything at all, it would seem. But his children grew up, and the world with each succeeding day became broader and higher than his 'mustn't'. They left him, and he stayed at home in the malicious confidence that they would return to seek his forgiveness. But his children did not return. His children preferred to die far from him.[3]

His sons and daughter grappled with life in various ways which infringed his narrow morality, and most of them came to grief in the harsh circumstances of political purges and war. One has survived, his daughter Antonina, now sacrificing herself, nearing forty and drifting into alcoholism, to look after her father. It is from her, and the change in her, that Pëtr learns the most.

In many ways Pëtr's Bolshevism is a secularized religious sectarianism of a stern moralist species, which enables him to divide everything categorically into the right and the wrong, the chosen and the rejected:

Over many years Pëtr Vasil'evich had, slowly and painstakingly, brick by brick, built up his own world. And, it seemed to him thus far, the edifice stood firm. In that world reigned law and order. Everything in it was checked and correct down to the smallest detail. Life was divided into two halves: 'yes' and 'no'. 'Yes' always turned out to be himself and his concept of the world; 'no' everything which contradicted that.[4]

This is Calvinist as much as it is Leninist. It gives Pëtr the criteria and the spiritual assurance to cast certain classes of people into outer darkness – the rubbish heap of history. At the same time the genuine moralism makes it impossible for him, as for Pasternak's Pasha Antipov, to accept the wholly selfish and amoral people who come to power on the backs of the revolutionary idealists, and it renders him potentially open to the kind of conversion he undergoes at the end of the novel.

His evolution away from confident Bolshevism started many years earlier, when he saw what was becoming of the Bolsheviks in power. His Civil War colleague, Paramoshin, guard on a trainload of White prisoners, had knocked out the teeth of one of his charges in order to purloin the gold fillings. When Pëtr writes a report on this incident to the head of the district Cheka, Avanesyan, the latter tells him bluntly:

'People like Paramoshin are the strength of the revolution. . . . Who do you think makes revolutions, Lashkov? Schoolboys, eh? Or bespectacled gentlemen who learnt their trade in émigré libraries, writing philosophical articles and sipping coffee? . . . Who whom. That's the only philosophy. The Paramoshins are the people we need for a revolution, Lashkov.'

This amoralism is reflected in Avanesyan's views about the use the new power-holders are entitled to make of their position:

'We didn't take power in order to live just like everybody else. We're not taking anyone else's property – it's our own. We're coming into our own as of right. The right of the victors. Let's leave asceticism to the idealists of Geneva.'[5]

Returning from this chilling interview, Pëtr refrains for the first time in his married life from interrupting his wife Maria at her prayers before the icons.

The cynical materialism of such people as Avanesyan is the natural forerunner of the life-style of modern officials, like the secretary of the *gorispolkom* (municipal council executive), Vorobushkin, whom Pëtr visits to obtain a residence permit for his godson, Nikolai, who has a criminal record. Vorobushkin sits behind a thickly upholstered door guarded by a secretary and is more interested in his coffee and newspaper than in helping the man who once, out of a sense of justice, saved him from being sentenced for railway sabotage which he had not committed.[6] Pëtr's encounter with such inheritors of the Bolshevik tradition, as well as the experiences of his family, make him receptive to the teachings of the underground church which Antonina joins. He begins to see materialist ideology in the light of an incident he suddenly remembers from the revolutionary years: crawling desperately hungry across a town square under fire because he could see a leg of ham in the shop window opposite – only to discover, when he got there, that the ham was made of cardboard.[7]

Gupak, the head of the church (and a man whom Pëtr thought he had shot in the Civil War for suspected sabotage), finds Pëtr vulnerable though not yet wholly defenceless to the insinuation that his colleagues, who have tried to change society, may not really have understood men very deeply:

'Each human soul is God's world created anew. How can you, with your deeply personal knowledge, comprehend another man, let alone compel him to live in your way? A man has to change himself for the better, not his circumstances. Now, you started with the circumstances. You have changed those circumstances, but man's soul remains hidden to you as it has always been. It is we who now take up the key to it.'

'How, with your fairy tales?'

'With the word. The good word.'[8]

Pëtr's conversion has also been prepared by his unassuming, industrious and pious wife. She died some years ago, but he recalls her uncharacteristic stubbornness over the question of the icons hanging in their home. Once, under pressure from militant party colleagues, he had tried to persuade her to part with them. Maria, normally so yielding, unexpectedly became immovable on this point. If the icons went, she would go too, she said. 'But from then on, in difficult circumstances, Pëtr Vasil'evich always felt the presence of something firm and consistent, beside which he felt secure. And for that he was grateful to Maria.'[9]

Pëtr's experience is replicated, amplified and reflected by other members of the Lashkov family: by Andrei, Pëtr's younger brother, when he is ordered to organize the evacuation of a large herd of cattle from the battle zone at the beginning of the war; by the third brother, Vasily, who as the concierge of a block of flats in Moscow, sees a procession of unhappy human fates pass before him until he succumbs to melancholy and drink; by his grandson, Vadim, failed actor and littérateur, who is confined in a mental hospital for his refractory attitudes; and by his godson, Nikolai, who marries Antonina, experiences comradeship and betrayal on a building site in Central Asia, and fathers the grandson who is the pledge that the cathartic experience of the Lashkovs will bear fruit. The peripetia of these members of the family is recounted in four separate novellas, forming four of the seven 'days of creation', and they are framed by two others, describing Pëtr's life and conversion. The seventh day – the day of hope and resurrection – is a blank page at the end from which the future begins.

Andrei's experience is illustrative. Though a member of a staunch Bolshevik family, accustomed by the forties to ruling over men, his task of evacuating cattle to Derbent is the first experience he has had of leadership. It tests his whole conception of life. His main discovery is that the Russian peasant, though he is submissive and will usually obey orders, has his own moral concepts and will not be driven against his own will beyond a certain point. His first confrontation with this force occurs when one of his most reliable peasants has a son born to him in the middle of the trek and refuses to go any further, knowing that his child would have no chance of survival in the harsh conditions of the journey, and wishing to save his life even at the price of remaining in German captivity. Andrei (unlike Solzhenitsyn's Gleb Nerzhin in his conversation with Spiridon) is horrified by the idea that preservation of the family can be more important than loyalty to one's nation.[10] He encounters peasant resistance even more sharply when, in cold weather that threatens the survival of the herd, he orders that the animals should be quartered overnight in a church. His peasants refuse to desecrate the temple of God in this way, and, when he insists, they decline to continue the journey with him, abandoning even their private cattle:

They stood before him, his best shepherds and drovers, impassive in their rectitude. He suddenly felt like a mischievous schoolboy and wanted, so much wanted to throw himself at their feet, if only they would not abandon him in the midst of that snowy waste, hundreds of miles from home. And Lashkov had almost made up his mind to abase himself and seek a compromise, but his blood ties with what in his family was always considered right and infallible took the upper hand, and he simply grated through his teeth: 'Get out of my way.'[11]

Ironically, when he arrives at his destination, the chairman of the receiving farm is short of hands and reproaches him for not bringing men with him to look after the cattle. The overvaluation of products at the expense of men defeats itself.[12] In the end Andrei takes a job as a forester, seeking an elemental peace as far away from Bolshevism as he can get, and marries a girl who had always loved him but had avoided him earlier because she didn't want to be seen chasing 'commissar's bread'.

Moved by the experiences of those closest to him, Pëtr realizes in old age that he has lived most of his life in vain, crawling, as it were, with infinite resolve and minuscule imagination across the square towards the cardboard hunk of meat. In his own modest way he has been one of the rigid, uncreative men, without skills, insight or understanding, who has brought the society to the spiritual devastation he sees clearly all around him. The exact opposite to him, in this respect, is the Gusev family, whose building repair work, craftsmanship conscientiously and joyfully carried out, helps to make his modest home ready at the end for the return of his daughter with her new baby. Installed with his new family, Pëtr feels he has reached a new understanding of the world:

Alone with himself Pëtr Vasil'evich was not afraid to admit that he was ending his life at the point at which he should have begun it. As in a dim negative newly developed, he began to understand in their fullness and richness the connections and causes of the world around him, and, struck by their mysterious sense of purpose, he started to see himself as he really was: a small particle of that well-designed organism, existing, perhaps, at the most sensitive of one of the living nodals of that organism. The realization that his 'I' was part of a vast meaningful whole afforded Pëtr Vasil'evich a sense of inner peace and balance.[13]

In many ways, though, whether or not the author sees this, this is no real change for Pëtr Vasil'evich: to feel himself part of a 'vast meaningful whole' is what he has always wanted, and for most of his life he has convinced himself that he was such a part. Now only the plus and minus signs have changed position. And the dawn into which he strides at the end holding his new grandson, Knowing and Believing, is the fully orchestrated Socialist Realist ending.

The inheritors of the earth are the Gusevs, believers and craftsmen who make things, who know their trade and are proud of it:

These people radiated an air of authority and reliability which he did not yet understand but beside which he felt more confident and lucid. Looking at them, at their strong, firm mouths, one could be certain that life on earth would never end. They would not let it end, so full and constant was the spring of activity and work which welled up within them.[14]

Their opposites are the uncreative, unskilled rulers of this world, men of no conscience whose arid word-mongering has cast the grey pall behind which the progressive demoralization of society has hitherto gone forward. Between these poles all the main characters move: and the movement is all in one direction, away from whatever truth and life Bolshevism may have once had towards the truth of the Gusevs. In fact the novel bears an overtly religious meaning. Maximov's beliefs cannot be confined within any particular church or denomination (and significantly, we are never told, or even allowed to work out, precisely which sect Gupak and the Gusevs belong to), but the meaning of *Seven Days of Creation* may be summarized unambiguously as follows: that man is a spiritual being created by God; that his essence is to love others and to use his faculties for creative work; that morality is determined by that essence and speaks from within in the form of conscience; that the Bolshevik revolution and the Soviet state result from a superficial understanding of man which sees him as a means and not as a free being, as subject to social laws and therefore amenable to social engineering; that the Soviet state has raised up a class of unskilled layabouts, incapable of creative work, and bearers of a concept of social solidarity which has nothing to do with love. The Lashkovs, originally staunch members of this class, feel the truths it professes turn to sawdust, and their sense of spiritual direction moves into opposite channels.

If *Seven Days of Creation* is a macrocosm, then *Quarantine* (*Karantin*, 1973) is a microcosm. The compositional principle is that of Camus's *The Plague* and Solzhenitsyn's *Cancer Ward*. An isolated, controlled environment threatened by disease and death shuts people away from their normal busy lives, and faces them with each other and with fundamental questions about themselves. The action, externally, takes place in only a few days, but flashbacks, dreams and visions draw in the whole of the characters' lives, and indeed the history of their country. In fact the materials of an epic are confined into quite small spatial and temporal boundaries. The cholera which catches the train up just short of Moscow is a kind of sickness of our times, like the month the two main characters, Boris and Maria, have just spent in Odessa, a month devoted to a loveless, passing and meaningless relationship. The quarantine compels them to spend more time together at a moment when they were about to part finally and with relief. This period of suspended animation turns back the process of their estrangement, ends their alienation from themselves and from one another, in a way which neither of them expects or looks for. As their immaculate co-passenger with the red tie-pin, Ivan Ivanovich Ivanov, tells Boris: '[The quarantine] will last long enough for you to return to yourself in full health.'[15]

Boris, an officer cadet at the prestigious Suvorov Academy, considers himself to be already absolutely healthy. The first discovery he has to make is of his own illness. As Ivan Ivanovich warns him, 'only dead men are healthy.'[16] To live is to be guilty: that is what Boris has to learn.

Maria is at least more conscious of her sickness. Seduced in early girlhood, and ever since an easy prey to lecherous and selfish men, she longs for 'real love', the 'perfect knight', and knows she has not found him. Counterposed to her usual experience of what language alone calls 'love', she has a memory of a boy who once used to worship her from afar, but who proved anguished and impotent when allowed to take physical possession of her. She needs a love which combines idealism with bodily passion: the true eros, in fact.

Her first advance towards self-understanding is a brief affair with the Georgian air force major Zhora Zhgenti, whose expansive southern temperament takes him beyond mere lechery to worship of this woman whom he possesses only once. His adoration gives her new strength and self-confidence – and this is vital for her, since basically it is her own low estimate of herself that degrades all her relationships. She purges this despised self in a dream of going with Zhora on a bombing mission, on which alone together they destroy the whole world, she being particularly obsessed with the need to eliminate innocent small girls before they are corrupted. This is a catharsis for her, which leaves her feeling tenderness towards those around her and conscious for the first time of growing life – Boris's child – within her.

Her new sensitivity is confirmed and deepened in Maria's relationship with a woman who is in some respects a kind of *alter ego*: Jeanne, the television actress whose life story parallels Maria's, but in even more riotous and humiliating form. When cholera is suspected on the train, Jeanne is the person who falls ill. When she is lying too weak to move, and the other passengers avoid her for fear of infection (including Boris who has had a fleeting liaison with her), Maria takes her into her own compartment and looks after her.

Maria did not feel the slightest fear of being infected, the dread of the deadly sickness did not even enter her mind: an unthinking faith in her own invulnerability had never left her from the moment she made the first step towards danger. Everything in her now was concentrated on caring for and saving the life which had been entrusted to her from the contagion consuming it.[16]

Through her sympathy – and the efforts of Ivan Ivanovich, who comes to assume a semi-magical role in the dual processes of healing and revelation – she has a vision of Jeanne's spiritual life, the lament of a Penelope who, for all her numerous lovers, has not discovered her Odysseus. (Here again the author, with his love for counterpoint and variation, puts in an account of the undying love of the White Civil

War leader Kolchak's widow for her dead husband, an experience opposite in every respect to that of Jeanne and of Maria herself.) She looks upon Jeanne at this stage with a mother's love:

Looking at her, Maria could not shake off the thought that before her lay not a woman formed by bitter experience, but only an unhappy child, who had not properly begun to live yet. With the intuition of her awakening motherhood, she sensed in the sleeping form her own defenceless 'I', and she began to weep quietly, calling on fate to show mercy and compassion. Maria was weeping for herself and Boris, for her lover and daughter, for those close to her and distant from her, for all who were grieving and suffering at that moment, and she had never in her life known tears to give such peace and relief.[17]

Boris's spiritual evolution is presented in an entirely different way. There is little inside him, or even in the events of the quarantine, to prepare him for his epiphany. It comes almost entirely from dreams and visions, which proceed partly from the admonitions of Ivan Ivanovich, and partly from the endless regime of drinking and sleeping with which the entrapped passengers while away their enforced idleness. Many of Boris's visions are ancestral memories, and lend the familial dimension of *Seven Days of Creation* a whole new extension, while also drawing into Maximov's range of themes an element less conspicuous there, namely a philosophy of Russian history.

The key to this view of Russia's evolution is betrayal. Three of Boris's four ancestors struggle for ideals in which they sincerely believe, and are betrayed by high officials of a government professing those same ideals. The devoted heathen sculptor, Il'ya, is abandoned, and his works destroyed, when his monarch converts to Christianity for reasons of state. Kirill, the monk, tries to warn Yavorsky (*locum tenens* Patriarch) of Peter the Great's planned abolition of the Patriarchate and subordination of church to state, only to find that Yavorsky betrays the secret of the confessional to the examining magistrate. And Valentin, the worldly drifter turned revolutionary, is shot in 1920 by a Cheka officer who – as an Okhrana agent – had originally advised him to enter the revolutionary movement. There is no limit to the duplicity and baseness of men who hold power, and in Russian history, both in their Tsarist and Soviet guises, they have violated everything their subjects hold sacred. As the fourth historical episode, that of the 1831 cholera, shows, the Russian people are superstitious and brutal, apathetically conformist in their bestial behaviour, but altogether less organized, effective and double-faced than their rulers.

Yet at the same time these men of power, quite without intending it – and indeed, in a moral sphere altogether remote from their understanding – have created the possibility of redemption for the mass of mankind. This is the theme dramatized in the 'Transfiguration of the Quiet Seminarist'. Structurally and in some ways thematically this is akin to Dostoevsky's Legend of the Grand Inquisitor, and one must expect in examining it to encounter something of the same multi-layered suggestiveness. We must note first of all that it is related by an Armenian priest, Akop, a former schoolmate of Zhora, who describes him as having been 'our leading atheist'.

The Quiet Seminarist is Stalin, presented here as an intelligent, diligent and shy youth, driven by an inferiority complex and an ambitious mother to endless achievement. At first he is satisfied by becoming the most brilliant scholar in the seminary, but before long he yearns for some altogether more exalted reward: to save humanity he wants to carry a cross 'that no one else can bear' (that is, if you like, to become a kind of perverted 'positive hero' in Christ's name).

In his zeal he thirsted to exceed everything which the holy fathers had wrought in the name of the Lord. The exploit of Judas, who had exposed himself to shame and execration for the greater glory of Christ, did not seem to him the ultimate in self-denial. He dreamt of achieving such things that at the feast of the saints he would sit at the right hand of the Lord.[18]

A holy man on Mount Athos advises him to go among those who, 'trampling God's commandments under foot, would turn Christ's children into a herd of obedient slaves, whose life and death shall depend on their will alone.'

'With sorrow in my heart I release you from all sins. You may practise betrayal and sacrilege, theft and murder, hypocrisy and lies. You must become the first among them. The first, no less. Their catechism is simple, their words empty and vain. Above all, forget God and conscience. When with God's help you attain the height of power among them, then your most grievous ordeal will begin. Those who have taken up the standard of lies and violence must die to the last man. And their death you will make a hundred times more terrible than the death of their victims. We shall save their souls, but let their bodies know the full measure of suffering which they have prepared for others!'[19]

The young seminarist carries out this formidable mission to the letter – as history bears witness – and finally in his death agony appears before Christ:

'Forgive me!' the former seminarist howled scarce audibly. 'Was it not for Thee that I betrayed my mother, wife and children, was it not for the sake of Thy truth that I transgressed the law and the commandments, was it not in Thy name that I plunged half the earth in blood?'

'No,' the Redeemer shook his head, 'but I forgive thee, for thou knowest not what thou didst. . . . I have come to bring peace to thy tormented soul. But thou didst not accept my gift, for it was not faith but pride that moved thee on thy path. And I have no greater reward: at my feast all are equal and all sit at the Lord's right hand. Farewell.'[20]

Akop, the narrator, interprets this legend as meaning that God has sent down a great affliction to test man and open his eyes. His conclusion is that 'the bitter experience of one nation is not enough for humanity' and that 'we shall have to go through it all again.'[21]

At times one is tempted to suppose that this is what the author himself believes. Perhaps it is sometimes. But it is not the only message that comes from the legend, especially when seen in its setting. Zhora, reassuring *homme moyen sensuel* in the midst of this elevated myth-making, protests: 'If he is right, then you and I are merely guinea pigs and nothing more. Why live then? Simply so that someone some time will at last see the truth? And you and I, then, are just so much garbage, ashes and dust?'[22] He hints at an alternative interpretation, taken up later: that God is not in fact a schemer and a controller, with tests to carry out to see whether humanity can live up to certain   Divinely imposed – ideals, but actually a co-sufferer, 'one of us', or at least sufficiently so that he has granted forgiveness and salvation to everyone, including (as Akop's legend explicitly states) Stalin.

A prisoner and a monk bring Boris his ultimate insights. The monk (the one who appeared to his pagan ancestor in Chapter 3) tells him that God 'through the sufferings of his Son on the cross learned the full measure of your sufferings and forgave you.'[23] The prisoner, still bound by the chains of the totalitarian state, sees the major temptations of humanity as 'blood and lies',[24] while the monk sees men as 'wallowing in blood and pride', 'possessed by bestial passions', but at the same time

'The measure of pain that has fallen to them is greater than their sins. Their earthly path has been saturated with such blood and tears that they can arouse nothing but pity and compassion. There is no retribution and no one to judge them. Who will venture to cast a stone at them? Who will say that in the night of fear and hatred which they had to come through, he would have remained cheerful and unsullied? Did they know what they did when they persecuted and tormented one another? They were all equally afraid, the persecutors and the persecuted. Through their common sufferings the Truth laid itself a path. With them is His love, with all of them.'[25]

Divine retribution is to be found 'here', not 'beyond'. Salvation is promised to all 'beyond', and can be found here too by those who have the wisdom, humility and insight to realize their sickness, to repent and then – as will follow naturally – to love. That is the very un-Calvinist message of the monk, and one which Boris takes up in his renewed relationship with Maria, moving out of quarantine into the 'healthy' world outside.

Quarantine is a flawed work, mostly as a result of being cast in two genres simultaneously. Whereas *Seven Days of Creation* is clearly an epic realist novel of a theological and philosophical kind, familiar from classical Russian tradition, *Quarantine* is only partly rooted in that tradition. The setting, the externals of the action and much of the language lead us to expect a realist novel, and by and large the handling of Maria (though brusque and over-concentrated by these criteria) is also of this kind. Boris, however, is treated allegorically. If his evolution is analysed from the viewpoint of the realist novel, then it is unmotivated and unconvincing. Essentially he is the hero of a spiritual biography of the *Pilgrim's Progress* type, with characters and scenes from the history of his ancestors woven into the story of his life to lead him to a goal he would be incapable of reaching on his own. Ivan Ivanovich must also be seen in this light. He is equivalent to Bunyan's Evangelist: the potions he offers, the calm he radiates are part of the *mise en scène* for the journey of the soul through temptation, bewilderment and danger.

In a way, indeed, Maximov is a kind of Bunyan of Soviet Russia. He speaks for the 'industrious sort of people', coming to terms with a literacy which opens to them the Bible (and also the Communist Manifesto), imbued with a sense of destiny, and bitterly resenting the status and privileges of the idle and unskilled parasites who claim to exercise authority. Like Bunyan, he gives a vivid picture of ordinary working men in a variety of situations; and his language affects a similar mixture of Biblical, secular, literary and colloquial styles. Above all, his principal concern is with men's pilgrimage through evil, suffering and temptation to ultimate redemption; and the structure and language of his works rest on the contrast between good and evil, light and dark, and on the perception (or lack of it) of the path and the goal ahead.

Not that, I imagine, Bunyan has been a direct influence on Maximov. On the contrary, his Bunyanesque features are probably derived rather from the Puritan side of Socialist Realism. More than perhaps any other writer mentioned in this book, Maximov is indebted to his country's official literary tradition – and this in spite of his complete rejection of that tradition's ideology. His conclusions are very different, but he has taken over in all its essentials the Socialist Realist *aesthetic*. Katerina Clark has characterized the Socialist Realist novel as 'a parable of quest, struggle, symbolic death and rebirth (i.e. initiation) whereby the life of a Soviet citizen parallels one stage in the reaching of History towards Consciousness in an ascending series of moments of epiphany, leading up to the ultimate leap into Communism.'[26] If one replaces the last word by 'redemption through love', then this is an excellent summary of the theme and structure of Maximov's two major novels, and to some extent of his other works as well. All his work is marked by a teleological drive which communicates itself through his narrative stance, his approach to his characters, his language and his thematic structures and plots. He knows the relationship of each character to the ultimate moving forces of history, can stand back and make judgements about them, and manoeuvre and manipulate them in accordance with those judgements.

Yet to call Maximov a Puritan or an inverted Socialist Realist does not quite do justice to the ambivalence of his anthropology. As a Puritan he fails to qualify fully because of his concern with collective rather than individual redemption. Furthermore, he specifically rejects the Puritan notion of the 'balance sheet' by which the sins and good deeds of the individual can be weighed against one another, or of the narrow road which leads through the conquest of temptation to the ultimate goal. In *Savva's Ballad* (*Saga o Savve*, 1974), Kirill rejects the judging God to search for his own God, of hope and forgiveness,[27] while, as we have seen, Boris's monk in *Quarantine* says of Boris's family and of the whole Russian people 'The degree of pain which has fallen to their lot is greater than their sins.' Sin and suffering do not indicate a state of alienation from God's grace, but on the contrary can be a means of self-knowledge and an advance towards redemption.

Maximov's work, then, exhibits a fundamental duality. As a thinker, he is compassionate and antinomian; but as an artist he is still a Calvinist (or Leninist) predestinarian. He is not prepared to allow his characters the freedom which his theology would accord them. As a philosopher, he disavows the Purpose, but emotionally and imaginatively he has not been able to rid himself of it. His writings, like those of Tendryakov and perhaps the later Solzhenitsyn, stand as a clear example of the contradictions which arise through partial emancipation from the Stalinist heritage.

7

Vladimir Voinovich, Georgy Vladimov

Every morning at a quarter to seven the alarm clock on my table goes off, to remind me that it's time to get up and go to work. Of course, I don't feel like getting up or going to work. Outside it's still dark, and the window, spattered with rain, is only just visible against the dark wall. I tug at the loop of the light switch, and then lie for several minutes with the light on, feeling the primeval desire to snooze for a while. Then I lower my legs to the floor – first one, then the other. From that moment the process of turning me into a modern man gets under way.

First of all I sit on the bed staring vacantly at some unspecified spot on the opposite wall, scratch myself, sigh and open my mouth wide. I have a bad taste in my mouth, and there is a kind of gurgling in my chest, probably because I smoke too much. My heart aches. Or rather it doesn't ache, it's just that I'm conscious of it, as if someone had inserted a round cobblestone under my skin there. Anyone lucky enough to observe me at this moment would get quite a bit of enjoyment from the sight. There can be few things on earth more ridiculous than my face, my person and the posture I adopt during these moments. Then I begin to wiggle my toes, wave my arms about and perform other gestures distantly reminiscent of gymnastic exercises. On the floor under the radiator lie a pair of dumb-bells that I bought last year. They are covered by a thick layer of dust and look bigger than they really are. I haven't used them for a long time, and the dust on them gives me a certain excuse – I don't want to make my hands filthy. But there was a time when I could do gymnastics and be out on parade within three minutes of reveille with my pack, my tommy-gun and all the other paraphernalia. Sergeant Shuldykov, who first taught me how to do it, he'd say: 'I'll have you up and ready to go in three minutes even when you get back to civvy street. I'll teach you how to do it. That's the aim of my life.'

If he had no other aims, then one must conclude that Sergeant Shuldykov lived in vain.[1]

Much of the essence of Vladimir Voinovich (born 1932) is in this passage, which opens his short story *I Want to be Honest* (*Khochubyt' chestnym*, 1963). The general tone is that of 'youth prose': the

136

somewhat self-deprecatory approach, the ironic use of words and phrases slightly too pretentious for the trivial subject, the insistence on minor and unprepossessing details of everyday life, the amused self-observation. The narrator, Samokhin, is a man without any evident motivation or ideal, the trivia of his life exist *per se* unilluminated by any purpose: he has simply to deal with them as they come. Why then is the story called *I Want to be Honest*? How does a man as vacant as Samokhin come to express any such sentiment? This is where Voinovich's individual features as a writer begin to assert themselves. We see something of them already in this opening passage in phrases like 'primeval desire', 'turning me into a modern man' and in the irony over the aim of Sergeant Shuldykov's life. There is something unusually gaunt in Voinovich's initial presentation of his characters: in *Two Comrades* (*Dva tovarishcha*, 1967), indeed, they are all naked, undergoing a medical examination at the military draft board. At the beginning of his stories, they nearly always appear as people without qualities, without apparent purpose or inner motivation, bewildered by the world, but still very open to experience precisely because of their inner emptiness. Often they are very young. The author begins by showing them in the midst of their everyday preoccupations, where their aims are strictly limited and short-term. Only gradually do more serious, long-term purposes emerge out of this daily friction with reality; only gradually do the characters discover themselves. Some of them never do so, or discover false, inauthentic selves, like Sergeant Shuldykov, whose sarcasm masks the fact that his life probably did indeed have little purpose beyond getting his platoon on parade in impeccable external order.

In a sense, Voinovich was rethinking the concept of the 'positive hero'. In his first published work, *We live here* (*Myzdes'zhivëm*, 1961) – note the bald, declaratory titles – Goshka, the unassuming, muddled chief character, is exhorted by his girl friend – who is thinking of leaving him for the attractions of the capital – to carry out some 'great deed' to prove his love for her. When he misses work – in order to revise for an examination – the chairman of his kolkhoz reminds him that in the Civil War Red Army cavalrymen were on horseback without a break for three days and nights. Even his friend Anatoly assures him that he is a 'negative hero'. But the point about Goshka is that he remains stolidly unimpressed by all these well served up literary and historical models and lives his own life as best he knows how, on the humbler values derived from a village childhood, and with the vague desire to improve himself by passing his exams and going into the town for further education.

An even more unlikely positive hero is Afanasy Ochkin, of *Half a Kilometre Away* (*Rasstoyanie v polkilometra*, 1963), a shirker of military service, a man who has spent most of his life with a criminal record in labour camps and has caused his wife constant distress and deprivation. His 'life path' is summed up in the last sentence of the story: 'Ochkin, who had been born half a kilometre from his grave, had travelled much and seen much – yet all the same he had covered only this half kilometre, had traversed in forty years a distance that for a normal person on foot takes only seven minutes.'[2]

There was clearly no Purpose to his life, only trivial, immediate, expedient purposes with a small 'p', such as the avoidance of trouble. But for Voinovich 'positive heroes' are not defined by any great Purpose, or even small ones. Two of his characters spend a great deal of their time arguing about how many columns there are to the portals of the Bolshoi Theatre. The argument has many variations, is often accompanied by drink and is resumed every time they meet. When one of them settles the question for himself in his own favour by getting hold of a postcard of the theatre, his triumph turns to dust in his imagination, and in the end he does not even claim the drink that is his due – he simply quietly tears the postcard up, so that the argument can continue. Much of Voinovich's work is a comic commentary on Nadezhda Mandel'shtam's distinction between 'aim' and 'meaning':

When I was young the question of the meaning of life had been superseded by the search for an aim. People are so used to this that even now they fail to see the difference between the two. In those years it was the revolutionary young who raised the question of an aim in life, and they had only one: to bring happiness to mankind. We all know where that landed us. The problem of meaning, as opposed to aim, is appreciated by very few people when they are young, since it can be grasped only through personal experience, and is tied up with the question of one's own identity. People are thus more inclined to think about it in their old age – and then only those who prepare for death and look back on their past life.[3]

For Voinovich's characters the situation is reversed: all aims have already been discredited, and there remains only the search for meaning.

Samokhin too is offered a purpose, in the usual party style: he is to hand over his section of an apartment block in time for the approaching Komsomol celebrations. He will then be promoted from mere senior foreman to the prestigious post of chief engineer, so that not only the party's purpose, but his own self-interest will be advanced. But something about this offer brings Samokhin up against his own rock-bottom sense of the things that are important to him. Everything that we have been told so far about him, his job and his work environment speak of a world completely without values. He has become a construction expert by sheer accident. He has no particular ambitions, and the building site on which he works is plagued by slovenly workmanship, poor quality tools, missing materials, and general cynicism amounting to bloody-mindedness. Samokhin, in his capacity as narrator, has recounted all this faithfully and clear-sightedly, but we have had no indication that he intends to stand out against it in any way. This offer of promotion, however, brings out his reserve of principle, for he knows there is no chance whatever of handing over the building in habitable condition by the deadline – and he suddenly realizes that he is not prepared to hand it over in any other condition. In the normal sense, in the sense in which his mother uses the term, he is a failure, because he has become 'neither a scholar nor a high-up boss' by the age of 42. So what remains?

My work is no better, but also no worse than anyone else's. Whether this is really my calling or not I still don't know, and frankly I'm not terribly interested. One's calling is only really put to the test in a job that requires a particular talent. A foreman doesn't need much in the way of talent – it's quite enough for him to be able to get hold of materials, read a set of plans and fill in the workers' job sheets in good time. There's no way, for example, I can build a house better than it is on the drawing-board.

But sometimes they want me to build the thing worse than I am capable of, and that annoys me. And when I object, that annoys the authorities.[4]

That is what motivates his decision: the realization that this is all he has left to sustain his own self-respect – 'whether my work is good or bad, it's all I have.' As so often in Voinovich's work there is an enormous gap between the formalities and the reality. The members of the inspection commission are not in the least interested in the quality of the work they are looking over: the sanitary inspector wants to get his suit from the dry cleaners before the queue gets too long, and the representative of the district executive committee has to buy provisions for his family for the holiday. They are both anxious to get the job over as soon as possible, without muddying their boots in the process, and are unconcerned by doors that do not close and even by a balcony railing that comes loose. They regard the Komsomol representative who insistently calls attention to the deficiencies as both naïve and a careerist. It is their negligent and slovenly attitude that finally stings Samokhin into refusing to sign the transfer document, when he was almost prepared to acquiesce out of weary cynicism.

Primary peddler of the appearances which mask reality is the newspaper reporter, Gusev, who comes to interview Samokhin, with his article about him and his promotion already almost completely written:

'I'd like to begin with the war. I need to show you blowing up houses, but dreaming of building new ones. The theme of the struggle for peace is very important just now. Were you an officer in the war?'

'No,' I said, 'in the war I was a sergeant-major, and I didn't blow up any houses because I was in intelligence.'

'It doesn't matter where you served,' he said. 'I want you blowing up houses for the principle of the thing. But tell me: when did you decide to become a construction engineer, during the war or as a child?'

'Well, I don't know what to say,' I hesitated. 'You see, after I was wounded I lived right opposite the construction institute. To get to any other institute I would have had to take a tram, but to get to that one I just had to cross the road. And I was on crutches then . . .'

'I see,' said Gusev, but did not write anything in his notepad.[5]

The 'magnificent prospects' of the distant future, the construction of communism, projected in official propaganda, have been allowed to smother present realities completely, leading most people to ignore the limited but genuine values that can still be preserved. In that respect Samokhin's irascible assertion of his sense of himself and the things he stands for is a reaction against the doublethink characteristic of public life. In his private life he goes through more or less the same evolution. His girl friend Klava is divorced, approaching middle age, and very dependent on him. She lies on Her sofa, reading countless novels and drawing from them effective phrases to use in her dramatic but never quite convincing appeals to him. He is impatient at her persistence, always on the point of leaving her, but never quite able to bring himself to do so. His image of Klava is clouded by the memory of Rosa, a beautiful Jewish girl whom he had loved chastely more than twenty years ago, and who had been killed by the Nazis at Baby Yar. She is still for him the ideal of womanhood, beside whom Klava seems a mere grey everyday comfort.

Klava, however, becomes pregnant, and a settlement of their uncertain relations becomes imperative. When Samokhin is injured (carrying an oxygen cylinder, trying to get the building finished quickly, even after it can no longer mean promotion for him), Klava visits him in hospital, and offers to take him home to look after him.

'No, no,' he says at first, 'I don't want you carrying my chamber pots after me.' This does not at all accord with his picture of Rosa, but he reflects all the same: 'Maybe that's what real love is, carrying chamber pots.'[6] At any rate he agrees rather hesitantly that the baby should be born and that he and Klava should make a family for it. In private as in public life, Samokhin finishes by standing up for the limited but real as against the distant or unattainable ideal.

The split between reality and ideal, between reality and appearance runs right through the work, and is explored in comic vein in the person of Ivan Adamovich, Samokhin's neighbour in the communal apartment. When appearances and the ideal are as dominant as they are in Soviet society, the individual is often tempted to doubt his own autonomous value, even his individual existence: this is the source of most of the cynicism with which this story is filled. Ivan Adamovich, who has been reading the old idealist philosophers, takes this one stage further and comes in one evening to Samokhin to announce: 'You think you exist. But in fact you don't. . . . You don't exist, neither does this room, nor this table   nothing. Everything is our imagination. A universal vacuum.' However, he too is brought up rudely against reality, in the shape of a two-year-old girl parked on him by a niece who has gone off for the night with her lover. When the little girl cries, he tries at first to comfort her, but soon loses his temper and shouts: 'I can't hear you crying. . . . Your crying doesn't exist. You don't exist and I don't exist. . . .'[7] This denial of reality collapses in the face of the evidence of dirty nappies:

Ivan Adamovich was holding up some little towelling panties in two fingers, and his face was a picture of complete discomfiture. 'Zhenya,' he said, 'look what the little horror has done.'
   'I can't see anything,' I said.
   'How d'you mean?' said Ivan Adamovich, taken aback.
   'Very simple.' I shrugged my shoulders. 'I can't see anything, that's all. It's all your imagination, Ivan Adamovich.'
   With his free hand, Ivan Adamovich thoughtfully scratched the back of his head. 'But it stinks,' he said uncertainly.[8]

Moral nihilism and philosophical solipsism are defeated by chamber pots and dirty nappies. Everyday reality and family life assert their rights with reassuring solidity, even in their least prepossessing forms. But in Soviet public life the last word remains with appearances. Gusev, having heard of Samokhin's refusal to hand over an incomplete building, has published on him, under the title 'High Principles', exactly the same article that he was preparing for

Samokhin's promotion to chief engineer. 'I was right about Gusev,' is the narrator's parting comment.[9]

The struggle to discover personal identity and to act in accordance with it is conducted not only against the pretences and chicaneries of public life, but also often against the love of one's nearest and dearest, as Voinovich shows in his *Two Comrades* (*Dva tovarishcha*, 1967). Valerka, the narrator and chief figure, lives alone with his mother and grandmother, his father having left with another woman. These two devoted women have marked out his entire future career for him: he is to study hard, pass his exams, go to an electrical engineering institute and become a successful electrical engineer. To this end, they try to supervise all his free time and his friendships:

I hadn't got a girl friend. I only had mother and grandmother, who for their own peace of mind wanted every incident in my private life to take place before their eyes. At nineteen I realized that restriction of the freedom of personality is a grave infliction, even if it is the result of someone's infinite love.[10]

By way of compensation he strikes up a friendship with the worldly and – by provincial adolescent standards – sophisticated Tolik, whom his mother cannot stand. 'I can understand it,' she says, 'when common interests bring people together, or when they become friends out of ideological conviction.'[11] But, as Valerka explains to the reader, neither he nor Tolik have any ideological convictions: it's just that they live in the same block of flats, and work in the same factory, which makes important and secret objects for the space research programme – but in the downbeat fashion of Voinovich's heroes, the two of them have no part in making the objects themselves, only the boxes in which the said objects are packed:

I think Tolik secretly hoped that they would launch the boxes themselves into space. For that reason, inside the boxes he sometimes pencilled in his surname, Bozhko, so that if any of them should reach another planet, his name would become known not only on earth but beyond it too.[12]

The early part of the work is taken up with various escapades of the pair, youthful pranks as a substitute for scrawling one's name on other planets. The last prank turns out to be much more important. Tolik, who is always the leader, takes them to an airfield, where they manage to wangle themselves onto a training flight. Afterwards Valerka cannot get the sensation of flying out of his mind. He resolves to become a pilot, even though – or perhaps because? – the best way for him to do this is to fail his exams and be drafted into the armed forces, taking just the road that his mother and grandmother most dread for him. The exams become in fact the moment of his self-assertion and self-discovery. He is supposed to be writing an essay on the 'Moral Character of Young Soviet Man', but what he does is to assert his own 'moral character' in his own way by writing a passionate description of his first flight in an aircraft. Ironically, the examiner who marks his paper is a woman with literary pretensions herself: she recognizes real quality in his writing, and gives him a five, the highest mark. She, though only briefly portrayed, is one of Voinovich's self-deceivers, and one who tries to mould others according to her image of them: she reads Valerka some of her dreadful verse, overloaded with alliteration, and enrols him for her literary seminar. Eventually Valerka has deliberately to take an exam in German instead of English (which he has been learning in school) in order to fail sensationally in a foreign language.

That was a real delight. I got my own back in full measure on everyone who was trying to push me into that institute, and on everyone who wanted to turn me into the local literary genius. The ancient walls of that institute had probably never heard such idiotic answers, and the examiner was so shaken that her pen broke as she wrote in my 'fail'.[13]

Compared with this, Tolik's worldly adroitness is now seen to mask an inner lack of genuine identity. He and Valerka are set upon by a gang of hoodlums. The maliciously inventive leader of the gang decides to add moral to physical injury by forcing Tolik to beat Valerka up. Tolik at first tries to escape, then to get away with a half-hearted swipe at his friend, but finally under pressure hits Valerka repeatedly and zealously.[14]

This is the turning point of the novel. From now on the relationship between Valerka and Tolik is reversed. Tolik seems reduced in stature, dependent on Valerka, and becomes obsessed with excusing himself for what he has done. 'It was better for you that way because *they* would have hit you even harder,' he pleads. 'There's a philosophy for you,' Valerka comments to the reader. 'I came across it later in other circumstances, heard almost those very words from people hastening to do what someone else would have done anyway in their place.'[15] Earlier on, he had felt sympathy for the fate of the apostle Peter because he denied Christ and then repented.[16] But faced with Tolik's analogous betrayal, he does not feel much sympathy. His attitude is not one of straightforward moral condemnation. it is just that Tolik now seems a smaller and less interesting person, and Valerka, having found his own feet, does not need a friend who has disclosed his inner emptiness so dramatically.

The society against whose background this friendship is struck up and then dissolved is sketched more sparingly than in *I Want to be Honest*, but one pervasive image keeps recurring, that of the enormous 'Palace' which divides the town in two.

To start with it was supposed to be the largest Palace of Metallurgists in the country, in the style of Corbusier. The Palace was almost finished, when it turned out that the architect was under the influence of western architecture. He got such a rocket for old Corbusier that it took him a long time to recover. Then times changed and they allowed the architect to return to his interrupted labours. But – once bitten, twice shy – he added to the building some hexagonal columns standing as though separately, just in case of anything. They called the edifice the Palace of Science and Technology, once again the largest in the country. After the erection of the columns they stopped building for a time, because under this largest thing in the country they had discovered the largest ever reservoir of sub-foundation waters. A few years went by – where the waters went I don't know – and they started building yet again, only now it was to be the largest Palace of Weddings in Europe.

The incongruity of this gigantism applied to the family and personal relations is underlined a little later when the narrator comments: 'Our flat was not the largest in the country: the three of us lived in two adjacent rooms.'[17] The unfinished Palace of Weddings, with its incomplete windows looking like dark baleful eyes, forms the background for the gang attack which is the climax of the work.

The story finishes with Tolik having become a poet, reading his banal verses to Valerka (like Gusev in *I Want to be Honest* he is a bearer of inauthentic experience), and then nervously fiddling with his string bag in his hand as he yet again pleads for Valerka's forgiveness.

In the end I managed to get away from him and walked on. After a bit I looked round. Tolik was standing in the middle of the road twisting his idiotic string bag first in one direction, then in the other. When he saw that I had turned round he hastily smiled and started to wave frantically. I couldn't help it – I raised my hand and made a non-committal gesture, half waving but at the same time half not waving. Its meaning was probably: 'OK, that's enough. Let's forget about it. The past is the past.'[18]

If that sentiment applies to the incident which so obsesses Tolik, then it probably also applies to their friendship. But even this is not certain: there is a gentle ambiguity about the ending. Voinovich very rarely consigns anyone to complete condemnation.

All of the works mentioned above show human beings finding themselves in a complicated world of corruption and duplicity, though also of love and understanding. Voinovich was asking in effect: how is principled action possible in the modern world? How is the good man formed, not ideally but in actuality? He was posing the traditional Socialist Realist questions in an entirely new form. In each case, it is not a purpose (still less the Purpose) which draws them on, but rather they discover by trial and error, even by accident, their own authentic forms of existence, the forms in which their own personality is most genuinely expressed, in which they can 'be themselves'. Their morality is based not on ideals or purposes, but on the concept of Solzhenitsyn's Spiridon: 'the wolfhound is right, the cannibal is wrong.'

The discovery of the authentic self lies, in fact, at the centre of Voinovich's work in general. In particular it underlies the satire in his novel *The Life and Extraordinary Adventures of Private Ivan Chonkin*, (*Zhizn' i neobychainye priklyucheniya soldata Ivana Chonkina*, 1975). The fundamental absurdity which the novel brings to light is the inauthentic existence forced on everyone in Soviet society by an overbearing system of authority and ideology, whose structures partly – in extreme cases completely – replace the human personality. The chief character, the red-faced, bow-legged soldier Chonkin himself, is the ideal catalyst for this satire because, though he is subject to the external coercion as much as anyone else, he does not internalize its ideology: indeed he is too good-natured and stupid even to understand it, and in that way remains spiritually free from it. When he stands up at a political education session and, incited by an unscrupulous colleague, asks if Comrade Stalin has had two wives, his naïvety releases a pent up complex of unmentionable subjects which reduce the political commissar to helpless silence. Chonkin is the innocent fool who gets everybody at cross purposes and in the process reveals their hidden motives. He is as good a touchstone for showing up the varieties of inauthentic existence as Chichikov in Gogol's *Dead Souls*.

He is of course an utterly unheroic hero, as the author admits to the reader early on:

'What a sorry sight he makes!' you will say indignantly. 'What kind of example is this for the younger generation?'... Couldn't the author have taken a military hero from real life, a tall, well-built, disciplined, crack student of military and political theory?' Of course I could have, but I was too late. All the crack students had already been grabbed up and I was left with Chonkin. At first I was disappointed, but then I accepted my luck. After all, the hero of your book is like your own child, you get what you get, you don't just fling him out of the window. Maybe some other people's children are a little better, a little smarter, but still you love your own more just because he's your own.[19]

This passage challenges the inherited Socialist Realist assumptions about literature in a number of respects. It is not only that the hero is different, but so too is the narrator, his relationship to reality and his attitude to the reader. Right from the beginning Voinovich has implied that his story is both reality and fantasy: 'It is impossible to say definitely whether it all really did happen or not, because the incident which set the whole affair in motion . . . happened in the village of Krasnoe so long ago that there are practically no eyewitnesses left. . . . I've collected everything I've heard on the subject and added a little something of my own as well, in fact maybe I've even added a little more than I heard.'[20] This ambiguity will persist throughout the novel, and is shown to arise out of the nature of Soviet reality, which (a) is fantastic, in the usual sense of the word, and (b) consists in large part of state-sponsored fantasy of one kind or another. Take the following activity of the chairman of the kolkhoz, from later in the novel, which is fantastic in both senses:

Ivan Timofeevich Golubev was sitting in his office, toiling over the composition of a report concerning haymaking in the last ten-day period. Needless to say, the report was a fraud, since there had been practically no haymaking at all during the last ten-day period. The men were leaving for the front, and the women were getting them ready – what kind of harvest could you expect? The District Committee, however, did not consider such reasons valid. Borisov would swear at him over the phone and demand that the plan be fulfilled. Of course he knew that at a time like this he was asking the impossible, but for him the papers reporting completed work were more important than the work itself – for his superiors were swearing at him too. So Borisov was collecting papers from all the kolkhozes, compiling the figures, and sending them up to the provincial level, where further reports were being drawn up on the basis of the district reports, and so on, all the way up to the top. And that's how Golubev came to be sitting in his office making his own modest contribution to the great cause of paper work.[21]

Most of the time Golubev is conscious of what he is doing and of the distinction between reality and fantasy, but just occasionally, looking over the immaculately tabulated figures he 'caught himself starting to half-believe them.'[22] Such is the insidious nature of consistently sustained fantasy. Fantasy has a grip on us beyond what positivist and scientist philosophies would lead us to expect. Man brings his own inner life to bear on his perception and interpretation of the outside world. On one level, what Voinovich is doing in *Chonkin* is showing up one set of fantasies, inhumane and harmful, and trying to replace them with another set, more gentle, fruitful and humane. He is asking the reader to make his own imaginative contribution to this process, to respond and add to his, the author's work, 'but if the story seems to you uninteresting, boring or even foolish, then just spit and forget I ever told it.'[23]

Chonkin is his ally in this process. A kind of 'anti-Socialist Realist hero', he springs from much earlier literary and even pre-literary roots: from Chekhov's little men, Tolstoy's simple peasants, Leskov's eccentric and slightly ridiculous 'saints', and above all from Ivan the Fool, the stupid peasant of Russian folk tales, who leads a charmed life in communion with animals and nature, and whose cheerful simplicity brings him miraculous victories over the rich, sophisticated and powerful of this world. There are all kinds of echoes and overtones in Chonkin's personality. His very origins are mysterious: rumour has it that he may be the illegitimate son of the last Prince Golitsyn. On the other hand, his father may have been an ordinary shepherd. Who knows? But he clearly springs from a twilight world of the prerevolutionary popular and literary imagination. The irruption of this unlikely (yet on another level very ordinary) figure into Soviet society provides the opportunity for a satire which reveals not only the absurdities of the system but also its deeper human mechanisms.

At the beginning Chonkin is under the external compulsion of the system. He leaps up and down in the hot sunshine under Sergeant Peskov's orders because he has no choice. But he is notorious for his untidiness and inability to perform the simplest parade ground manoeuvre without tripping over himself. More than a year of army training has made not the slightest impression on him, and he is doing the duty most suited to his personality – managing the stable, where he can collect firewood, cart dung, and talk to horses who, unlike human beings, don't answer back. Summoned to unexpected sentry duty, however, Chonkin is suddenly freed from all immediate surveillance and compulsion. Rather quickly he sloughs off his forced existence as a soldier and resumes his natural existence as a man and a peasant:

Chonkin stopped and, resting against the plane, started to think. They had left him alone for a week with no one to relieve him. So what was he to do? According to the regulations a sentry was forbidden to eat, drink, smoke, laugh, sing, talk or relieve himself. But could he really just stand there for a week? In the course of a week, try as you might, you couldn't help breaking the regulations! Having come to that conclusion, Chonkin walked back to the tailplane and broke the regulations there and then. He looked around. Nothing happened.[24]

He begins to sing songs, and exchanges ribald remarks with some women passing in a cart:

All this had the pleasantest effect on Chonkin. He leaned on his rifle and was overcome by thoughts of the opposite sex, such as were not at all permitted by the regulations. He looked around again, but not as he had done before, with nothing in mind, just for the sake of a look; now he had something quite definite in mind.

And he found it.

In the vegetable garden closest to him Chonkin caught sight of Nyura Belashova, who, after her afternoon rest, had come out again to mound her potatoes. Her chopper moved in measured rhythms as she turned various sides to Chonkin, who watched her closely, evaluating her ample forms at their full merit.[25]

Having made this transition from regulation-bound soldier to natural man, Chonkin more or less renounces his sentry duty altogether, not from slovenliness, but because there does not seem any point in elaborately guarding a plane miles from anywhere. He moves in with the plump Nyura, helps her in house and garden plot, and in fact resumes his proper existence as a peasant – in which capacity he exhibits a competence and intelligence that would have astounded his sergeant. Indeed as a peasant he goes on in later parts of the novel to become what he never was in the army, a first-rate soldier, and to win miraculous victories over the most powerful institution in the land, the NKVD.

It is worth making the point, since the comparison suggests itself, that in this respect Chonkin is entirely different from the Good Soldier Schweik. Schweik is a born shirker, lazy, foulmouthed, often actively malevolent. He achieves his victories by wilfully obstructing the system or at best by negligence and slovenliness. Chonkin, by contrast, is unfailingly good-natured, loyal and conscientious. He believes in Stalin, seeing him as a father figure, and he wants to do his duty by him and the motherland. Indeed, it is excess of zeal that leads him to defend his plane against the NKVD troops, whom he mistakes for Germans. It is by his very devotion to the system that he defeats it and shows it up: an irony altogether more profound than that we find in Hasek's work – for all the latter's qualities.

Chonkin's good-hearted devotion to the system, coupled with his complete failure, through stupidity and good nature, to understand its doublethink, show up every other character in the book, both by contrast and as a direct result of Chonkin's actions. Take Golubev, for example. We have already seen the kind of enforced make-believe he has to take part in. His life is a hell of personal indecision and mute brow-mopping obedience, softened only by the liquor he keeps in the farm strong-box. For every decision – or indecision – he can be held responsible. His colleague, Kilin, the village party organizer (*partorg*), is in the same position. Their situation is summed up in the scene at the beginning of part two when the news of the outbreak of war reaches the village and all the villagers rush to the farm office to find out what has happened. Kilin, who has been told to organize a 'spontaneous meeting' to explain the military-political situation, is delighted that they have gathered so quickly. However, when he phones district party headquarters for further instructions about how to conduct the meeting, he is severely reprimanded for having allowed a 'spontaneous meeting' to assemble spontaneously:

'You have unleashed anarchy, that's what you have done!' Borisov let his words fall like drops of lead. 'Who ever heard of people assembling all by themselves, without any direction from the leadership?'

Kilin went cold inside.

'But listen, Sergei Nikanorich, I mean, you said yourself: "A spontaneous meeting"' . . .

'Spontaneity, comrade Kilin, must be directed!' rapped out Borisov.[26]

Borisov's last pronouncement can stand on its own as a summary of the doublethink that dominates the lives of all the party officials, and on whose twin prongs they go in fear all their lives. This is the old conflict between 'spontaneity' and 'consciousness', now reduced to burlesque: Kilin has forcibly to disperse the inquisitive crowd to their homes, and then laboriously recall them from their everyday concerns.

The speech which Golubev reads at the meeting thus perversely convened reveals much about the relationship between words and reality under this system.

'Comrades!' the partorg began his speech and immediately heard the sound of sobbing. Displeased, he looked down to see who was causing the disturbance. All he saw was people's faces.

'Comrades!' he repeated, and suddenly felt that he could not say another word. It was only at that moment that he really took in everything that had happened, the grief that had come upon them all, himself included. Seen against this grief all his recent fears and cunning moves seemed absolutely trivial. And the text on the paper in front of him also seemed trivial, empty and stupid. What could he say to these people who, at this very moment, were waiting for words which he did not have in him? Only a moment before, he had been thinking of himself as someone special – a representative of a higher power that knows and understands when, what and how everything should be done. Now he knew nothing.

Soon however he gets a grip on himself:

'Comrades!' he began for the fourth time. 'The treacherous attack by Fascist

Germany . . .'. He felt some relief as soon as he had spoken the first phrase. Gradually he took possession of his text and the text took possession of him. The familiar word patterns dulled his sense of grief, distracted his mind, and soon Kilin's tongue was babbling away all by itself, like a separate and independent part of his body: 'We shall stand our ground . . . we shall return blow for blow . . . with heroic labour we shall meet . . .'.

The weeping from the crowd stopped. Kilin's words caused vibrations in people's eardrums but did not reach their minds. Their thoughts were returning to their ordinary concerns.[27]

So crazy is this world of authoritarian fantasy, mumbo-jumbo and doublethink that Golubev gets it into his head that Chonkin is some kind of 'inspector-general' come to unmask all his fabrications and contrivances – just about the unlikeliest character imaginable to have been cast in this role. For some days he goes around tense, fearful and irritable, afraid to do or say anything openly. Eventually he can stand it no longer, and decides to challenge Chonkin directly. The resulting conversation is a comedy of misunderstandings, but Golubev finishes up by losing his temper and pouring out at the bewildered Chonkin years of pent-up spleen and frustration. This is the one time in the novel when he breaks out of his world of servile word-bound make-believe, expresses his real feelings, and enjoys a moment of 'authentic existence'. He thinks that his daring will cost him years in a labour camp, but all the same he 'returned home in a good frame of mind that day. He stroked the heads of his sleeping children and even said a tender word to his wife, who was so unused to affection from her husband that she went out into the hallway and shed a few tears.'[28]

Golubev and Kilin are ordinary corrupt, lazy, timid, uncomplicated human beings, who find the authoritarianism and duplicity of the system difficult to adjust to, and resort to the bottle when the strain gets too intense. Not so Revkin, the first secretary of the district party committee (and hence Borisov's superior). His personality is entirely made up of official attitudes, and for that reason, when Chonkin (in one of his 'extraordinary adventures') captures the entire local branch of the NKVD, he feels their absence as an *internal* malaise:

Comrade Revkin gradually began to sense that something was missing in the world around him. This odd sensation gradually grew stronger; it stuck in him like a splinter, and wherever he was he could not help thinking about it – in his office at the District Committee, at a conference of outstanding workers, at a session of the District Soviet, even at home. Having failed to come to any understanding of his condition, he lost his appetite, grew distracted, and once he even went so far as to put his long johns on over his riding breeches and was about to go to work like that, but Motya, his personal chauffeur, tactfully restrained him.[29]

The most extended portrait of an authority figure is that of the NKVD Captain Milyaga, whose suave, smiling exterior masks (or perhaps reveals?) a personality entirely formed by the inauthenticity of power. This personality is first revealed in its dual poles of lordliness and servility in the encounter with the Jewish trader, Moisei Solomonovich, whose surname turns out to be – genuinely – Stalin. The disintegration of Milyaga starts when he goes out to the village of Krasnoe to discover what has happened to the NKVD platoon he sent to capture Chonkin. Taken prisoner in his turn, he remains for some days isolated from the world in Nyura's hut, and for the first time in his life feels unneeded, not part of any smooth, well-ordered organization. He contrives to escape, but this makes things worse, because he does not know whether perhaps the Germans have occupied the area, whether (horror of horrors) the NKVD has ceased to exist locally

> He couldn't understand now why he had escaped. It had been warm and comfortable back in the hut, but out here there was the rain and the cold and it was pitch black and he did not know where to run, or for what. . . . If someone had come up to him and asked: 'Hey, what are you crying for?' Milyaga could not have answered. From joy that he was free again? But he felt no joy. From fury? From the desire for revenge? At that moment he felt neither. All he felt was complete indifference to his fate, hopelessness and the utter futility of anything he might do.[30]

This breakdown of his personality is followed by a grotesque revelation of its real nature. When he is captured by a patrol from the Red Army regiment sent to liquidate 'Chonkin and his band', he is mistaken for a German paratrooper, while he himself takes his captors for members of a German occupying force. The resulting interrogation, with its double-entendres, in which Milyaga tries to pass himself off as someone who might be useful to the Gestapo, and finishes screaming 'Long live comrade Hitler!' is a masterpiece of satirical revelation.

The peculiar kind of society that Voinovich is examining needs not only its authority figures, but also at least a few true believers. Such is the home-grown village scientist, Gladyshev, a figure with more than a touch of Lysenko about him, and the man who actually betrays Chonkin's presence in the village to the NKVD. Drawing his erudition from a prewar run of popular scientific journals, and 'inspired by the progressive teachings of Michurin and Lysenko', he tries by selective breeding to produce a hybrid combining the fruit of the tomato with the roots of the potato (which plant he proposes to call a *puks* – short for 'Road to Socialism' in Russian, but also suggesting the word for 'fart'). 'So far these experiments had not produced any actual results, although certain characteristics of the "puks" had already started to appear: the leaves and stems were rather like those of potatoes, and the roots were absolutely tomato-like.'[31] He also has an elaborate and improbable project for solving the problem of Soviet agriculture. Since, as he observes, dung is the fertilizer which starts food growing, and since all food, having been digested, returns to the state of dung, one could simplify the natural cycle and do away with the need for agriculture altogether by living on dung alone. In pursuit of this project he fills his house (to the utter despair of his wife) with pots containing different varieties of excrement in order to investigate their properties, and even concocts a home-brew from dung to offer to his guests.[32]

Given the name of the tomato plant, one cannot help but feel that for the author these coprophilous schemes are a kind of Rabelaisian *reductio ad absurdum* of the whole Purpose of using science to build a communist society. Gladyshev is the only person in the village who not only accepts the existing power system, but also accords it genuine devotion, out of belief in its progressive and scientific nature. The capacity some people have for building their whole lives out of illusion and ignoring even insistent realities is essential to a lasting totalitarian system, and this capacity is one which has always fascinated Voinovich. In *By Means of Mutual Correspondence* (*Putëm vzaimnoi perepiski*, 1973) he shows how a whole marriage is built out of some innocent pen-friend flirtation, exploited by a woman determined to get her hands on a man and settle down with him. The mixture of allure, cunning and brute force with which she ensnares her partner is in its own homely way reminiscent of the means used by the totalitarian state, and substitutes for love in holding the family together. In his novel *Degree of Trust* (*Stepen' doveriya*, 1973) – a portrait of the nineteenth-century revolutionary Vera Figner – there is one figure, the failed writer Skurlatsky, who wants to imagine himself a leading revolutionary, close to those who assassinated Tsar Alexander II, and who carries through his assumed role, even when arrested by the security police, interrogated and confronted with his supposed colleagues. Again, these are cases of people without their own genuine inner life, their own authentic existence – the woman who wants a husband, the writer who cannot write a novel – and who therefore fill their emptiness with grandiose and absurd substitutes. The implication is inescapable that the most zealous supporters of the totalitarian state also act out of inner emptiness.

Fantasy and imagination are eternal human faculties which can work in a variety of directions. They can tell us much about our own nature. In dreams men and animals operate on the same level and interact on each other. Ivan's dreams frequently tell him more about reality than his waking perceptions. It is in dreams, for example, that he sees Stalin as a vengeful leader, ordering him to be shot for dereliction of duty. It is in a dream too that he sees society as a company of pigs, all snorting away in identical fashion, and demanding that he snort too, not reluctantly or forcedly, but 'with pleasure'.[33]

In *Chonkin* Voinovich shows us perverted and inhuman fantasies enslaving a whole society; but he also indicates the kind of fantasies which are fruitful and liberating. Gladyshev's pseudo-scientific imaginings are unwittingly punctured by Chonkin himself. One of Gladyshev's confident 'scientific' assertions is that in the course of evolution the monkey became human by hard work. Chonkin is puzzled by this statement and contends that, in that case, then the horse would appear to have a better claim to human status. After this altercation Gladyshev dreams (or thinks he dreams) that the kolkhoz workhorse has turned into a man and wants to go into town, join the party and make a career for himself. As the action of the novel develops, this horse keeps cropping up in situations which suggest it *did* in fact disappear and go into the town on its own; and after the battle which concludes the novel Gladyshev comes upon its corpse:

There was a scrap of paper crumpled on the ground under the horse's hoof. Seized by a premonition of something extraordinary, Gladyshev grabbed the piece of paper, lifted it to his eyes and froze, dumbfounded.

In spite of the gathering dusk and his none-too-keen eyesight the home-grown village scientist was able to make out the large wavering scrawl beneath the caked mud and bloodstains: 'If I perish, I ask to be considered a Communist.'

'Good Lord!' shrieked Gladyshev, and for the first time in many years crossed himself.[34]

The generally accepted theory of evolution – the kingpin of positivist and scientistic thinking – is thus, in its Gladyshevian version overthrown, and we are led back to religion, fairytales and folk culture, which may be fantastic too, but are at least harmless fantasies compared with those of the Gladyshevs and super-Gladyshevs of this world.

It is Voinovich's peculiar triumph in *Chonkin* to have written a satire which is far more than negative. The novel does everything that a satire should do, and very powerfully, in showing up the pretences and evils of the society it depicts. But at the same time it is remarkably good-humoured and gentle. On the whole even the negative characters awake some sympathy in the reader's mind, as though the author, from some position of assured humanity, were able to feel unthreatened by their vices and to see them as merely foolish and misguided. This comes partly from the nature of his hero: Chonkin is not a positive hero in the sense that anyone would want to take him as a model for social behaviour. But at the same time his image does awaken the reader's humanity: he points to the essentials of human existence camouflaged by the gross and inflated inessentials of the system. Partly also it comes from Voinovich's narrative style: he has taken the affectionate irony which he and others developed as part of the 'youth prose' style of the early sixties, and applied it to his characters so that we identify with them even while understanding very clearly their foibles and faults.

* *

This capacity for affectionate irony, illuminating uncertain personalities groping for their path in life is something which Voinovich shares with his contemporary Georgy Vladimov (born 1931), who, like him, started out from a conscious re-examination of the 'positive hero'. His Viktor Pronyakin stands at the beginning of *The Great Ore (Bol'shaya ruda*, 1961), a truly Socialist Realist figure, looking out over the crater of a quarry near Kursk where iron ore is being sought. He is a man who wants to work, to excel, to take part in the great discovery of ore which is expected at any time. Though initially refused a job at the quarry, he takes over and repairs a small, clapped-out tip-up truck, then uses it to beat others, better equipped, in removing earth from the floor of the quarry up to the dump at the top. Finally, working alone in the pouring rain, when all the others have given up, he raises the first load of genuine ore, but skids in the mud on the rise and plunges to his death. What end could be more appropriate for a builder of communism?

But in the early sixties when this story was published, other influences were in the air. From the west, the stoic, laconic heroism of Hemingway, from the Soviet Union, the gentle, self-deprecatory irony of 'youth prose'; and Vladimov's portrait of his hero is far more ambiguous and psychologically penetrating than it could have been even a few years earlier. The contrast is the more striking in that Rita, the first girl he meets at the site, is willing to regard him, in the full glow of the inherited tradition, as one of those who 'live for a real cause, working with their own hands'. 'They can sometimes be rude,' she admits, 'and I have seen them drinking, fighting and swearing. But that's because it doesn't occur to them to take a look at themselves. How much real, working-class nobility they have in them. You're like that, too.'[35]

Pronyakin, however, comes over to the reader as a man driven to achieve partly by internal doubt, even self-hatred, and partly by the child's need to have everything *now*, without waiting for it. The incident (revealed in a flashback) of his betrothal is revealing. Having been away from his bride in the war, he returns to her and expects her to welcome him as a conquering hero and to yield totally to him on the first night back. When she hesitates, he storms out of the house and off to the railway station, where he shacks up with the waitress in the buffet, and marries her instead. He wants a wife, sex, someone he can love, all at once. His colleagues observe and resent – the same impatience in his approach to his work. As Matsuev, his brigade leader, remarks, 'You're in too much of a hurry, Viktor . . . you want everything at once.' His colleague Kosichkin takes an altogether more leisurely view of life:

'"The ore! The ore!" Well, what about the ore! Of course it would be nice to shift a load of iron rather than earth. . . . But why get steamed up about it? Suppose you're destined to discover the ore on Friday, then it's not going to turn up on Monday, is it? Well then, for God's sake. Why ruin your life for it?'[36]

The notion that things will be as they will be is quite foreign to Pronyakin, as indeed it was to the heroes of Soviet fiction for thirty years. That is an alternative philosophy which has no meaning for him.

He has another reason for working hard, and that is to bring some degree of stability and comfort into his life. Hitherto he and his hastily acquired wife have been wanderers, much needed in the fast changing and growing Soviet industrial scene: he moves into a workmen's hostel and she joins him later. Now he wants to settle down:

'I need to earn some money, buy things and settle down to a human existence. Then OK, then I'll turn out ten production norms for nothing. You may get irritated with me' – he was thinking of Matsuev and Fedya and probably of the whole brigade – 'but when *you* get home your wife greets you like a warm currant bun, and your house is like a department store, and you've probably got a motor cycle in the shed. So why should I have to sleep around, listen to other people snoring? . . . No, I'll burst every vein in my body, but I'll get there. And then I'll be as kind and nice as all of you. Get me?[37]

This restless monologue betrays much of Pronyakin's personality: his desperate need for security and warmth, his envy of others, his impatience and the urgent ambition inside him. This is what in the past has driven him to alcoholism, a degradation which still haunts him and to which he dreads to return. This too is what his colleagues sense, and what makes them suspicious of him. More interestingly, his reflections are remarkably similar to the public morality proclaimed by the Soviet government during the building of communism: that only when material security has been finally achieved will it be possible to observe moral and humane standards. Pronyakin, the obsessive, the alcoholic, the wanderer, the man who causes his own death in a burst of overweening ambition and genuine achievement, almost stands for the whole of a society in the throes of exaggerated modernization.

Would it be extravagant to suggest that Ruslan, the discharged labour camp guard dog, is no less than Pronyakin a Socialist Realist hero? That at any rate is the opinion of Abram Terts.[38] And like Pronyakin, Ruslan is representative of a whole society. But in his second novel, *Faithful Ruslan* (*Vernyi Ruslan*, 1975), Vladimov has adopted a much more complex standpoint. Ruslan is a caricature of the Socialist Realist hero – and in part of the Socialist Realist narrator too, in the sense that the point of view adopted throughout the work is ostensibly his. He watches uncomprehendingly – but we, the readers, through the narrator's intermediacy, understand what is happening – as the labour camp which is his physical and spiritual universe is broken up, the prisoners are dispersed and he himself is kicked out into the wider world, which bears the traces of Gulag but lives by different laws.

Good, simple-minded but deadly Ruslan performs first of all the service of making familiar Soviet scenes strange, thus indirectly commenting on them. Here, for example, are Lenin and Stalin on a pedestal:

Two inanimate figures, the colour of aluminium feeding bowls were for some reason standing on pedestals. One of them, the bareheaded one, had his arm stretched out and his mouth open, as though he had just thrown a stick and was about to command 'Bring!' The other one, dressed in a peaked cap, was not pointing anywhere, but had one hand slipped inside his uniform; his whole posture seemed to say that whatever was 'brought' should come to him.[39]

Both what Ruslan takes for granted and what he finds unusual present us with an image of the whole penitentiary world in all its horror, yet also in its logic, its rationality, its orderliness, even its sacrality. More than this, observing the human scene as an intimate but also as an outsider, Ruslan can make penetrating observations about human beings in general.

At the same time he is half a human being himself: he is a vital and functioning part of an all-too-human institution. The qualities that have been instilled into him are those required also of the rank and file camp guards. He gets 'high marks for malevolence', 'excels in mistrust towards outsiders', qualities generally prized in Soviet subordinates. When a prisoner steps out of line, it is Ruslan who deals with him; given one additional order, he will tear him to pieces. Ruslan's world is one in which all relationships are those of guard and prisoner. He has his own primitive cosmology and sociology:

Our poor globe, girded and scarred with boundaries, frontiers, enclosures and prohibitions, flew spinning towards the pin-points of the stars – and there was not an inch of its surface where somebody was not guarding somebody else. Where one set of captives, with the aid of another set of captives, was not carefully watching over a third set of captives   and over themselves – to preserve everyone from the danger of a deadly overdose of sky-blue freedom.[40]

This is Ruslan's version of the Ptolemaic heavenly spheres, and when the amnesty reveals to him another, hitherto unsuspected, as it were Copernican, world, he is not impressed with it, for its 'freedom' seems to him mere slovenliness, indeed inhumanity: at least in the camp 'people were not indifferent to one another, everyone was closely watched – and man was considered the highest value, even if he didn't see it that way himself. Sometimes this value had to be protected from the men themselves, when they tried to squander it in escape attempts.'[41] The Service for which he has been trained is his highest ideal, and indeed 'It was strange that the masters, for all their intelligence, did not understand that, and considered it necessary to encourage the dogs with additional rewards.'[42] They treat dogs entirely as human beings, assuming they will need a little low bribery to maintain their loyalty, forgetting that in this respect at least dogs are higher creatures. What distresses Ruslan about the closing of the camp is not only the breakdown of old habits but also of the faith that had sustained them. As he observes his colleagues lapse from their high calling to seek other homes, other duties and even – horror of horrors – to accept food and caresses from non-guards, 'what hurt him was not so much that they had grown tired of waiting [for the Service to return], but that they had grown tired of believing.'[43]

In all these respects Ruslan is, in slightly superhuman, exaggerated form, the model Soviet subordinate. In other respects he remains an animal, with his own view of the world and – more important – of human beings. In this capacity he is able to make astute observations about men in general and *homo Sovieticus* in particular. Through his devoted but perceptive gaze we see his master, an average obtuse, suspicious, callous guard: 'His master . . . might not be too brave, but on the other hand he knew no pity; he might not be too intelligent, but at least he never trusted anybody; he might not be too well loved by his friends, but then he would shoot any of them, if the Service required it.'[44]

A straightforward, healthy, simple creature like a dog recognizes without difficulty that men are flawed and divided beings, seized by contradictory and often destructive impulses. Ruslan sees, for example, Scruffy (a newly released prisoner) drinking:

That foul liquid, Ruslan already knew, was affectionately called 'vodka' or 'vodochka' – but was also known as 'that bloody substance' – and he couldn't make out whether Scruffy enjoyed drinking it or not. In the evening he longed for it with his whole being, but in the morning he hated it and suffered from it. This was not the first time Ruslan had noticed bipeds do things that they didn't like doing, without any compulsion – which no self-respecting animal would ever dream of. It was for good reason that in Ruslan's hierarchy dogs were placed just below the masters, who always knew what was good and what was evil, but ahead of the camp inmates.[45]

The latter category Ruslan regards as human beings normally do animals:

They were really feeble-minded: they persisted in thinking that somewhere beyond the forests, far away from the camp, was a better life! No camp dog would ever entertain such foolishness. And, as if to confirm just how hare-brained they were, they would escape and wander around for months starving, instead of eating their favourite food, *balanda*, for a bowl of which they were prepared to cut each other's throats, and then they would return with a shamefaced look on their faces – only to devise new escape attempts later! Wretched, deranged souls! Nowhere could they find peace.[46]

The baleful influence of the labour camp does not last only while its inmates are still inside it. Even when released, many of them are still under its spell and cannot find real freedom, or even in many cases return to their pre-camp existence. Scruffy finds refuge with a certain Styura, one of the countless unattached women living near the site. He shares board and bed with her, and does odd jobs for her round the house. Ruslan assumes that this is all a continuation of the Service, in new circumstances, and escorts him scrupulously everywhere he goes. Eventually Scruffy makes an attempt to return to his own family, but he knows that much has changed there, that his wife has been with other men; to him it is unknown territory by now. At the last moment he jumps off the departing train and returns to the safe, homely arms of Auntie Styura. Ruslan interprets this as another failed escape attempt, and who is to say he is wrong?

It is this divided nature of men which, in Ruslan's eyes, makes possible their highest achievements, as well as their sometimes inconceivable baseness.

Every animal knows how great man is, and realizes that his greatness extends equally far in the directions of both Good and Evil, but an animal cannot always follow him the whole way – not even one who is ready to die for him – cannot accompany him up to every peak, across every frontier: somewhere on the way he will stop and dig his heels in.[47]

Thus Ruslan feels something akin to remorse at having zealously sniffed out the murderer of a 'squealer'. More seriously, when a particularly vicious commandant orders the hosing out of prisoners who refuse to leave their barracks on a day of minus 40 degrees weather, the dogs revolt. Their leader is the skilful, artistic, even aristocratic Ingus, the dog who has learned effortlessly to do everything the training requires whilst preserving a certain inner detachment. The other dogs now all follow *him*, even the ferocious Dzhulbars, on whom the guards normally rely to carry out the harshest commands. When it comes, in fact, to the extremes of inhumanity – what in any other context one might call 'brutality' – animals cannot follow humans all the way in their trampling of the moral law.

For most purposes, however, dogs (and rank-and-file human subordinates) will do anything they are trained and commanded to do. This is not entirely a matter of habit: it is also, as we have seen, devotion and even faith. The habits indeed are built on devotion and faith:

Ruslan was more than half way through his life, and the whole of the first half he had been used to never being without people, to obey, serve and love them. Aye, there was the rub: to love them. For no one lives without love in this world, neither wolves, nor sharks in the sea, nor snakes in the swamp. He was permanently poisoned by his love, by his acquiescence in the world of men, by that sweetest poison which kills the alcoholic more than alcohol itself – and even the rapture of the hunt would not replace that yet greater rapture, of obedience to the loved one, happiness from his slightest word of praise.[48]

This is something which applies to people no less than to dogs. They too are 'poisoned by their love', willing cogs in a terrible mechanism simply because they have been brought up and trained to it, have received their (deliberately restricted) measure of warmth and affection from it.

It is for this reason that the shadow of the labour camps still hangs over the Soviet Union. Vladimov paints the retreat of the penitentiary system as provisional only. The sceptical Scruffy has heard the 'little bell' sound for him, but knows that the 'great bell' has not sounded for the nation as a whole. It is not only that people like Ruslan's master are sorting and filing away archives in boxes marked 'for eternal keeping' (restoring a transcendental concept of time which Soviet ideology otherwise rigidly denies), but also that human beings, like dogs, long for the master's hand when once they have felt it and received their modest rations from it. The point is underlined by the dramatic ending to the novel. One day Ruslan's patient vigils at the railway station (where he is waiting for a prison transport to arrive and resume the familiar routine) are rewarded by the arrival of a team of Komsomol volunteers to open a plastics factory on the site of the camp. They are a motley and undisciplined mob compared to the grave and proper zeks of yore, and Ruslan is not at all impressed with them, but still they form up on the station square and march off five by five up the road to the camp in the old familiar way. At first they sing and laugh and even pat and stroke the dogs who greet their coming. But gradually they realize that more and more dogs are joining them – Alsatians who since the amnesty have sought shelter in the nearby settlement and lapsed into slack ways but who, on seeing a column marching up the familiar road, hear the renewed call of the Service and imagine that the great days have returned.

Those watching the column from windows, boarded sidewalks or over fences, seeing that strange procession of people and dogs, were for some reason not smiling any more but began to look silent and grim. Gradually, those in the column itself stopped laughing, shouting, teasing and patting the dogs, and eventually a hush descended, broken only by the measured tramp of the people and the warm breathing of the dogs.[49]

Thus the final tragedy, and Ruslan's death, is prepared. Cheerful, open-minded Komsomol enthusiasm yields to the laws of the labour camp, in which 'a step to the right or to the left is considered an attempt to escape'. 'Poisoned by love', a society falls again into its old bonds.

Vladimov's vision is tragic, Voinovich's on the whole comic, but they have much in common all the same. They are both describing a world in which limited but attainable values have been disdained in order to reach out for unattainable ones. This hubris has had profound consequences both for public discourse and for the individual personality. The mass media are filled with ringing phrases and with statistics that conceal more than they reveal; individual human beings feel themselves to be tiny cogs in the majestic machinery of history, and doubt their freedom and even their independent existence. This schizophrenia of the political and the personal is what Voinovich and Vladimov uncover through their characters and through their narrative personae.

8

Vasily Shukshin

A prominent feature of the life of the Soviet people in the last generation or two has been sheer uprootedness. People have been torn from their moorings by war, urbanization, political oppression and the creation of a modern industry and a collectivized agriculture. In their millions they have been swept into factories, building sites, army barracks, labour camps, and then often pushed back out again into a world ill prepared to receive them. Their education has been scrappy, their work experience harsh, and little in the way of culture or settled family life has cushioned them against the bewildering peripetia of this existence.

These are the people for whom Vasily Shukshin (1929–74) speaks. Indeed, he was one of them himself (like many writers of the 'middle generation' born in the late twenties and early thirties). Born in the Altai region of Siberia, he worked as a lad on a Kolkhoz, but soon migrated to the building sites of the town, and then did his military service in the navy. His education came in dribs and drabs in the interstices of these peregrinations. Not until the age of twenty-five did he finally settle in the town, and for all his later successes, both in the cinema and in literature, he remained to the end of his life with the feeling that he was a latecomer to urban culture, lacking confidence that he had really established himself in it. A few years ago he wrote:

Now that I'm nearly forty it turns out that I'm not yet really a citizen of the town, but I don't belong to the country any more either. . . . That's worse than falling between two stools: it's like having one leg on the shore and the other in a boat. You can't stay where you are, but you're afraid to jump into the boat.[1]

He was also torn between the worlds of literature and the cinema, and towards the end of his life he was trying to bring himself to give up

162

the cinema and settle down to writing. He admired Belov for staying in Vologda and doing just that.[2] But arguably he could never have done it himself: indeed, his widow has described how at the end of his life he had plans for further films, especially the long cherished project of one on Sten'ka Razin.[3]

Most of his literary creations have the same ambiguity about them. They are the children of the Soviet Union's whirlwind years of social change, in which tens of millions of people were torn away from their backgrounds and homes. Shukshin's heroes are the uprooted, who have left one milieu and never quite settled in another: village lorry drivers and chauffeurs, construction workers, demobbed soldiers, taxi drivers, *shabashniki* (odd job men), all members of a raffish social stratum which is neither of the country nor of the town. Even where his characters are firmly rooted in the village, then the village itself is changing, as urban culture, habits and concepts take hold, imperfectly understood and reflected in distorted forms. Neither proletarian nor peasant, Shukshin's people strive after a goal or an ideal without having the strength or confidence, the inner personal resources, to attain it. They are disoriented and bewildered, by turns aggressive and timid, arrogant and insecure; and their relations with parents, spouses, children, work-mates and superiors are correspondingly unstable.

Not surprisingly, therefore, the archetypal Shukshin situation is the *skandal,* the all too human conflict situation which brings out in raw and painful form the deepest feelings of the actors. One or two plot outlines will give an impression. A young man discovers that his unmarried sister is pregnant and goes like a medieval knight to demand satisfaction from her boyfriend – but lights upon the *wrong* boyfriend.[4] A shop assistant mistakes a customer for a drunk whom she threw out the previous evening, and the other customers, sick of waiting in the queue, add their own insults, until in the end he goes to get an axe to kill someone and has to be forcibly restrained by his wife.[5] An elderly widower, anxious to propose marriage to a pious old lady in the village, asks a girlfriend of his youth to act as matchmaker, but she uses the occasion to vent years of frustrated loneliness by denouncing both the prospective partners for immorality.[6] A country woman comes to visit her son in a prestigious urban hospital, but is not admitted by the concierge because it is not the right day for visiting; her son, instead of bribing the concierge or appealing to his doctor for help, discharges himself from the hospital in protest, and thus misses a vital operation.[7] A middle-aged man takes his prospective bride to a family feast to introduce her, but constantly, almost obsessively, seeks quarrels on well-worn themes with his relatives until she walks out in embarrassment.[8] This is the stuff of Shukshin's human comedy: human feelings thrashing about, spilling out in all sorts of inappropriate, ridiculous and hurtful ways. People dream of the impossible and use unsuitable means to attain it. Semi-coherent words and phrases tumble out and form up in uncertain sentences. One sometimes has the impression that both society and language are being torn apart.

One can see Shukshin's world in microcosm in the story *In Profile and Full Face* (*V profil' i anfas*, 1967).[9] A young man, Ivan, faces a turning point in his life. A qualified mechanic, he has returned to his native village to work for a while as a chauffeur after the break-up of his marriage in Eastern Siberia. He has just lost his driving licence after the director of the sovkhoz reported him to the militia for being drunk in charge. He has to decide whether to leave the village or not. He plays out his internal drama before two audiences: first an old man, then his own mother. Both dialogues are examples of imperfect communication: with the old man because the latter has had an entirely different life experience and does not understand what is biting Ivan; with his mother because of her desperate desire to persuade him to stay in the village with her. The old man, who has struggled all his life to have enough to fill his belly, does not understand why Ivan cannot be satisfied with the modest but sufficient living he would make as an ordinary farm worker. Ivan refuses to do this, not only out of professional pride as a skilled worker, but also because he wants his work to have some purpose: 'I don't know what I'm working for. . . . Just so that I can fill my belly? All right, it's full. What next?' The old man's generation he sees as 'cavemen' (*dremuchie*) with no 'horizons'. The two of them conduct a dialogue which fails to meet in the middle. Ivan's declaration of his own identity, '*Ya ne fraer*' (I'm not a dilettante / I'm a serious person), goes over the old man's head because it is couched in labour camp slang he does not understand. Ivan's real feelings break out in snatches of song accompanied by explosive chords on the guitar. The two of them have only one thing really in common: the bottle of home-brewed vodka. Their drinking together constitutes a minimal human contact.

Ivan's dialogue with his mother is no more coherent, this time because the emotional charge is so great that it constitutes a barrier to communication. The mother's conception of the world, like the old man's, is that one yields to authority, begs and bribes where necessary, but takes one's lot and does not assert oneself. Her son's abrupt sense of his own worth she sees simply as an unfortunate mode of communication, not as part of his essence – especially since her aim for him, as a quiet and loving companion to her old age, is quite different from his own. Ivan, for his part, responds sufficiently to her love to want to shut himself off still further and not take any part in the dialogue beyond the muttering of discouraging monosyllables. Only once does he break out with 'Mum, this is hard for me too'.

At the centre of Ivan's personality – what we see here in these two dialogues, as it were, 'in profile and full face' – is an alienation which he expresses in the following image:

I was a witness once: one fellow punched another in the glasses and ruined his eyesight. So there I was sitting in the courtroom and couldn't understand what I was doing there. All for an absurd punch-up. All right, so I saw it happen – so what? I was in a terrible state throughout the trial.... It's just like that now. I sit here and think 'What am I doing here?' The trial was a long one, but at least eventually it came to an end and I was able to go. But where can I go from here? There's nowhere to go.

Characteristically, the old man understands this image in the light of his own concerns: 'There's only one way out: to the other world.' But the image actually captures much of contemporary Soviet society: indeed it is the one which Terts uses in *The Trial Begins* (1961). The leading positions in the Soviet power hierarchy and in the media are occupied by people who see life as a kind of trial conducted by those who are in the right against those who are in the wrong. The majority of the population, not feeling themselves to be in either category, can only stand by and observe with a strong sense of non-involvement. Ivan, for his part, embraces this non-involvement as his fate, and strides out of the village, kicking aside, metaphorically and literally, the only two beings who care for him in the world, his mother and his dog. 'One must live alone in this world. Then it will be easy.'

Shukshin's technique as a narrator is largely to let his characters speak for themselves. But he does not entirely remove himself from the text. Indeed, the very opening paragraph is unequivocally an authorial comment:

An old man was sitting on the bench by his front gate. He felt as weary and dull as the warm evening which was drawing on. Long ago he too had known his morning sunshine, when he had stepped out boldly and felt the earth light beneath his feet. Now, however, it was evening and peaceful, with a touch of mist over the village.

Having established this explicit correspondence between the old man's mind and the state of the external world, Shukshin can allow the acrid smoke and the occasional bursts of flame from the bonfire to suggest the mood of his personages. Similarly, the smell of the morning smoke, dry, wooden and unstoked, corresponds to the overnight change in Ivan's mood as he faces the prospect of immediate departure. These authorial interventions, like Solzhenitsyn's in *Ivan Denisovich,* are couched in a language which the characters would not actually have spoken but which they would have understood, and whose image content is wholly within their comprehension and experience.

The best known of Shukshin's uprooted heroes by now is certainly Egor Prokudin, the chief personage of *Snowball Berry Red (Kalina krasnaya,* 1973) which as a film has made a name for Shukshin as its author, director and principal actor all over the world. Egor is a classic victim of Soviet social experimentation. Brought up as a small child in a Siberian village, he became separated from his mother during the terrible famine of 1933, and has never seen her since (till the events of the story). When the old people of the villages round about get together, they discuss the fates which befell their families at the time of the 'dekulakization', so that we know this is a memory which is still living, indeed dominant, in the villagers' lives, rather as the unemployment of the thirties continued to dominate the social and political outlook of British working people long after the Second World War. The collectivization, dekulakization and famine form the setting in which Egor's life must be seen.[10]

We do not know what Egor has done since early childhood, except that he fell in with a gang of criminals, and, when we first meet him, is just finishing a spell in labour camp. We first see him awkwardly but conscientiously booming out the line of the bass bell in a chorus: a kind of foreshadowing of his subsequent clumsy efforts to find harmony in social life outside. The main plot is concerned with his attempt to break away from the life of crime and settle down, in a village not far from his birthplace, with a woman to whom he has been writing from the camp. He fails. The gang catches up with him and murders him. But even apart from the harsh laws of the underworld, he has not the inner constancy to tolerate a settled way of life. The roots, the traditions, the sense of identity, are lacking.

This is apparent from the very start, when, in conversation with the camp commandant, he reveals that he knows virtually nothing about cows.[11] His desire to settle down with a cow and a plot of land sounds simply quixotic. Later on he shows that he has not the faintest idea how to take a bath in a village bath-house – one of the fundamental rituals of the Russian peasant way of life: instead of pouring boiling water on the stones in order to produce steam, he pours it directly over the shoulders of his bathing companion, who rushes out naked into the yard shrieking.[12] His country childhood was so brief and broken off so prematurely (we are not told at precisely what age) that it has left him with none of the peasant's customs or skills, only with a few memories that form the one untroubled portion of his mind. He finds a certain distant echo of this serenity when he is ploughing on the tractor, but he does not believe he can really find peace again – as indeed he does not: the birch copse at the end of the furrow is the place where the gang kills him.[13] He resumes his unity with the soil, in the narrator's eyes, only after death: 'And he lay there, a Russian peasant, on his native steppeland, near his home. . . . He lay there, pressing his cheek to the earth as though listening to something that he alone could hear.'[14]

For most of the story, Egor is seen as a person perpetually unable to form stable relationships with others, though he has a yearning for such stability, and even a distant inkling of what it might be like if he could attain it. He talks throughout of looking for a 'festival of the soul' (*prazdnik dushi*) – a phrase as vague in Russian as in English. He tries to find stability with Lyuba, the woman to whom he has been writing from the camp, but it is symptomatic that he goes to see her only after his criminal associates have been raided by the police and he has not found anyone else to take him in. Half-measures and sharp changes of direction characterize all his actions. Furthermore, when Lyuba declines to let him into her bed on the very first night, he rushes off to the nearest town, not necessarily intending to return, and organizes a 'debauch' with his release money and the help of a friendly waiter. This is just another variant, another attempt to find what he is looking for. And it does not work, because the fellow debauchees whom the waiter finds for him are so repulsive. 'The attractive people,' he tells Egor, 'are all married, with families.' Egor sees the force of this and rushes back again to Lyuba who, a forgiving woman battered already by life with an alcoholic husband, takes him in once more.

Egor's attempt to find stability in a job is no more successful. He has a great piece of luck, landing the prestigious job of chauffeur to the sovkhoz director, but abandons it on the first day because he cannot stand the limited and convention-bound relationship of driver and passenger ('I felt as if I was kind of smiling at you the whole time.').[15] The tractor-driving job which is broken off by his murder does at least have the advantage of solitude, and who knows. . . . We are left to speculate whether he could have found peace that way. It seems unlikely.

Most painful of all is Egor's relationship with his mother. When he goes with Lyuba to see her, he has to do so incognito and in dark glasses: without these protections the return of feeling would be too agonizing. Strong emotions express themselves in him not in tears, but in a steely set expression of the face (which Shukshin as actor conveys excellently on the screen) and a vice-like grip of the hand. (The film unfortunately had him beat the earth and weep after leaving his mother, which is quite inconsistent with the rest of his character, and does not figure in the published text.) Tears he cannot stand in anybody, and he gives his feelings dynamic expression only in occasional snatches of song, or in ridiculous professions of love addressed to birch trees.

Egor does not, then, really succeed in breaking out of the pattern which has dominated his life. Good relationships for him are brief ones, as with the taxi driver who drives him out of the prison settlement. The criminal community, with its tense goal-oriented relationships, embroidered by a little non-committal sex, is his logical home, and the fact that it reclaims him violently at the end is not simply the intervention of an external force.

*   *

Some of Shukshin's stories take us further than the portrayal of personalities torn about by rapid social change. Indeed a changing society is not necessarily essential to their peculiarities. This becomes clear if one reads Shukshin's two long novels, *The Lyubavins* (*Lyubaviny*, 1965) and *I Have Come to Give You Freedom* (*Yaprishël dat' vam volyu*, 1971),[16] which, though springing from very different periods of Russian history, also portray restless, explosive personalities. *The Lyubavins* depicts an Altai village in the twenties, where the Soviet system has as yet scarcely even taken hold. Traditional village life continues more or less as it has for generations, and the major changes are still to come. Yet the impression one has is not of harmony and mutual cooperation as, say, Belov might have described it (compare his *On the Eve*). It is true, there is a long description of communal hay-making and of the evening singing and dancing which follow it, so that one is given some idea of the solidarity of inherited rural culture. But by and large it is the divisions within the village that are emphasized. Routine agricultural life is seen as austere and restricted, demanding from the peasants a degree of self-denial such that from time to time lusty and violent impulses cannot but break out. After the particularly hard labour of the harvest period the peasants 'imperceptibly turned into animals. There was a thudding of clubs and a crashing of broken crockery. An evil spirit welled up and broke out. At one end of the village sons rose against fathers, at the other end fathers against sons. Grudges going back a year were dredged up.'[17]

What the peasant yearns for is *volya*, freedom from work, from cares and from the continuous repression which his way of life demands. This *volya* can take many forms. At times a sunset, or the sounds and smells of spring, can lift the grey pall which hangs over peasant perceptions to reveal something beyond. At one stage the villagers are shown rehearsing a play for presentation at the village club (with the purely utilitarian purpose of shaming rich peasants into parting with their grain), but, in the course of acting, the imaginary world they are thinking themselves into takes on a life of its own: 'They did not want to leave the village Soviet building. They wanted to stay on and think up ever new twists, to go on laughing and playing the fool. They were all in such a good mood. They had suddenly discovered a source of joy.'[18]

But these interludes are rare. In general, the continual self-imposed privation leads to an accumulation of longing for freedom and spontaneity which makes the peasant a subconscious brother of the bandit. And indeed, whenever there is trouble in the village, violence flares up and someone gets killed, so that the murderer has to go off to the hills and become an outlaw. There is a persistent mutual symbiosis between the village community and the gang of bandits in the hills: each is necessary to the other for its way of life. The party and the Soviet government are trying to break into this vicious circle by building a village school and eradicating illiteracy, but the progress they make in the course of the novel is not encouraging. Indeed, Kuz'ma, the youth who is supposed to be representing the party, gets himself involved in the old round of feuding by marrying a village girl whom others have coveted.

The more one reads Shukshin, the more one discovers that most of the heroes of his short stories share, in one way or another, this longing for *volya*, or for something analogous to it. They are seeking to break out of the here and now, the immediate and empirical, the always imperfect, into some other, imagined world, of freedom and perfection. This transcendent world can appear to them in many different forms. For the peasants of *The Lyubavins,* singing, dancing and play-acting offer moments of release. For other characters such release takes different forms: for young men love, a worthy job, dreams of the future, of building a better world (the form of transcendence appropriate to the traditional Socialist Realist hero), for old men reflecting on death and musing about the past, for all men story-telling, art and religion. If there is nothing else, then there is, of course, always drink, a very prevalent form of the search for transcendence.

In this sense, an archetypal Shukshin character is Stepka (from the story of that name)[19], who escapes from prison a mere three months before his sentence expires (though he knows he is bound to be caught and sentenced to two further years) simply because it is springtime and he wants to see his village and family. He spends an intoxicating afternoon and evening among his loved ones, and then tells the policeman who comes to arrest him: 'It doesn't matter . . . I've charged up my batteries now [*podkrepilsya*], and I can take prison for a bit longer. My dreams were tormenting me – every night I would dream about the village . . . It's fantastic here in spring, isn't it?' But of course he has not taken into account the suffering his premature dash for freedom will cause his family. The pain of joyful celebration followed by instant parting is expressed at the end in the large eyes and clumsily passionate gestures of his dumb sister.

This search for freedom is an amoral force. Another of Shukshin's springtime escapees is the unnamed youth of *The Desire to Live* (*Okhota zhit'*, 1966). Like Stepka he has given no forethought to his escape, and finds himself wandering through the *taiga* without a gun, facing certain death if he should chance upon a bear. An old forester gives him haven in his hut, they talk together, and the young man tells him what induced him to make his break:

'You don't know how bright the lights are in a great city. They beckon to you. There are such dear, sweet people there, and it's warm and comfortable, and there's music playing. People are very civil there – and very afraid of death. Now, when I walk through a city, it belongs to me, see? So why should they be there while I am out here? . . . It's me who ought by rights to be there, because I'm not afraid of anybody. I'm not afraid of death, so life belongs to me.'[20]

This outlook (reminiscent of Kirillov in Dostoevsky's *The Possessed*) has its own terrifying logic. The old man feels compassion for the young man's youth, strength and beauty, and lends him a gun so that he can shoot his way out of the *taiga* if necessary. This gun the lad uses to kill the old man, so that there will be no danger of his escape being reported. The lad may not be afraid of his own death, but other people's certainly gives him no pause either.

The search for transcendence can also be funny, as in the case of Bron'ka Pupkov, the incongruously named hero of *Mille Pardons, Madame* (1968). Bron'ka is the eternal *neudachnik,* the man who makes a mess of everything. The missing two fingers on his right hand ought by rights to be an honourable war wound, but in fact he blew them off when trying to get a drink in winter by breaking the ice on the river with the barrel of his rifle. Now, in his fifties, he has only one serious occupation in life: taking tourists on hunting expeditions from his village in the *taiga*. The culminating point of each expedition comes when Bron'ka recounts to his charges, in luxuriant profusion of detail, how he was selected by the Soviet High Command to assassinate Hitler. He sets the scene with a fine instinct for suspense, inducing his listeners to ply him with vodka at each stage of his narrative. He tells how he crossed the German lines, made his way to the bunker, brushing aside German generals with a casual 'mille pardons, madame', came up to Hitler, raised his revolver, spitting out words of vengeance for the suffering of the Soviet people, fired at point-blank range and . . . missed! After his recital Bron'ka sits for hours by the riverside, in an almost mystical trance, and thereafter has to drink continuously for two days in order to recover. But the story deeply impresses his urban listeners, not brought up on the rich rural traditions of *vran'ë*, and this is a catharsis for him, a public acting out of his nagging sense of personal failure which perhaps is all that preserves him from permanent drinking. It is arguable that *vran'ë* is a characteristically Russian mode of seeking the transcendent. As Terts has commented: 'The Russian people drink not from hardship and not from grief, but from an age-old need for the miraculous and the extraordinary – they drink, if you will, mystically, striving to transport the soul beyond earth's gravity and restore it to its sacred non-corporeal state.'[21] And, in its most creative form, *vran'ë* lies at the basis of much imaginative literature.

The theme of creative art is one which Shukshin explores in the story *The Craftsman* (*Master*, 1971). Sëmka Rys', a village joiner, discovers a beautiful little church in a nearby village. He admires its position down in a valley where it presents itself all of a sudden in its entirety to the traveller coming round the spur of the hill. He admires the glazing of some of the brickwork on the eastern side of the dome, where the sun's rays strike it in the early morning, and the buttresses against an interior wall which relieve the otherwise unimaginative right angles. Haunted by the church, he reflects on the aspirations of its original builder:

What did the unknown builder think of when he left us that graceful fairy tale in stone? Was he glorifying God or was he showing off? But show-offs don't look for out-of-the-way places, they stick to the high road or even the market square where crowds of people will notice them. No, this one had something else on his mind – beauty, you might say. He sang his song – a good one, too. And went on his way. What made him do it? He didn't know himself. Something inside him demanded it [*dusha prosila*]. . . . That's how it goes: if you know how to give happiness, then give it. And if you don't, then make war, give orders, that sort of thing, and you can destroy this fairy tale. Just stick a few pounds of dynamite under it, and the whole thing'll go up: that's all it needs. Each to his own.[22]

This extended reflection contains the kernel of the whole story. The transcendent world of the artist and the empirical world of the soldier and politician are directly counterposed to one another, and their collision is played out in the rest of the story. Sëmka proposes to the local Soviet that he should restore the church in his own free time, without pay, completing the glazing work round the dome which the original craftsman was unable to finish. But the chief architect of the Soviet tells him kindly but firmly that experts from Moscow long ago described the church as being of 'no artistic value', being a mere seventeenth-century copy of a twelfth-century model. For that reason permission for restoration is refused, and no materials can be made available. The buttresses Sëmka admired aesthetically have a simple utilitarian reason for their existence: they were put there relatively recently to strengthen the walls after the latter had been undermined by gravedigging. The effect of this judgement on Sëmka is shattering. His creative impulses are thwarted, what he had thought to make partly his own is taken away from him altogether. What he had considered beautiful and pristine is officially stated to be merely derivative and expedient. Sëmka takes offence as against a living person, never goes again to look at 'his' church, and even avoids the village in which it is situated.

For old men, release and greater understanding come with looking backwards. Reflections, memories reveal the meaning of a whole life, and sometimes uncover an unexpected beauty in it. *Musing* (*Dumy*, 1967)[23] portrays the reminiscences of an elderly kolkhoz chairman, provoked by the nightly recurring (and initially infuriating) serenade of a village lad courting his girl. This sound inexplicably lifts Matvei right out of the everyday world of work and worry, and back to a night in his early teens when he had rushed on a horse from the meadows back to the village at night to fetch milk for his sick brother.

Man and horse became one and sped together into the dark night. And the night sped towards them, the heavy scent of dew-damp grass meeting their face. A kind of wild rapture seized the lad, the blood coursed thumping through his head. . . . He wasn't thinking about his brother's being ill at that moment. He wasn't thinking about anything at all. His spirit soared, and every vein in his body thrilled.

In his memories of that night, Matvei is conscious of penetrating into a strange region which has little in common with his ordinary life as chairman of a farm:

He would hear the accordion playing far off down a side street. And immediately a kind of malaise would come over him. A strange, even welcome malaise. Without it something was missing.

This mood leads to reflections on love and death, subjects which either do not exist for him in his everyday life, or have turned into prosaic equivalents: love into marriage, death into the mere cessation of life, a dull fear at the back of everyone's mind. This dichotomy is suggested in Matvei's intermittent attempts to convey his feelings to his sleepy wife.

Then, when the accordion player duly gets married and no longer uses public means to woo his beloved, the vital trigger disappears, and Matvei loses touch with his malaise, relapsing into the everyday world where he smokes, sleeps badly and drinks too much.

Death is an important theme in Shukshin's work, a final frontier which forces – and enables – the old and sick to understand more about their lives. It is presented in its simplest form in *An Old Man's Death* (*Pomiraet starik*, 1967).[24] The old man dying is concerned with practical, this-worldly things: instructions to relatives, the question of who will dig his grave in the frost. At the same time, he is already abstracted from this world in a way that gives its affairs a new meaning.

He has a 'severe' and 'solemn' expression on his face, a look of 'other-worldly peace'. He is not a believer, and refuses extreme unction, but nevertheless an utterance that'starts as a routine profanity turns into an invocation: 'Lord, lord ... Lord, perhaps you do exist, forgive me, a sinner.' Not something he would have said in the prime of life: whether it is weakness or insight we are left to speculate.

In death the real meaning of a man's life, his work, his beliefs, his worth, stand out with greater relief. In *Uncle Ermolai* (*Dyadya Ermolai*, 1971)[25] the narrator stands at his uncle's grave and remembers how as a boy he once lied bare-facedly to him, thinking him fussy and officious. Now his thoughts about his uncle's peasant existence are altogether more appreciative and lead on to a reappraisal of his own life:

He was an unsparing worker, and a good, honest man. Like everybody here, when you come to think of it. ... Granddad, grandma. Simple enough, really. But somehow I can't think it through, what with college and all my books. *Did* their life have some great meaning? Can it be found in the way they lived it? Or was there no meaning, just work and more work. ...? They worked and they bore children. I've seen lots of different people in my life since then, not idlers, no, but. ... Somehow they all see their life differently. And so do I. Only, when I look at these grave mounds I wonder which of us is right, which of us has really understood things better.

In *Rain at Dawn* (*Dozhd' na zare*, 1966)[26] death brings the final confrontation of two long-established enemies, Efim, a party activist and former dekulakizer (now dying in a village hospital) and Kirill, a peasant whom he once expropriated and exiled. Their dialogue is bitter. Kirill is not a believer – he understands man's peace of mind in terms of a purely secular conscience: 'he who has hurt people in his lifetime does not die easy'. From the position of moral superiority this implies he asks Efim what *he* had lived for. Efim replies: 'So that there should be fewer fools around.' Kirill counters:

'You're a fool yourself. You used to keep on and on about a "new life", "a new life" ... You didn't know how to live yourself, and you prevented others from living. You made a mess of your life, Efim.'

This judgement is delivered with cheerful, unrancorous finality. Some kind of attraction, even compassion, brings Kirill back to the hospital to see how his old enemy is getting on, and in fact he is present when Efim dies. He feels a certain genuine sorrow for him, and as he goes off into the early morning, a warm rain breaks a long sustained drought. There is no real reconciliation between the two men, but the ending (reinforced by the story's title) suggests the author's hope that the burning hatred which has parched so much of the Soviet Union's social and political life may be passing as death takes away some of the old enemies and helps to bring others together. This is a hope which Shukshin has not been alone in feeling: it underlies the semi-senile reconciliation of Olesha Smolin and Aviner Kozonkov in Belov's *A Carpenter's Tales*. On the other hand, Shukshin himself denies it in a later story, *Autumn (Osen'yu*, 1973),[27] in which the central figure is another former activist, Filipp. Filipp in his youth refused to marry the girl he loved, Marya, because she insisted on a church wedding, and that was against his principles. Now, in his old age, he meets Marya's funeral procession and quarrels bitterly with her widower, till they have to be almost forcibly separated by the other mourners.

If death throws new light on the meaning of life, then it naturally poses religious questions. In facing this dimension, however, Shukshin's touch is less sure. This, one may surmise, is an area which he was probing tentatively through his characters. His vision of human beings certainly makes religious answers natural, yet for the most part he actually presents religion in eccentric or neurotic forms. A kind of manichean pantheism seems to emerge as a corollary of Shukshin's selection of plot and character, and it is directly expressed by one or two of his heroes. In *I Believe! (Veruyu!*, 1971)[28] Maxim is affected by what might be called a distillation of the ills of Shukshin's 'seekers', a world-weariness which he calls '*dusha bolit*' (my soul aches), and which will not be appeased by getting into a fight or drinking or attempting suicide, or any of the other palliatives which Shukshin's characters normally apply. In the end he goes to a priest – but a highly unusual priest – who lays before Maxim a vision of life which excludes neither belief in God nor acceptance of communism, a kind of exuberant pantheism, in which good and evil coexist eternally, and in which each man does his own creative thing as best he can. The apotheosis of the story comes with the priest dancing a wild gopak, singing, clapping and yelling incoherent Credos:

'I believe . . . in aviation, in the mechanization of agriculture, in the scientific revolution, in space and weightlessness! For they are objective! . . . I believe that soon everyone will gather in huge stinking cities. I believe that they will suffocate there and rush back to the open fields. . . .'

There is certainly here an element of satire on the implicit official Soviet religion, yet the vision also fits Shukshin's own outlook. He is a Soviet man aware of and uneasy about his own limitations. The same vision is repeated in more pessimistic form in *Bird of Passage(Zalëtnyi*,

1970).[29] Sanya, a sick man in his early fifties from somewhere unknown, has settled in a hut at the edge of the village, where most of the time he drinks and looks out over the river to the hills beyond. 'He had a way of talking wisely about life and death. . . . And he was a genuinely good man. People felt drawn to him as to a lonely, mortally sick close relative.' Sanya's philosophy, worked out in sickness and repose, is one which sees both beauty and bitterness in the foundation of human life:

'Man is a . . . fortuitous, beautiful and agonizing attempt on Nature's part to become conscious of itself. But a fruitless attempt, I assure you, because Nature harbours alongside me a canker. Death! And death is unavoidable, but we can ne-e-ever take that in. Nature will never understand itself. . . . So she gets furious and seeks vengeance in the form of mankind.'

This vision illuminates the vigorous yet tormented characters who people Shukshin's stories. Man appears as a flaw in the universe, and the conflicts of Soviet society as just another confirmation of this inescapable incongruity.

Towards the end of his life, Shukshin was preoccupied with the problem of literature as society's reflection upon itself (standing towards society in the same relationship as man to nature?). The preoccupation led him to seek a new form, which he was still elaborating when his evolution was cut short. In place of the anecdotal type of story, related in close identification with the principal character, he was introducing strong elements of fantasy and satire, and distancing himself from his characters. To emphasize this he gave his story *Point of View* (*Tochka zreniya*, 1974)[30] a deliberately unusual genre name, *povest'-skazka*, which implies a mixture of novella and fairy tale. It is a satire on the Soviet literary process. The framework is the presentation of a matchmaking from the opposed points of view of two writers, one an Optimist and the other a Pessimist, who cannot settle their differences by themselves and go to a magician who stages the two scenes as a kind of competition. The Pessimist shows the two families obsessed with material problems, especially that of living space (*zhilploshchad'*); besides this, the young couple accuse each other of looking for extra-marital liaisons, and the match falls through. In the Optimist's version both the families are too principled to be bothered by material questions. They are the soul of generosity: indeed the bridegroom's father proposes to give the couple a second-hand Pobeda car. The only trouble is that the son's unrestrained joy at this prospect brands him as a 'property-lover' in the eyes of the bride, and so, once again, the match falls through. In each case the bride's hand is won by a certain Neponyatno Kto (It's Not Clear Who), who silently accompanies the bridegroom's party, ignores the match-making, and contents himself with businesslike questions about the size of the apartment. Each side of the story is presented, largely in dialogue, in a cliché-ridden language appropriate to its narrator: on the Pessimist's side ragged, slangy, abusive, on the Optimist's replete with the overblown sentiments of ideological journals.

The external authority to whom the two writers appeal to settle their differences, the Magician, for his part needs an 'assistant for organizational matters', a grey Certain Someone who looks like a secret policeman to the Pessimist but to the Optimist is a 'tranquil, perspicacious, kindly man'. The two writers' ultimate banalities and contradictions are poured out to this administrative genius. He it is who turns out in the end to have been It's Not Clear Who, the figure who in each episode pulled the chestnuts out of the fire while the writers were busy distorting people's fates in their own preconceived ways. In the final scene a neighbour drives out the writers and the Magician, the family settles down to its matchmaking undisturbed, and the Certain Someone, clearly superfluous, makes his apologies and goes. As an indictment of the distortions which writers have imposed on society this could hardly be clearer.

Till the Cock Crow Thrice (*Do tret'ikh petukhov*, 1975)[31] continues this satire, this time more unequivocally through the medium of the traditional *skazka*. The main personalities are some of the most familiar fairy tale heroes, Ivan the Fool, Baba Yaga, the Wise Man, but they are reinterpreted in the light of the contemporary Soviet social and cultural situation. One night, after lights-out in the library, some of the principal figures of classical Russian literature jump down off the shelves and hold a meeting to discuss whether they can allow Ivan the Fool to remain one of their number, or whether they should expel him. The heroes of classical Russian literature wish, as it were, to repudiate their folk origins. (The most decided in her opposition to him is Poor Liza, who shares his peasant origins, but has since moved up in the world.) Eventually they take a compromise decision: that he must go and obtain from the Wise Man a note certifying that he is 'intelligent' (*umnyi*). This posing of the problem indicates the direction of the satire: it is not wisdom (*um-razum*) that Ivan seeks, as in the traditional tale (and the subtitle of this work), but merely a piece of paper, a formality. Such is the nature of contemporary cultural life.

And in the event, he does not even get that: he succeeds instead in purloining a rubber stamp which satisfies the formal requirements of his quest, though nobody knows what to do with it when he brings it back. The Wise Man in the monastery turns out to be a time-server whose citadel has just been taken over by devils dressed in blue jeans, singing pop songs, dancing shameless modern dances, and hanging their own portraits in place of the ikons. He is busy adapting himself to his new masters, and makes cautious statements about 'the possible beneficial effect of ultra-diabolical tendencies on certain well-established norms of morality. . .'. In his spare time he visits a circle of decadent youth, headed by his world-weary 'queen', Nesmeyana, to whom he takes great pleasure in presenting Ivan as a specimen of something really folksy (*narodnoe*)!

On his journey Ivan also meets Baba Yaga, who tries to use him as free labour to build herself a new hut, her daughter, who tries to seduce him, and Gorynych the three-headed serpent whose wily use of his authority nearly thwarts Ivan's quest: he regards him alternately as food to be eaten, as a peddler of folk-tales with improper endings, and as a harmless subordinate whose caprices can be satisfied along with a kick on the backside – he is in fact a kind of composite personification of censorship and literary bureaucracy.

The one sane person in this fairy tale is Misha the bear (always a good-humoured and commonsense figure in the *skazka* – see Belov's *Vologda Whimsies*). But he has been ousted from his traditional lair by the devil's batterings, and has taken to drink, abandoned his family, and is now preparing to leave the countryside altogether, go into town and sell himself to a circus as the only way to survive in the modern world.

Everything speaks here of the corruption of inherited customs and culture by literary administrators and commentators, by the incursion of 'diabolical' ideology and cheap mass culture, and by the natural pliability of man. Ivan himself has no defence against these influences, and if he survives it is only because he is rescued from outside: the one element which has remained unchanged from the traditional *skazka* is the *deus ex machina*.

In these late works Shukshin directly attacks a society which has lost its ideals or distorted them beyond recognition. But the vacuum which this loss entails is felt as a haunting presence in most of his work. In a society that has repudiated religion and then lost its own Purpose, what remains for men to dream about? As Mikhail Geller puts it: 'They say that people who have lost an arm or a leg continue to feel pain in the amputated limb; Shukshin's characters feel pain where man's soul used to be.'[32] In his whole portrait gallery of human types, there is only one man who finds what he is looking for. That is 'Alësha beskonvoinyi' (literally: 'Alësha the unescorted'), who always takes Saturday off work, whatever his wife or the kolkhoz brigade-leader may say, and spends the entire day preparing and taking a bath in his bath-house.[33] In the simple sensations of chopping wood, heating the water and sweating in the steam he finds what all Shukshin's other characters search for in vain.

What does all this searching amount to? Geller and Le Fleming[34] both see the goal as *volya,* freedom in the old peasant understanding (rather than the modern civic one) of that term. This is true, but partial; it does not cover, for example, Shukshin's old men or his craftsmen. Perhaps it is Egor Prokudin's term, 'a festival of the soul', which best describes what they are looking for, something beyond the immediate and empirical, the contingent and imperfect. In fact Shukshin has rediscovered and dramatized man's drive towards the transcendental, which Marxism denied and Socialist Realism distorted.

9

Yury Trifonov

In 1950 Yury Trifonov won the Stalin Prize with a novel called *Students*, about life in Moscow University after the war. It depicts a happy time of returning to normal, affluent peacetime life for young men who have been at the front and young women who have served as nurses: they are discovering themselves and each other, choosing a mate and taking their first steps on the party and career ladder. Most of them live in a world of lace curtains, black limousines, chauffeurs and vacations on the Black Sea coast; and those who were not born to this world are plainly about to enter it. Their moral dilemmas do not go much beyond the questions of whether all the buttons of a jacket should be done up, and whether boys should pay for girls when they go to the cinema together. Even the denunciation and dismissal of a professor is a straightforward and not particularly controversial matter, since he is so obviously 'backward looking' and 'not in touch with the times'.[1]

A quarter of a century later Trifonov returned to this setting, in *The House on the Embankment* (*Dom na naberezhnoi*, 1976).[2] The externals of the action are rather similar, but the style, the characters and the narrator's outlook are totally unrecognizable. The gentle, plush world of the Stalin Prize novel has become bitter, harsh and violent. There are yawning differences in status, power and privilege between the different characters; and the main plot now hangs on intrigues and denunciations. The only feature that the two novels have in common is the meticulous and detailed description of everyday life, of *byt*, as the Russians call it. Even here, there is a great difference: in the first novel, *byt* is the red carpet that leads into the future, its smoothness and attractiveness a proof that it is indeed the highway to

180

'magnificent prospects'; whereas in the second, *byt* is a viscous fluid, a sticky, invincibly present here-and-now that overwhelms and drowns nearly all the characters. In the first novel, the Purpose is so close and assured as to be taken for granted; in the second, it has disappeared without trace. No wonder that quite a number of critics have attacked Trifonov's recent works with the charge that the author is unable to raise his head from the dust to the broader and more rewarding perspectives that offer themselves when *byt* is regarded in the light of its 'revolutionary development'.

The wounds that Trifonov strikes are exceptionally painful for an entrenched literary bureaucracy, for the life he is describing is that of the Moscow intelligentsia of the sixties and seventies, with flashbacks going back to the twenties and thirties. It is a panorama which is relatively full and frank, and deeply pessimistic. Trifonov portrays the interrelationships of his characters as a closed and vicious system out of which there is no escape, at any rate in the course of normal social existence. While his moral attitude is generally negative, however, he leaves sufficient ambiguity and sufficient sympathy for the plight of his characters as to refute any attempt to see him simply as an unmasker of the petty bourgeois life style, *meshchanstvo*.

Trifonov himself has commented on the habit of disdaining *byt* in a way which illuminates his work:

Byt is the great test. One should not speak slightingly of it, as though it were a base side of human life, unworthy of literature. *Byt* is after all just ordinary life, the ordeal of ordinary life, where the morality of today manifests itself and is put to the test.

People's relationships with one another are also *byt*. Our element is the muddled, complicated structure of *byt,* at the intersection of a multitude of connections, outlooks, friendships, acquaintanceships, antagonisms, psychologies, ideologies. Anyone who lives in a large town senses every day, every hour, the magnetic streams of that structure, and sometimes they tear him apart. Constantly one has to make choices, decide things, overcome things, sacrifice things.[3]

This is why Trifonov plunges with such single-mindedness into the apparent trivia which make up the everyday life of the urban middle class: apartments, furniture, clothes, children's education, in-laws, family quarrels, love affairs, the whole interlaced with a dense network of relatives, friends, acquaintances, and even odd individuals who drop in for a sentence or two, are briefly characterized, and then disappear never to re-emerge.

Byt, of course, has many aspects, but there is one which particularly interests Trifonov, and that is the crisis of middle age. It can come not only in one's forties and fifties, but at almost any time of life, according to temperament and circumstances. It is the time when a man finally realizes that he is *never* going to write his *magnum opus,* discover the philosopher's stone, or find the ideal, all-consuming love – that he is not going to fulfil the promises that lit up his youth. It is a time for 'preliminary stocktaking' (*Predvaritel'nye itogi*[4]), for a 'long goodbye' (*Dolgoe proshchanie*[5]), while one adjusts to 'another life' (*Drugaya zhizn'*[6]). It is a time when a man's sense of the absolute, the transcendent, is lost, and he is left with only the immanent and the contingent; this is the dark side, if you like, of the spiritual movement which we have noted earlier, away from absorption in the Purpose to absorption in the here-and-now. A whole society is going through middle age. Most of Trifonov's works involve a surrender – of love or principle in favour of the tangible and the expedient.

The Long Goodbye (1971) is characteristic. It relates the breakdown of an imperfect but functioning relationship, that of a young actress, Lyalya, and her former schoolfriend, Grisha Rebrov, a gauche and neurotic scholar trying to write a drama about a Populist revolutionary by burying himself in the Lenin Library. The relationship has long attracted the disapproval of Lyalya's mother, the ambitious, snobbish, gossipy Irina Ignat'evna, who is constantly holding her daughter back from formalizing the liaison and advising her to have abortions. Lyalya is a complex personality: both an ambitious performer, weary of her secondary roles, and an outgoing, compassionate young woman.

Lyalya felt she possessed the mysterious something necessary for happiness. She could not have explained precisely what it was, but she knew she had it. Because, whenever others were unhappy, she felt she wanted to pity them and ease their lot, to share something with them, and if she felt such a wish, then she must have something to share.[7]

It is her pity which initially attracts her to Smolyanov, who first appears as a provincial dramatist, a pathetic figure mocked by the actors of Lyalya's troupe who have to perform his play. Lyalya wants to comfort him and make up for the humiliations caused by her colleagues. However Smolyanov, though a mediocre playwright, turns out to be very good at providing himself with connections where he needs them – a head waiter in the Moskva restaurant, the director of a shoe shop, and so on. He also gains political support by writing plays on the currently fashionable theme of 'forest zones' to be planted as windbreaks in the steppes. He gets these works performed in Moscow despite the opposition of both the stage manager and the literary adviser of Lyalya's theatre. He becomes useful to Lyalya in her career, and this artificially prolongs the liaison until an evening when he tries to pass her off as a courtesan for a superior whom he is trying to please. At that point Lyalya suddenly realizes the depth to which she has fallen, and breaks with Smolyanov in horror. It is then that Grisha finds out about the affair, becomes disgusted at Lyalya's pregnancy that had delighted him only a few days earlier, and decides to break away from everything and everyone and go off on an expedition in the Siberian *taiga*, from which he returns to a more successful, but inwardly more empty life writing film scripts. Lyalya capitulates once more to her mother, has an abortion, and later becomes the wife of a senior army officer.

In its picture of people caught up in social and professional connections they cannot abjure, struggling for a love they dimly perceive but cannot entirely believe in, allowing themselves to choose the second best because they have little faith in themselves, this work encapsulates Trifonov's overriding concerns as a writer.

The House on the Embankment is also a clear example of moral capitulation, of a much more degrading kind. The nub of the action is the pressure brought on a research student, Vadim Glebov, to denounce his supervisor and prospective father-in-law, Professor Ganchuk, so that he may be eased out and replaced by younger, more ambitious colleagues. The whole work is an interesting case study in the way party, and even security police, connections are exploited in the interests of intrigues involving career promotion. Vadim's surrender to the pressure put upon him is paralleled by the fading of his love for Ganchuk's daughter, Sonya, who is unfailingly sympathetic and protective towards him, even when his treachery becomes clear. She eventually has a nervous breakdown, falls seriously ill and dies. Vadim in fact destroys both Ganchuk's career and his family, but since much of the story is told through his eyes, the process is revealed to us in passing, undramatically, filtered through his unwilling memory and distorted by his retrospective desire to interpret his own role in the most favourable possible light. This is the opposite procedure from that of the Socialist Realist narrator, who dramatizes the action and underlines the moral lesson: here the action builds up in a rambling manner, and the narrator does his best – but unsuccessfully – to point up ambiguities and to distract the reader from the moral lessons which suggest themselves.

One very obvious lesson is that, as Trifonov sees it, in this kind of society, Vadim's behaviour is easily understandable: indeed, it would be taken for granted by most people, and this is what makes the morality of it so easy to evade. This is a society which has come to look upon denunciations and unmaskings as a matter of course. Ganchuk himself, in a sense, helped to prepare his own downfall. In the twenties he was a member of one of the numerous groups that used unscrupulous – but still purely literary – methods against one another. He is proud of having struggled whole-heartedly against 'petty bourgeois elements', and indeed regrets only that he did not 'finish them off altogether'. For a time, in the Civil War, he even worked for the Cheka. 'Ganchuk was', we are told, 'a name to put fear into enemies.'[8]

As Trifonov presents it, the style of these relatively gentlemanly literary battles of the twenties coalesces with the methods of the security services (investigation, denunciation, dismissal, even arrest) and with another social phenomenon of the period, street gang battles, to produce the peculiarly murderous factional. intrigue which characterizes academic life in the late forties. As a small boy Vadim remembers that he and his colleagues used to be ambushed by street hooligans, and had to try and organize themselves for self-defence. The leading figure in their 'home guard' was Anton, a rather weakly, artistic boy, who used to steel himself consciously to play the role of hero which he felt was required. He formed a Secret Society for the Testing of the Will, which met to practise ju-jitsu and prove its strong nerves by walking on balcony rails high above the street. This Anton, with his aspirations to be a painter and his home 'where in a secret desk drawer there lay a pile of thick 55 kopeck notebooks, covered in minute handwriting',[9] was killed in the war, and only his memory remains, an example of what will-power can achieve. He does not live to see the moral decay of his comrades after the war.

Another influential person in Vadim's life is Levka Shulepnikov, who before the war lived in the large grey apartment block of the title, towering over Vadim's modest house; here important party and state officials lived, including Levka's father, an officer in the NKVD. The Shulepnikovs' large, luxurious, single-occupancy apartment used to intimidate Vadim, and he went there reluctantly. Other children felt the same about Levka, who remained isolated, but aloof and proud, with a touch of willed mystery and violence about him. Hints of the real character underneath come only when, in uncontrollable fury against a teacher, he shouts 'I will violate her!' The brutality of the sentiment, combined with the strange formality of the word chosen to express it, produces an odd frisson.

Vadim's uncle is arrested, evidently in the late thirties, and Vadim intercedes for him with Levka's father. Shulepnikov profits by the occasion to ask which schoolboys have been bullying his son. In the hope of easing his uncle's lot, Vadim mentions a couple of names – and therewith his first betrayal is accomplished, as part of a routine transaction. No salvation is forthcoming for his uncle, but as a result of his denunciation (though the narrator smooths this over a bit) both boys are expelled from the school and the family of one of them is exiled from Moscow.

So the precedent is set, the habit of mind painlessly and naturally inculcated. After the war, when Vadim wants to make an academic career, he uses his acquaintance with Sonya, and then her growing affection for him, to worm his way into Ganchuk's confidence. He continues his pursuit of Sonya partly out of the pride of conquest, and partly because he is tickled with the thought of inheriting the professor's pleasant country dacha. But when his association with Ganchuk becomes a hindrance to his advancement, when the head of the academic section of the Institute (a former military procurator) asks him to speak at a public meeting and make his attitude clear, Vadim is tormented by what he has to do. He tries to calculate precisely the pros and cons of each 'variation'. What would acting in a principled manner give him?

The gratitude of Ganchuk and his whole family, Sonya's even more extravagant love. A few people would shake his hand for half a minute and tell him what a fine person he was and how well he had spoken. . . . Then work as a minor clerk somewhere. A life of taking the suburban train out to Bruskovo every Saturday, laden like a pack-horse. The losses would be devastating, the gains meagre.[10]

He manages also to convince himself that Ganchuk in his time has acted in a high-handed manner, that he is old-fashioned, no longer in touch with the times, with progress. Anyway, if he does what is demanded of him, he will soon be able to rise in the world to the point where he need no longer worry about those who will reproach him with the price of his graduate studentship, his 'thirty pieces of silver'.

This is the moment at which his selective memory gives out, but the narrator fills in for us:

Perhaps things had not been quite like that, because he tried not to remember it. What he didn't remember ceased to exist. It had never been. There had never been a second, crowded meeting in March, when there was no longer any sense in allowing his conscience to gnaw at him and he had no choice but to go along and, if not speak himself, at least listen to others. Actually, he must have said something at it. Something very brief and trivial. He had quite forgotten what. It was of no importance.[11]

So betrayal, though more or less a social norm, is still not easy. Something inside Vadim resists it, causes him inner turmoil and subsequently represses the memory.

We finally see Vadim as an established middle-aged man, travelling abroad to literary congresses, with health and family problems. Ganchuk, in his old age, is deserting Gor'ky, in whom he had always believed, as a result of seeing his methods degraded and turned against him, and moving uncertainly towards a Dostoevskian position, again seen through Vadim's uncomprehending eyes:

He said something about how the thought that had tormented Dostoevsky – that *everything is permitted* if nothing exists except the dark room with spiders – still existed today in a trivial, everyday form. All the problems had become incredibly petty, but they still existed. Today's Raskol'nikovs did not kill old money-lenders with an axe, but they still worried about whether to cross that same line. And anyway, what was the difference whether you did it with an axe or by other means? Whether you killed or just gave a little shove, so that the place was vacated?[12]

This of course is Ganchuk's comment on Vadim, but also an oblique authorial comment on the whole action, on the way in which fundamental moral questions are decided in *byt*. Trifonov's own debt to Dostoevsky probably goes deeper than Ganchuk's by this time: the only character who comes with real credit out of the story is Sonya, the self-sacrificing compassionate woman destroyed by her love for an unworthy man. As if her name and character did not speak for itself, Trifonov has added the direct reference to *Crime and Punishment*.

The House on the Embankment shows up many of the features that have become typical of Trifonov's work in the seventies. He winds the reader gradually into the fates of his characters, following step by step the apparently trivial moments out of which their failures and abdications are constructed. He likes to plunge in at the centre of the plot, just where the vital decisions are about to be taken, as though it were the centre of a knot, and then, in a series of flashbacks, traces the various strands which lead to this nodal moment. The technique produces a sense of ineluctability: the strands seem like so many tentacles of intrigue, gossip and enmity which catch up the protagonists and engulf them. It is as though there were really nothing else in life and therefore no hope of redemption for ordinary, fallen, social man. Trifonov's language accentuates this impression: he lays the details of each transaction, each intrigue exhaustively before us, piling them together into sentence constructions not even graced by subordinate clause connectors. He is like an inexhaustible gossipy letter writer for whom every punctuation mark is a comma because there is so much to tell and it is all interlinked.

His narration is usually conducted in the third person, except in *Preliminary Stocktaking* (and a rather shadowy first person narrator in *The House on the Embankment*, who shows up only occasionally). The narrator, however, stands very close to the characters, understanding their thought processes, observing and judging them from only slightly above their heads, as it were. At times he seeks the safety of objective judgement or aphorism, but mostly he attempts to mingle his own opinions with those of his characters – most strikingly in the case of Vadim, *against* whom he is telling the story. He offers us sometimes several alternative views of a person or an action, from different angles, without choosing between them. His moral judgements, for that reason, often have a touch of the hesitant or ambiguous about them.

A striking example is *Preliminary Stocktaking* (*Predvaritel'nye itogi*, 1970). The family life of the translator Gennady, Rita and their son Kirill is an offence to the ideals of either a Christian or a socialist society. Yet the clearest condemnation of that family life comes through Gennady, who is himself part of it, and therefore in a position to do something about it if he really wished. He reproaches Rita with the hours and rubles she spends on currently fashionable acquisitions, rare editions of Aquinas, Leont'ev and Berdyaev:

I told her I found it profoundly repulsive. That her pseudo-religiosity was sheer hypocrisy and affectation and that the first commandment of any religion – and especially of Christianity – was love for one's fellow men. What was she doing about it? She didn't give a damn, she stayed out at all hours, she proudly showed off her books. Her husband was neglected, and her son was growing up like a wild thing in the forest.[13]

The egotistical side of Gennady's sermons is clear enough. But there is much in the plot and in the presentation to justify this moral position. Earlier he has reflected:

You can be ill or do uncongenial work all your life, but you must feel yourself to be a human being. And for that one thing is essential – an atmosphere of simple humanity. As simple as elementary arithmetic. No one can cultivate that atmosphere autonomously, all on his own, it arises from others, from those who are close to one. We don't notice how sometimes we lose sight of that eternal truth: we must be close to those who are close to us. Well, honestly, you may say, what sort of threadbare philosophy is that: love your neighbour? Biblical mumbo-jumbo and idealism. But if a man does not feel the closeness of those around him, then, no matter how intellectually elevated he may be, no matter how ideologically well equipped, he begins to squirm and suffocate spiritually.[14]

The placing of this passage (which ends, note, with a direct Soviet equivalent of a famous passage from Paul's Letter to the Corinthians) makes it clear that it is part of a self-pitying meditation on Gennady's part: his family, he is thinking, has not really let him develop his humanity. On the other hand, the moral reflection has a validity of its own – one which is, moreover, corroborated by the whole work. Gennady is a weak vessel to be bearing such pronouncements, but this is precisely the ambiguity which makes Trifonov's work fascinating.

The nodal point of the novel concerns an old icon which Rita has asked her housemaid, Nyura, to procure for her from an old aunt back in the village. Nyura is a key figure. She is a country girl who lost her parents and suffered permanent damage to her health in the famine of the thirties. Prematurely ageing and almost deaf, and abandoned or exploited by most of her relatives, she was glad to get a steady job with the family, and her slow, obtuse but dogged devotion constitutes the one force that holds them together. Gennady feels no particular responsibility for her, but values her because her presence enables him to get his work done. Rita, for her part, uses her to obtain the valuable old icon from her aunt. When Nyura falls ill and asks for the icon in hospital, Rita entrusts it to Kirill, who instead of taking it to Nyura sells it on the black market. Readiness to exploit human relationships in the parents degenerates into criminal activity in the son, their implied morality re-emerging in him with a brutal directness which they would never have permitted themselves. The reaction of the two parents is indicative: Gennady feels a certain responsibility for what his son has done, but also feels helpless to do anything about it or even to confront him directly. Rita, on the other hand, refuses to get excited about the morality of the issue, and is merely worried about which strings to pull so that Kirill will not get into serious trouble.[15]

Nyura's illness is also a test of their humanity. When she goes into hospital, the family almost falls apart: 'We all started to go our own way, each of us sought his own room, his own affairs and secrets, his own silence. She alone had been our *home*, the guardian of stove and hearth!'[16]

The illness turns out to be a chronic form of schizophrenia, from which there is likely to be no cure. This raises the question of whether the 'guardian of their stove and hearth' is a member of the family and ought to be taken back when discharged from hospital, perhaps incapable of much work and requiring nursing. Gennady reads Rita yet another sermon on 'love for one's neighbour', but does not feel bound by it himself, since he after all does not read Berdyaev. Each prefers to take no responsibility, tacitly leaving the other to take the decision. As Rita says with the flaccid self-insight of so many of Trifonov's characters, 'when three egoists live together, no good can come of it' [17]

Is there any alternative to this egoism in human affairs? Amongst the middle-class Moscow community we are not given much hope of one. Only Nyura, with her sympathy for the neurotic and lazy Rita ('What will you do without a help?' she worries) is unselfish, and that is not because she has conquered egoism, but simply because she has never developed it. Similarly, in Turkmenia, where Gennady is working in a writers' dacha after escaping from his family, the caretaker, gardener and janitor, Atabaly, attracts Gennady as a man who is 'hard working and well disposed towards people',[18] always ready, in spite of his eleven children and numerous duties, to have a quiet chat. His children and children-in-law have the same troubles that all families have, yet he is somehow able to rise above them and offer help and support. Perhaps that is circumstance:

Egoism [Gennady reflects] is a deficiency of love. Our woes derive from that monotonous cause. But can a man who has eleven children be an egoist? It's inconceivable! However much you might want to and no matter what your inborn personality traits, you just couldn't be one.[19]

Certainly both Nyura and Atabaly have had very hard lives. Yet, if we allow that unselfishness, goodness, the capacity to love others are formed largely by circumstance, then what becomes of man's project to create by his own will-power a more humane society? Especially since, on the evidence presented by Trifonov, the kindest people tend to be the old-fashioned ones, while up-to-date intellectual Moscow offers a thankless soil for the development of kindness. Modernization seems to be hard on the circumstances which allow or encourage it.

Trifonov has a strong sense of history, and is deeply pessimistic about the direction in which his society is moving. *The Long Goodbye* is framed by an evocation of the transition of a Moscow suburb from dachas behind yellow fences, foliage and lilacs to rows of eight-storey apartment houses with large, convenient shops on the ground floor. As the novel advances, so do the apartment houses.

In those days, in the era of lilacs, the inhabitants of the little yellow-fenced house used to go a long way for their meat – by tram to the Vagan'kov market. Nowadays they would find their shopping much more convenient. But nowadays, unfortunately, they do not live there any more.[20]

Lyalya's capitulation to her mother and to expediency is paralleled by the failure of her father to save his garden, with its celebrated collection of numerous varieties of dahlias, from the bulldozer.

But it is not just a question of optimism or pessimism. History enters into every facet of Trifonov's characters through families. He has a strong sense of the way families are built up, evolve, meet each other, collide, become entangled and coalesce with each other. The whole structure of *The Exchange* (*Obmen*, 1969) is built around this. Viktor comes from a family of 'hereditary revolutionaries', the Dmitrievs: his grandfather was a law student at St Petersburg University, was imprisoned and exiled for subversive activities, was acquainted with Vera Zasulich. Now seventy-nine, the grandfather finds the modern world totally incomprehensible: how can one call an electrical repair man by the familiar *ty* or grease the palm of a shop assistant in order to have a specially good radio set put aside for one?[21] Viktor's wife Lena calls him a 'well preserved monster'. Viktor's uncles were Red Partisans and then officials of the OGPU, while his father was a railway engineer with unfulfilled literary pretensions. It was through the uncles (purged though they were, as we discover between the lines) that the Dmitrievs obtained the pleasant dacha in Pavlinovo, where much of the action takes place and which gives way at the end to a new football stadium. Kseniya Fëdorovna, Viktor's mother, is the last representative of the cultured side of the Dmitriev family: she is well-educated and gentle, but now ill and inclined to passivity. The Dmitrievs lose out to Lena's family, the Luk'yanovs, in the struggle for Viktor's soul. Lena's father was above all a fixer, the kind of man with connections and know-how who has always been necessary in Soviet society to offset the rigidity of its official principles. He can manage everything from getting a cesspool repaired to finding Viktor a job in an Institute. Lena's mother, Vera Lazarevna, comes from a working-class family, and is still rather surprised by, and conscious of, her rise in

the world. The central point of the novel is the discovery that Kseniya
Fëdorovna has incurable cancer. Lena immediately thinks up a plan:
to get round the appalling and general housing shortage by arranging
an exchange of apartments, in such a way that she and Viktor will gain
a large one, moving into it with Kseniya Fëdorovna, who is entitled to
her own living space, and – the unspoken assumption – take it over as a
whole when the latter dies. Viktor, who is capable of gentler and finer
feelings, eventually falls in with this plan to exploit the expected death
of his mother. He is, in a word, finally Luk'yanovized, as his sister Lora
puts it. He is by now worlds removed from his grandfather – and
significantly it is his grandfather's funeral that causes him to reflect
most deeply on the irrevocable nature of change.

What pained him most sharply was the feeling of irretrievability, of being cut
off, which accompanies funerals – something had gone, never to return, and
what continued was something not quite the same, mixed in new
combinations. That was stronger even than his grief over his grandfather.
After all, grandfather was old and bound to pass on, but something else, not
connected with him, existing independently, was disappearing along with
him: something that tied him to his mother and sister.[22]

In some ways it is the grandfather himself who has the last word on
the theme of historical relativity. When Vera Lazarevna recalls what a
refined dacha resort Pavlinovo was before the Revolution ('They were
respectable people here then: stockbrokers, merchants, lawyers,
actors') and how it has deteriorated, only the grandfather has the
breadth – and the historical memory – to point out how each
generation has its own aspirations.

'Let us imagine, my dear Vitya, that your mother-in-law's uncle had lived to
see the time when those people in their goatee beards and pince-nez were taking
the air. What would he have said? Probably "Look at the kind of society we get
in Pavlinovo today! The most incredible riff-raff, in loose-fitting tunics and
pince-nez." Eh, don't you think? I mean, before that there was a landed estate
here, but then the owner went bankrupt, sold the house, sold the land, and half
a century later, when his heir looked by, out of morbid interest, he might have
said, looking at the merchants' and officials' wives, at the gentlemen in top hats
and (bowing to Vera Lazarevna) at your respected uncle arriving in a hired
cab, "Ugh, disgusting! What awful people!"'[23]

For Trifonov, time and 'progress' destroy as much as they create.
The only lesson to be drawn from the passage of history is perhaps the
one which the formerly revolutionary grandfather draws, that 'it's
stupid to despise people. You shouldn't despise anyone.'
In *Another Life* (*Drugaya zhizn'*, 1975) the understanding of

history becomes an existential problem. Ol'ga Vasil'evna's husband, Serëzha Troitsky, is a historian, an unsuccessful one, at least in the sense that he can never finish his dissertation before dying from a heart attack at the age of forty-two. He is opposed to the ideas of historical inevitability and historical expediency such as dominate official Soviet scholarship. In his view the individual is the centre of the historical process, the 'subtlest nerve of history' and one that stretches from generation to generation. Serëzha's rather muddled ideas come close to a theory of metempsychosis and certainly envisage for the individual a kind of immortality:

Man will never reconcile himself to death, because he carries within him a sense of the infinite length of the strand of which he forms a part. It is not God who confers immortality on man, and not religion that suggests the idea to him, but the sense, encoded into the genes, of belonging to an infinite series. . . .[24]

This theory generates Serëzha's research method, which he calls 'digging up graves': namely, the painstaking and detailed rediscovery of every possible fact about the life of the individual under study, including visiting any surviving relatives or those who might have known him. The method lays him open to the criticism of not being able to see the wood for the trees – where the selective qualities of 'historical expediency' would save him a lot of work and enable him to finish his dissertation. Partly because of this, and partly because of the harsh way he always expresses his disagreements with others, he becomes the victim of intrigues designed to force him out of the Institute. Feeling his historical work slipping away from him, he pursues the same dimly perceived goals by means of spiritualist seances, another way of communicating with past individuals, of *understanding*:

We are surprised that we don't understand one another. And why don't people understand us? We feel that all evil springs from that cause. If only people understood us! There would be no quarrels, no war. . . . Parapsychology is a dreamlike attempt to penetrate into another person, to give oneself to another person, to be healed by understanding. One could go on for ever about that. . . . But how can we go on desperately trying to understand others, when we don't even understand ourselves? Yes, of course, my God, we've got to understand ourselves first! But no, we're not strong enough, or we haven't enough time, or perhaps we aren't intelligent or courageous enough. . . .[25]

These thoughts (presented here through his wife reflecting on them after his death) lead to his decision to resign from the Institute, to give up gathering insignificant crumbs from the long-deserted feast-table of history, and to devote himself to the knowledge that really matters.

Through the wood he has previously not been able to see for the trees he begins to discern 'another life', but in what it consists he does not find out, for the heart attack comes before he has had time to get very far.

Ol'ga Vasil'evna, herself a biologist and — of course — a convinced materialist, intellectually rejects her husband's speculations about personal immortality.

She knew for certain that everything began and ended with chemical particles. There was nothing beyond those formulae in the universe or beyond its bounds. He had several times asked her quite seriously: 'No, do you really think you can disappear from the world without trace? Or that I can?' And she would answer in genuine surprise: 'Why, do you really think you can't?' And he would reply that, no matter how hard he tried with his imagination or understanding, he couldn't conceive it. . . .

And now he *had* disappeared. He was nowhere, he had joined the eternity of which he would sometimes lightly talk while smoking a cigarette. But, my God, if everything begins and ends with chemistry, then why does pain exist? After all, pain is not chemistry, is it?[26]

But – and this is perhaps the main point of the work – what her mind cannot grasp is quite accessible to her feelings. Indeed, it is she, through her love for him, who achieves what Serëzha, with his ratiocination, exhaustive research and experimental parapsychology, could never achieve: the breakthrough to 'another life'. At the beginning, two months after his death, she is obsessed with thoughts of suicide. Death to her is a less painful thought than memory and the attempts to understand the past, to understand who was at fault in his premature death. All this leads nowhere, to a dream in which the 'other life' appears to her as a pathetic woodland bog, containing nothing and leading nowhere.[27] All her life she had protected him, his weakness, his neurosis, and that had been the meaning of her life, a kind of continuous compassion compensating for the aridity of her intellectual life. And now the only way she can find out of her suffering is another such love – which she does find at the end, again for a weak and sick man. At the end we see her with this other dimly sketched figure, standing in the belfry of an old church just outside Moscow, looking out over the city gradually disappearing in the twilight.

It was windy up there, and a gust suddenly hit them. She reached for him to shield him and save him, and he embraced her. And she reflected that she was not guilty. Not guilty, because there was another life all around, inexhaustible like those chilly expanses, like that boundless city, dimly seen as it awaited the evening.[28]

There are in Trifonov's work many women of the type of Ol'ga

Vasil'evna, who love out of pity a man who, from 'objective' criteria, is not worthy of it: Lyalya in *The Long Goodbye*, for example, or Sonya Ganchuk in *The House on the Embankment*. The effect of reading his work, however, is not to awaken our condemnation of such 'blind' love, but on the contrary to cast doubt on the value of the 'objectivity' of the judgement. In other words, the reader undergoes something of the same intellectual process which the 'unworthy' Serëzha Troitsky lives through.

Just in the same way, Grisha Rebrov, in a brief moment of happiness when he thinks Lyalya is going to have a baby and their family stability is to begin at last, mutters to himself: 'Not *cogito ergo sum*, but *I love ergo sum*. That's how it is! Why don't people realize that? Why won't they understand? Why, it's blindingly obvious!'[29]

Trifonov's break with traditional Socialist Realism has in the end been a fairly radical one. First of all in his subject-matter, his concentration upon *byt*. *Byt* was everything that was despised and rejected by the Bolsheviks of the twenties and thirties: it was the element of the petty bourgeoisie, not worthy of heroes fighting for high civic ideals. They despised mere creature comforts, comfortable apartments, social position. The Purpose drained all meaning from *byt*. Trifonov's characters are no longer living in that kind of world: they inhabit a relatively normal, rather conservative society where the aspiration for a comfortable, cultured, not too demanding existence is pretty general. Just as, in Balzac or Dostoevsky, men's passions spoke in terms of money and social position, so here, in Trifonov's socialist society, they take the form of struggling for an apartment, a place in the Institute, a promotion in the official hierarchy.

In this kind of society, history once again reclaims its usual role. Families grow, coalesce, break up and re-form. Marriages last unbroken, even unsatisfactory ones, for decades, as Gennady reflects in *Preliminary Stocktaking*:

We shouldn't have lived together for twenty years. *Also sprach Zarathustra*: it's too long. Twenty years is no joke. In twenty years forests disappear and soils are eroded. The best built house needs repairs. Turbines are written off. And the enormous progress science makes in twenty years, why it's terrible to think about. . . . Not to mention the fact that new African states have arisen. Twenty years! That's the kind of stretch that leaves no room for hope.[30]

So people change, institutions change, even moral concepts change. Trifonov's style and mode of presentation are designed to give us a strong sense of this changeability. He deliberately aims at 'density',[31] never giving us a whole dialogue but only the immediately relevant part of it, passing over whole periods in an individual's or a family's life in a sentence enumerating a few characteristic, selected details. Characters are presented from different points of view, sometimes because they are seen by different observers, sometimes because time has passed and they have changed.

In his choice of narrative viewpoint Trifonov faces a major dilemma. What he values and wishes to present is the way people see each other. For this, third person narration, through internal monologue, by a variety of characters, is the natural procedure, and the one he usually adopts. But at the same time, he wishes to achieve a certain unity of approach, to ensure that certain perceptions do not escape the reader (this is perhaps a lingering legacy from Socialist Realism, where the author left the reader in no doubt about his views): for that reason he sometimes intervenes in the first person in a rather gauche and unsatisfactory way (for example in *The House on the Embankment* and at the end of *The Exchange*), when actually the reader has already, through structure and other internal evidence, been able to form his own opinion of the characters.

There are perhaps three stages in reading a Trifonov work. At first one thinks, what a terrible world to live in! Then one reflects that certain positive values are expressed, but usually by people in whose judgement one feels no confidence, and who are using them often as weapons in the petty battles of *byt*. Finally, one notices that the plot and narrative method do in fact uphold these values, in spite of the weak vessels that give utterance to them.

The values are those which Gennady expresses in his lachrymose appeals to the reader, which Ganchuk gropes for in old age, which Serëzha Troitsky believes in theory and Ol'ga Vasil'evna fulfils in practice. That human beings have access to another world, to a kind of immortality, through love for their neighbour, that this can be attained only through the daily testing, the purgatory which is *byt*, and that this is what gives *byt* its meaning and renders it tolerable.

10

General Conclusions

Here we have been, breaking our backs for years at All-Union forced labour. Here in slow annual spirals we have been climbing up to an understanding of life – and from this height it can all be seen so clearly: it is not the result that counts! It is not the result – but the spirit! Not *what*, but *how*.[1]

These words from *The Gulag Archipelago* are almost a summary of what most of the writers presented in this book have been working towards. And, though based on Soviet experience, what they say applies not only to the Soviet Union. The notion that results are what really count has been for centuries a commonplace of the various western forms of empiricism and positivism, of which Marxism is merely an example – albeit the only one that has succeeded in submitting millions of people to its rule. What the Soviet people has suffered under is in fact an extreme form of attitudes widely taken for granted in the west: materialism, atheism, scientism, belief in progress. Rufus Mathewson (whose work on the 'positive hero' is otherwise so illuminating) is surely wrong when he dubs as 'anachronistic' the battle against 'the extension of scientistic systems to areas of experience not susceptible to scientific reduction'.[2] Far from being a symptom of 'Russia's arrested intellectual development in Stalin's Fourth Rome', it is something that is going on all around us in the west, not least in the social sciences.

However, there is no question that the process has been unusually intense and destructive in the Soviet Union. What has happened there is that the scientific view of man has been raised to the status of an official myth, propagated with all the resources of the state, and unchallenged by any alternative view. Articles in the Soviet press, government pronouncements and party resolutions are still underlain

196

by the image of human beings as cogs in a social mechanism directed by the expert few who are in a position to rise above it and control it. This image is a powerful determinant of the way most Soviet citizens see themselves and understand their own lives. Especially this is so for intellectuals, who have the most intensive regular contact with official propaganda. The image tends to produce apathy and caution, a feeling of the futility of protest or resistance, so that, paradoxically, Marxism-Leninism becomes a distinctly conservative ideology.

One of the profoundest recent diagnoses of the state of Soviet society is D. Nelidov's *samizdat* article, 'Ideocratic consciousness and the personality'.[3] He argues that the inhumanity of totalitarian society is generated not so much by the rulers' excess in the use of power, as by their projection of an impoverished image of man which is, in large measure, accepted by the oppressed themselves – though never entirely accepted, because a residue of 'irrational' belief in human freedom somehow remains. The resulting confusion combines with pervasive fear to produce that divided state of mind which George Orwell aptly called 'doublethink'. Everyone's thinking, including that of the party leaders themselves, is formed and dominated by the ideology. In effect this ideology is a system of coded signs to which the population is (never entirely satisfactorily) programmed to respond. The leaders may change some of the external details of the ideology, even quite abruptly, as they did, for example, after Stalin's death, but they cannot change the image of man that underpins it, nor can they change the signs which are the ideology's link with the public. In that sense they are themselves in the grip of the ideology. That is why Nelidov uses the term 'ideocracy' – rule by ideology – to describe the system.[4]

Physical resistance to such a system is worse than pointless, because it lends some genuine meaning, however tenuous, to the concept of 'enemy', which is one of the key signs in the ideocratic code. Even peaceful political opposition is of limited value. Probably real change can only come about in totalitarian society when the image of man fostered by the regime breaks down from within. In its day the Socialist Realist novel did real service for the political leaders in providing a literary myth consonant with the official ideology and also capable of inspiring at least some readers some of the time. What we have seen in this book is the breakdown of the image of man projected in those novels. The revival of non-Marxist, non-Chernyshevskian philosophy and the re-emergence of popular language and (in

Bakhtin's sense) of 'serious-comic' folk culture have made that image no longer tenable. The novelists discussed in this book have, each in his own way, sketched out the first honest internal chronicle of the tragedies of Soviet society. They are their country's most serious historians. In Solzhenitsyn's words, they have 'preserved the nation's lost history' and thereby 'preserved both the national language and the national soul'.[5] They have rejected the reductionist totalitarian image of man and its attendant myths, and have moved towards an alternative image which, in different ways in each individual author, recalls the Christian personalist outlook which they have discovered in Dostoevsky and in the rich prerevolutionary religious and philosophical tradition exemplified by *Problems of Idealism* and *Vekhi.*

These novelists are realists in literary method, that is to say, they attempt to give an authentic and usually quite detailed picture of the social life they describe. This is not what might have been expected. Twenty years ago, Abram Terts, in the first serious analysis of Socialist Realism, claimed that the realist method had been discredited by the abuse to which it had been put in the service of ideology, and he called for a 'phantasmagoric art, with hypotheses instead of the Purpose, and the grotesque replacing everyday life'.[6] In fact, this prescription did not turn out to be appropriate. Recent Soviet fiction of the 'fantastic' type, intriguing though some of it is, has proved less penetrating and revealing than the best works of the relatively familiar realist type. The reason for this is not far to seek: when all values are in doubt and no one is quite certain what the nation's real history is, then there is no fixed landscape against which the fantastic and the grotesque can be viewed in perspective. Terts's own *Fantastic Tales* (*Fantasticheskie povesti,* 1961), probably the best of their kind in recent Soviet literature, do have an elusive and unanchored feeling about them as a result. Indeed, I would say that, since Soviet reality has itself in many respects been so fantastic and grotesque, what the Soviet reader came desperately to need was a restored sense of *reality* and a framework for understanding what had happened to him and to those around him. This is where the sobriety, the cognitive drive, and the 'serious-comic' approach to the world characteristic of the realist novel have shown themselves so healing. By the same token, however, if this realist literature has been successful in restoring a framework for self-understanding, then the groundwork may have been laid on which Terts's 'phantasmagoric art' could flourish in the future. As has been shown, some of the recent work of Belov, Rasputin, Voinovich and Shukshin points in this direction.

Some will find it surprising that the censorship should permit recognizably truthful descriptions of the recent Soviet past. This, however, is to misunderstand the nature both of the censorship and of the Soviet literary system. Most censorship is carried out by writers themselves: by the author in self-censorship, by editorial boards and by the various commissions of the Writers' Union. The doctrine of Socialist Realism, though imposed by the party, was generated from the literary practice of writers themselves, and therefore the practical development of the doctrine, and its ultimate transmutation into new and ever less recognizable forms, also lies in the hands of writers. The state censorship merely defines what is formally unmentionable, and the party sets general guidelines and limits. The *dynamic* comes from writers themselves, and in general, certainly in the last generation, has been in the direction of more frankness, of unprejudiced 'inquiry into the nature of man, of man as he is and not as he might be constructed', as A. Borshchagovsky put it at the very revealing discussion of Solzhenitsyn's *Cancer Ward* held in the prose section of the Moscow branch of the Writer's Union in November 1966.[7] That being so, the onus has been on the party, through its cultural department, to intervene and forestall what it views as excesses. This it has evidently done from time to time, though in ways that were and are very difficult to predict. The result has been that writers do publish comparatively honest statements about Soviet society, but that some of them then get into political difficulties which may lead to their expulsion from the Writers' Union, or even from the country. Of the writers examined in this book, all started their writing career in Soviet journals, and all at least ostensibly shared the stated aims of the Union of Soviet Writers. Four of them, however, Solzhenitsyn, Maximov, Voinovich and Vladimov, have been driven into *samizdat* in pursuit of their own interpretation of the demands of 'realism', as their growing frankness made them less acceptable to the loyalist writers in whom the party places its trust. Two of them, Solzhenitsyn and Maximov, have actually been expelled from the Soviet Union (though admittedly in Maximov's case the actual crossing of the frontier was voluntary) and deprived of their Soviet citizenship. Voinovich was expelled from the Writers' Union, and Vladimov resigned from it, calling it a branch of the KGB.[8] The relationship between the KGB and the Writers' Union is probably not quite as direct as Vladimov describes it, but it is entirely understandable that he should see it that way. The KGB does indeed have considerable *negative* power in the Writers' Union, influencing very strongly what does *not* get published, as was shown by Voinovich's experience in the spring of 1975, when two KGB officers interviewed him at the Hotel Metropol and offered to remove the obstacles to the publication of his *Chonkin* if he would agree to cooperate with them by making reports about other writers. Voinovich's refusal to enter into this bargain provoked them to have recourse to their wider repertoire of non-literary forms of pressure: they threatened him with possible physical violence and gave him a doctored cigarette that made him feel ill for some days afterwards. The whole incident suggests that the KGB likes to intervene in literary matters, but does not always feel certain how best to do so, particularly when well-known writers are involved.[9]

The process described in this book has not taken place, then, without major tragedies, each of which means a writer deprived of his natural audience and ultimately perhaps of his homeland. And no one can tell where the blow may fall next. But in the struggle to publish more honest works writers have experienced victories as well as defeats. The rejection of the totalitarian image of man has been taking place in officially published literature as well as in *samizdat*. In this sense there is one Soviet literature, not two, as some observers have suggested.[10] Solzhenitsyn, not normally an apologist for those who compromise in any way with the Soviet establishment, has praised the writers who have 'dragged through the meat-grinder of censorship ... the little artistic details [which] preserve and communicate to us a whole area of life whose depiction is forbidden.'[11]

Moreover the writers examined in this book attract not only criticism[12] in the official Soviet media: hardly a single survey article on recent Soviet prose appears without favourable mention of Belov, Rasputin, Shukshin or Trifonov. Nearly every critic recognizes them as being among the most important contemporary prose writers and indeed as constituting at least part of the current mainstream of Soviet fiction. The contortions which the critics execute in order to demonstrate that these writers are still faithful to (a renovated, flexible and updated) Socialist Realism would be worthy of a chapter to themselves. Suffice it to say here that I do not myself think the exegetical gymnastics will work: characters, language, narrator, and indeed the underlying myth have all changed so much that the term

Socialist Realism, unless it has become genuinely meaningless, can no longer be applied. These novelists have far more in common with the familiar 'critical' realists of the nineteenth century, both in Russia and elsewhere – Stendhal, Eliot, Balzac, Tolstoy. They differ, however, from them in one important respect. Nineteenth-century novelists (even in France, which had its share of political revolutions) worked in societies whose institutions and values were quite securely established. To portray human beings in those societies fully, novelists worked in the direction of 'unmasking' those institutions and values, showing up their precariousness and relativity, or even falsehood. Recent Soviet novelists, on the other hand, have been operating in a society whose values were completely overturned in the revolution of 1917, and whose new ones were then subjected to a searing re-examination after 1953. These novelists start, in fact, on the whole, from man uncertain of his identity, or having what he thought was a stable identity severely challenged, and being compelled to construct a new one for himself as he goes along. This is true even of Belov's and Rasputin's peasants, let alone of Maximov's outcasts, Shukshin's misfits, Trifonov's middle-aged and disillusioned intellectuals and Vladimov's disoriented young men (and dog!).

This process of self-discovery (or failure in self-discovery) has something in common with the quest for inner meaning traversed by many Socialist Realist heroes: only now there is no certainty and no social utopia at the end of the path. Modern Soviet man must be content with fragmentary insights, must renounce any ultimate goal, and must become accustomed to the idea that the way is more important than the Purpose, the spirit than the result. All he can be said to discover for certain is that man is an end, not a means, that he is free to take his life into his own hands, and that his essence consists in love and creativity, understood in the broadest sense. That understanding of man is, of course, a fundamental European tradition. It badly needed reasserting in the Soviet Union. Who can say that we in the west today have a surer grasp of it? Can we perhaps learn something from those who have tried to chronicle the Promethean experiment of Soviet society?

Notes

Chapter 1: The Socialist Realist Tradition

[1]Carl R. Proffer, 'Writing in the shadow of the monolith', *New York Review of Books,* 19 February 1976.

[2]Edward J. Brown, *Russian literature since the Revolution,* New York: Collier Books, 1969, p.33; Gleb Struve, *Russian literature under Lenin and Stalin, 1917–53,* Norman: University of Oklahoma Press, 1971, p. 393.

[3]Marc Slonim, *Soviet Russian literature: writers and problems, 1917–77,* 2nd ed., New York: Oxford University Press, 1977, pp. 164–5.

[4]Brown, p. 33.

[5]Slonim, p. 167.

[6]Rufus Mathewson, *The positive hero in Russian literature,* 2nd ed., Stanford: Stanford University Press, 1975, p.4. Mathewson's book has probably done more than any other to make us aware of the context in which Socialist Realism should be studied. Its overall negativism is therefore all the more discouraging.

[7]This description, derived directly from A. Zhdanov's speech at the First Congress of the Union of Soviet Writers in 1934, is found in a standard textbook, *Russkaya sovetskaya literatura,* Moscow: Uchpedgiz, 1963, pp. 315–16.

[8]Zhdanov's speech is reproduced in H. G. Scott (ed.), *Problems of Soviet literature,* London: Martin Lawrence, n.d., pp. 21–2. The best description of the *theory* of Socialist Realism (though it has little to say about the *practice*) is C. Vaughan James, *Soviet Socialist Realism: origins and theory,* London: Macmillan, 1973. Lenin's 1905 article can be found translated in this book, on pp. 103–6.

[9]A. Ovcharenko, 'Osnovnye tipy sotsialisticheskogo realizma', *Moskva,* 9/73, p. 200.

[10]For a full discussion of recent modifications in the theory, see Max Hayward, 'The decline of Socialist Realism', *Survey,* Vol. 18, no. 1 (1972), pp. 73–97.

[11]A useful exposition of these programmes is H. Ermolaev, *Soviet literary theories, 1917–34: the genesis of Socialist Realism*, 1963, Berkeley: University of California Press, 1963.

[12]The exception is the research of Katerina Clark, to which I am indebted more than I can possibly acknowledge in detail. Some of it is now published: '"Boy gets tractor" and all that: the parable structures of the Soviet novel', in R. Milner-Gulland et al. (eds), *Russian and Slavic literature*, Cambridge, Mass.: Slavica Publishers, 1976, pp. 359–75; 'Utopian anthropology as a context for Stalinist literature', in R. C. Tucker (ed.), *Stalinism: essays in historical interpretation*, New York: Norton, 1977, pp. 180–98; 'Little deeds and big deeds: literature responds to the First Five-Year Plan', in Sheila Fitzpatrick (ed.), *Cultural revolution in Russia, 1928–31*, Bloomington: Indiana University Press, 1978, pp. 189–206.

[13]Vaughan James, pp. 86–7; Ermolaev, chapters 6 and 7.

[14]Vaughan James, p. 120.

[15]M. Dewhirst and R. Farrell (eds), *The Soviet censorship*, Metuchen, NJ: The Scarecrow Press, 1973, p.2. Arkady Belinkov was a novelist and critic who left the USSR in 1968 after a long non-conformist literary career which earned him repeated prison and labour camp sentences. A detailed list of the organizations involved in censorship is given in E. Etkind, *Zapiski nezagovorshchika*, London: Overseas Publications Interchange, 1977, pp. 319, 322–3.

[16]C. Milosz, *The captive mind*, New York: Vintage Books, 1953, pp. 10–11.

[17]Nadezhda Mandelstam, *Hope abandoned*, trans. Max Hayward, Harmondsworth: Penguin Books, 1976, p. 39.

[18]The difficulties Marxists get into when they try to formulate a positive aesthetic are well illustrated by the relatively sophisticated attempts of Plekhanov and Trotsky, both of whom recognized the autonomy of art without being able to explain it in their theories. See Mathewson, chapters 9 and 10, and Margaret M. Bullitt, 'Towards a Marxist theory of aesthetics: the development of Socialist Realism in the Soviet Union', *Russian Review*, Vol. 35, no. 1 (January 1976), pp. 53–76.

[19]Mathewson, pp. 251–2.

[20]M. Bakhtin, *Problemy poetiki Dostoevskogo*, 3rd ed., Moscow: Khudozhestvennaya Literatura, 1972.

[21]Ian Watt, *The rise of the novel*, 1957; M. Bakhtin, 'Epos i roman', in his *Voprosy literatury i estetiki*, Moscow: Khudozhestvennaya Literatura, 1975, pp. 447–83.

[22]Y. M. Sokolov, *Russian folklore*, Hatboro Pa.: Folklore Associates, 1950, pp. 321–2.

[23]Although the *zhitie* was almost certainly a direct influence on Soviet writers (mediated through Gor'ky's *Mother*), it is very doubtful whether many of them had read even Bunyan, let alone obscurer Puritan writers. All that can be hypothesized is that 17th-century English Puritans and 20th-century Russian Bolsheviks had a good deal spiritually in common, and tended to produce the same kind of literature. The resemblance in the two personality types has been noted by a number of historians: see especially Christopher Hill, *Society and Puritanism in pre-revolutionary England*, London: Secker

& Warburg, 1964; M. Walzer, *Revolution of the saints*, London: Weidenfeld & Nicolson, 1966.

[24]W. Haller, *The rise of Puritanism*, New York: Columbia University Press, 1938, pp. 130–1.

[25]N. Valentinov, *Encounters with Lenin*, London: Oxford University Press, 1968, pp. 63–4.

[26]H. Segal (ed.), *The literature of 18th-century Russia*, New York: Dutton, 1967, pp. 273–4 (quoted in Dewhirst and Farrell, p. 19 n.).

[27]By S. Babaevskii, later the butt of much sarcasm. But he has survived and is still adapting himself to more recent trends.

[28]Abram Terts, *On Socialist Realism*, New York: Pantheon Books, 1960, p. 77. An excellent survey of the novels of the late Stalin period is Vera Dunham, *In Stalin's time: middleclass values in Soviet fiction*, 1976.

[29]Note the stolidly Russian surnames. This is a Russian, not a multi-national empire, that the Zhurbins are building.

[30]V. Kochetov, *Izbrannye proizvedeniya*, Moscow: Gosudarstvennoe Izdatel'stvo Khudozhestvennoi Literatury, 1962, Vol. 2, p. 541.

[31]ibid, p. 503.

[32]Unpublished research.

[33]This tightening of party control is exemplified in great detail, as are the methods employed by the party and KGB, in the recent memoir of Efim Etkind, *Zapiski nezagovorshchika*, 1977.

[34]V. Pomerantsev, 'Ob iskrennosti v literature', *Novyi Mir*, 12/53.

[35]I. Ehrenburg, *Ottepel'*, Moscow: Sovetskii Pisatel', 1956, p. 93.

[36]Katerina Clark shows in her unpublished work that the imagery of the 'garden', the longing for the organic, was present in much Stalinist fiction. Here too, then, Ehrenburg is strengthening one aspect of the Socialist Realist tradition at the expense of another, that associated with machines and mechanical imagery.

[37]V. Tendryakov, 'V zashchitu polozhitel'nogo geroya', *Novyi Mir*, 11/54, p. 210. A. Makarenko's *Pedagogicheskaya poema*, a semi-autobiographical work, was published in 1934, and has figured on most subsequent lists of approved Soviet classics.

[38]V. Aksënov, 'Zvezdnyi bilet', *Yunost'*, 6/61, p. 20.

[39]V. Aksënov, 'Kollegi', *Yunost'*, 7/60, p. 80.

[40]*Yunost'*, 6/61, p. 12.

[41]*Yunost'*, 7/60, p. 80.

[42]*Roman* means 'novel'; *rasskaz* 'short story'. *Povest'* has no equivalent in English: it corresponds roughly to the German Novelle, but in fact a Russian *povest'* can be appreciably more complex in its plot and structure than the Novelle. For this reason, I use the word 'novel' throughout this book to denote both *povest'* and *roman*.

[43]*Yunost'*, 7/57, p. 6.

[44]A. Gladilin, 'Pervyi den' novogo goda', *Yunost'*, 2/63, p. 35.

[45]A. Bitov, 'Bezdel'nik', in his *Aptekarskii ostrov*, Leningrad: Sovetskii Pisatel', 1968, p. 51 (the story was written in 1961–2).

[46]A. Steininger, *Literatur und Politik in der Sowjetunion nach Stalins Tod*, Wiesbaden: Otto Harrassowitz, 1965, pp. 127, 185; Helen von Ssachno, *Der*

Aufstand der Person, Berlin: Argon Verlag, 1965, pp. 283–4. Good analyses of the language of 'youth prose' can be found in J. Holthusen, 'Stilistik des "uneigentlichen" Erzählens in der sowjetischen Gegenwartsliteratur', *Die Welt der Slawen,* 3/68, pp. 225–45; in the articles of A. Kozhevnikova and V. Odintsov in *Voprosy yazyka sovremennoi russkoi literatury,* Moscow: Nauka, 1971, pp. 97–163; and in Deming Brown, 'Narrative devices in the contemporary Russian short story: intimacy and irony', *American contributions to the Seventh International Congress of Slavists,* Vol. 2 (*Literature and folklore*), The Hague and Paris: Mouton, 1973, pp. 53–74.

⁴⁷Yu. Kazakov, 'Stariki' in his *Goluboe i zelënoe,* Moscow: Sovetskii Pisatel', 1963, pp. 113–29.

⁴⁸'Otshchepenets', translated as 'Oh, Forget it!', in Yu. Kazakov, *The smell of bread,* London: Harvill Press, 1965, pp. 23–37.

⁴⁹*Goluboe i zelënoe,* pp. 162–3.

Chapter 2: Two Key Works: 'Doctor Zhivago' and 'One Day in the Life of Ivan Denisovich'

¹The major exception to this was Mikhail Prishvin, who represented almost single-handed a kind of alternative line of development, based on appreciation of nature and genuine, not synthetic, folklore.

²Abram Terts, 'The literary process in Russia', *Kontinent 1,* London: André Deutsch, 1976, p. 91.

³Gene Sosin, 'Magnitizdat: uncensored songs of dissent', in R. L. Tökés (ed.), *Dissent in the USSR: ideology, politics and people,* Baltimore: Johns Hopkins University Press, 1975, pp. 276–309; Gerry Smith, 'Underground songs', *Index on Censorship,* Vol. 7, no. 2 (March/April 1978), pp. 67–71.

⁴Erich Auerbach, *Mimesis,* 1957; M. Bakhtin, 'Epos i roman', in his *Voprosy literatury i estetiki,* Moscow: Khudozhestvennaya Literatura, 1975, pp. 447–83.

⁵Bakhtin, p. 466.

⁶A. Piatigorsky, 'Remarks on the metaphysical situation', *Kontinent 1,* pp. 51–2.

⁷*Politicheskii dnevnik, 1964–70,* Vol. 1, Amsterdam: Herzen Foundation, 1972, pp. 503–8.

⁸E. Crankshaw, *Khrushchev's Russia,* Harmondsworth: Penguin Books, 1959, p. 168.

⁹loc. cit.

¹⁰ibid., p. 159.

¹¹See his remarks on his translation of Shakespeare's 'Romeo and Juliet': 'Love is as simple and absolute as consciousness and death, nitrogen and uranium. It is not a state of mind, but the basic principle of the world. Love, then, is a keystone and foundation, equivalent to creativity. . . . The highest that art can dream of is to listen for love's voice, and to render its ever fresh, unprecedented language.' *Sochineniya,* Ann Arbor: University of Michigan Press, 1961, Vol. 3, p. 198.

[12]Boris Pasternak, *Doctor Zhivago,* trans. Max Hayward and Manya Harari, London: Fontana, 1961, p. 71 (Russian edition, Milan: Feltrinelli, 1957, p. 66).
   [13]pp. 17–18 (10).
   [14]p. 148 (148).
   [15]p.248 (256–7).
   [16]p.388 (407).
   [17]p. 394 (412).
   [18]p. 313 (327).
   [19]pp. 346–9 (363–6).
   [20]p. 292 (306–7).
   [21]p. 444 (466).
   [22]p. 463 (486).
   [23]p. 74 (68).
   [24]loc. cit.
   [25]p. 95 (91).
   [26]p. 427 (448).
   [27]p. 147 (148); p. 347 (363); p. 368 (385).
   [28]p. 441 (463).
   [29]p. 386 (404).
   [30]p. 387 (405).
   [31]p. 489 (513).
[32]Nadezhda Mandelstam, *Hope abandoned,* trans. Max Hayward, Harmondsworth: Penguin Books, 1976, p. 60.
   [33]Pasternak, *Doctor Zhivago,* p. 506 (530).
   [34]Terrence des Pres, *The survivor: an anatomy of life in the death camps,* New York: Oxford University Press, 1976, p. 69.
   [35]A. Solzhenitsyn, *One day in the life of Ivan Denisovich,* trans. Max Hayward and Ronald Hingley, New York: Bantam Books, 1963, pp. 66–7. (Throughout quotations from this translation I have amended the words 'gang' and 'boss' to 'brigade' and 'leader' respectively.)
   [36]p. 50.
   [37]p. 31.
   [38]pp. 84–5.
   [39]p. 112.
   [40]See R. Luplow, 'Narrative style and structure in *One day in the life of Ivan Denisovich',* *Russian Literature Triquarterly,* no. 1 (fall 1971), p. 401. In an analogous way, Abram Terts's voice both emerges from and blends with that of other zeks in his *Voice from the chorus,* London: Collins & Harvill, 1976.
   [41]Solzhenitsyn, p. 142 (p. 103 in the Sovetskii Pisatel', 1963 edition).
   [42]p. 128.
   [43]p. 15.
   [44]p. 196.
   [45]A. Solzhenitsyn, *Odin den' Ivana Denisovicha,* Moscow: Sovetskii Pisatel', 1963, p. 77. The *Novyi Mir* (11/62) text, on which the Bantam translation is based, is much shortened at this point, one of the relatively few instances of censorship – or self-censorship – in this text.
   [46]Solzhenitsyn, Bantam ed., p. 45.

[47]p. 169.
[48]p. 38.
[49]p. 90.
[50]p. 198.
[51]Roman Gul', 'A. Solzhenitsyn, Sotsrealizm i shkola Remizova', *Novyi Zhurnal*, no. 71 (1963), p. 83.
[52]George Lukacs, *Solzhenitsyn*, London: Merlin Press, 1970, p. 33.

Chapter 3: Vasily Belov and Valentin Rasputin

[1]Some Soviet sociologists have recognized this as the principal division in Soviet society. See Yu. V. Arutunyan, *Opyt sotsiologicheskogo izucheniya sela*, Moscow: Izdatel'stvo Moskovskogo Universiteta, 1968, especially p. 45.
[2]Yu. Kazakov, *The smell of bread*, London: Harvill Press, 1965, pp. 39–46.
[3] *Literaturnaya Moskva*, no. 2, Moscow: Khudozhestvennaya Literatura, 1956, pp. 404–14.
[4]S. Zalygin, *Interv'yu u samogo sebya*, Moscow: Sovetskii Pisatel', 1970, p. 10.
[5]B. Shragin, *Protivostoyanie dukha*, London: Overseas Publications Interchange, 1977, Chapter 2.
[6]Ian H. Hill, 'The end of the Russian peasantry', *Soviet Studies*, Vol. 27 (1975), pp. 109–27; E. Starikova, 'Sotsiologicheskii aspekt sovremennoi "derevenskoi prozy"', *Voprosy Literatury*, 7/72, pp. 11–35.
[7]V. Ovechkin, *Trudnaya vesna*, Moscow: Sovetskii Pisatel', 1956, p. 319.
[8]D. Pospielovsky, 'The "link" system in Soviet agriculture', *Soviet Studies*, Vol. 21 (1970), p. 415.
[9]Gleb Zhekulin, 'Efim Dorosh', in R. Milner-Gulland et al (eds), *Russian and Slavic literature*, Cambridge, Mass.: Slavica Press, 1976, pp. 425–48.
[10]A. Solzhenitsyn, *Stories and prose poems*, London: Bodley Head, 1970, p. 54 (a sentence omitted in this translation has been restored).
[11]*Ogonëk*, 13/63, p. 30.
[12]'Lyudi kolkhoznoi derevni v poslevoennoi proze', *Novyi Mir*, 4/54.
[13]The first three novels of the series (*Brat'ya i sestry*, *Dve zimy i tri leta*, *Puti-pereput'ya*), as well as *Pelageya* and *Al'ka*, can be found in F. Abramov, *Izbrannoe*, 2 vols, Leningrad: Khudozhestvennaya Literatura, 1975. The last Pekashino novel, *Dom*, is in *Novyi Mir*, 12/78.
[14]'Pisatel'' i Sibir',' in his *Literaturnye zaboty*, Moscow: Sovremennik, 1972, p. 63.
[15]*Nash Sovremennik*, 9–11/75.
[16]*Sever*, 2/68, pp. 59–61.
[17]'Bobrishnyi ugor', in Belov's *Kholmy*, Moscow: Sovremennik, 1973, p. 531.
[18]'Literatura i yazyk', *Voprosy Literatury*, 6/67, p. 99.
[19]Kholmy, p. 216.
[20]pp. 251–3.
[21]p. 314.

[22]p. 361.

[23]Note the northern *okan'e* implied in the spelling.

[24]The contrast between Olesha and Aviner is further analysed in Gleb Zekulin, 'The contemporary countryside in Soviet literature: a search for new values', in James R. Millar (ed.), *The Soviet rural community,* Urbana: Illinois University Press, 1971, pp. 376–404.

[25]*Novyi Mir,* 7/68, p. 20.

[26]pp. 12–13, 19.

[27]pp. 52–3.

[28]p. 53.

[29]pp. 25–8, 45.

[30]p. 49; cf. Boris Pasternak, *Doctor Zhivago,* p. 37 above.

[31]*Novyi Mir,* 8/69, p. 159.

[32]p. 167.

[33]pp. 174–7.

[34]pp. 178–84.

[35]Presumably for this reason, the novel seems to have had a difficult history: see below, p. 216n.

[36]V. Belov, *Kanuny,* Moscow: Sovremennik, 1976, Part 1, Chapter 10.

[37]ibid, p. 146.

[38]Just before the taxation campaign Sopronov is actually expelled from the party, but continues to masquerade as a party activist because his primary cell has not been informed of the expulsion. This kind of irregular expulsion (only primary cells are supposed to carry out expulsions) was not all that uncommon at the time, but in this case it looks like a device to enable Belov to continue presenting Sopronov in a highly unfavourable light. I do not think we shall be distorting Belov's intentions if we regard Sopronov as a party member throughout. Certainly his aims are identical with those of Erokhin, the slightly more sophisticated but no less ruthless district party secretary.

[39]p. 314–15.

[40]p. 109.

[41]p. 218.

[42]p. 244.

[43]*Nash Sovremennik,* 8/70, p. 13.

[44]p. 26.

[45]p. 48.

[46]*Nash Sovremennik,* 7/70, p. 27.

[47]p. 37.

[48]See below, p. 166.

[49]*Nash Sovremennik,* 10/74, p. 5.

[50]p. 69.

[51]p. 40.

[52]*Nash Sovremennik,* 10/76, p. 22.

[53]pp. 54–5.

[54]p. 68.

[55]p. 25.

[56]pp. 43–4.

[57]p. 44.

[58]p. 30.
[59]pp. 48-9.
[60]*Nash Sovremennik*, 11/76, p. 40.
[61]p. 42.
[62]10/76, pp. 14-15.
[63]*Literaturnaya Gazeta*, 22 November 1967, p. 4.
[64]ibid., 31 January 1968, p. 5.
[65]ibid., 17 January 1968, p. 6.
[66]V. Chalmaev, 'Neizbezhnost'', *Molodaya Gvardiya*, 9/68, pp. 259-89; I. Dedkov, 'Stranitsy derevenskoi zhizni', *Novyi Mir*, 3/69, pp. 231-46; A. Dement'ev, 'O traditsiyakh i narodnosti', *Novyi Mir*, 4/69, pp. 215-35. For a general discussion of these disputes, see V. N. Pavlov, 'Spory o slavyanofil'stve i russkom patriotizme v sovetskoi nauchnoi literature, 1967-70gg', *Grani*, no. 82 (1971), pp. 183-211, and Alexander Yanov, *The Russian new right: right-wing ideologies in the contemporary USSR*, Berkeley: Institute of International Studies, University of California, 1978.
[67]L. Anninskii, 'Tochka opory', *Don*, 6/68, p. 179.

Chapter 4: Vladimir Tendryakov

[1]J. G. Garrard, in an article published in the mid-sixties, gave special attention to these two works, and to Soviet criticism of them. His conclusion was that Tendryakov had essentially abandoned Socialist Realism, and had moved on to concern with abstract personal and moral issues. See *Slavic and East European Journal*, Vol. 9, no. 1 (spring 1965), pp. 1-18.
[2]V. Tendryakov, *Podënka – vek korotkii*, Moscow: Molodaya Gvardiya, 1969, pp. 351-2.
[3]V. Tendryakov, *Perevërtyshi*, Moscow: Sovremennik, 1974, p. 161.
[4]p. 162.
[5]p. 183.
[6]p. 283.
[7]p. 353.
[8]p. 354.
[9]*Nauka i Religiya*, 8/71, p. 71.
[10]See below, p. 114.
[11]*Nauka i Religiya*, 8/71, p. 79.
[12]loc. cit.
[13]P. I. Novgorodtsev (ed.), *Problemy idealizma*, Moscow, 1902, p. 2, from S. N. Bulgakov's article 'Osnovnye problemy teorii progressa'.
[14]*Nauka i Religiya*, 8/71, p. 72.
[15]p. 82.
[16]pp. 79-80.
[17]*Problemy idealizma*, p. 23.
[18]*Nauka i Religiya*, 8/71, p. 76.
[19]B. Pascal, *Pensées*, Harmondsworth: Penguin Books, 1966, nos 199-200, pp. 90, 95 (translation modified).

[20] *Nauka i Religiya,* 8/71, p. 76.
[21] p. 80; italics and capitals as in the original.
[22] p.81.
[23] *Nauka i Religiya,* 10/71, p. 83.
[24] *Perevërtyshi,* p. 554.
[25] p. 555.
[26] p. 587.
[27] p. 564.
[28] p. 573.
[29] p. 604.
[30] p. 606.
[31] 'Lyubit' inykh tyazhëlyi krest', in B. Pasternak, *Stikhi i poemy, 1912–32,* Ann Arbor: University of Michigan Press, 1961, p. 337.
[32] *Perevërtyshi,* p. 568.
[33] His later novel, *The Eclipse (Zatmenie),* does not continue this evolution. It is a deeply gloomy work and seems to suggest a final loss of hope in the old heritage, without turning towards anything new.

Chapter 5: Alexander Solzhenitsyn

[1] L. Rzhevskii, *Tvorets i podvig,* Frankfurt am Main: Possev, 1972, pp. 141–62.
[2] G. Nivat and M. Aucouturier (eds), *Soljenitsyne,* Paris: L'Herne, 1971, p. 118.
[3] A. Solzhenitsyn, *The first circle,* trans. M. Guybon, London: Collins & Harvill Press, 1968, p. 296.
[4] p. 14.
[5] p. 40.
[6] p.39.
[7] p. 38.
[8] p. 37.
[9] p. 421.
[10] p. 187.
[11] p. 418.
[12] pp. 95–6, 511.
[13] p. 7.
[14] p. 124.
[15] p. 126.
[16] p. 132.
[17] p. 109.
[18] This important little section is omitted from the English translation of M. Guybon (which does not state that it is abridged). It is in the Possev, 1969 edition of Solzhenitsyn's complete works, Vol. 3, p. 139.
[19] Trans. Guybon, p. 120.
[20] pp. 172, 223.
[21] pp. 102, 238.
[22] p. 363.

23In an extra chapter written some years later Solzhenitsyn even has Nerzhin try to take up the idea that language is the most powerful instrument for *overthrowing* tyranny: 'Slovo razrushit beton', *Vestnik Russkogo Khristianskogo Dvizheniya*, no. 114 (1974), pp. 193–203.

24 *The first circle,* trans. Guybon, p. 247.

25pp. 497–8.

26'Tverskoi dyadyushka', *Vestnik Russkogo Khristianskogo Dvizheniya,* nos 112–13 (1974), pp. 160–73.

27 *The first circle,* trans. Guybon, p. 346.

28p. 87.

29p. 505.

30See Herbert Eagle, 'Existentialism and ideology in *The first circle',* *Modern Fiction Studies,* Vol. 23, no. 1 (spring 1977), pp. 47–62.

31 *The first circle,* trans. Guybon, p. 555.

32p. 323.

33p. 519.

34pp. 388–9.

35p. 402.

36p. 40.

37See V. Krasnov, 'Mnogogolosost' geroev v romane Solzhenitsyna *V kruge pervom', Grani,* no. 103 (1977), pp. 155–75.

38A. Shmeman, 'Reflections on *The Gulag archipelago',* in J. Dunlop et al. (eds), *Aleksandr Solzhenitsyn: critical essays and documentary materials,* New York: Collier Books, 2nd ed., 1975, pp. 520–1.

39 *The Gulag archipelago,* trans. T. P. Whitney, London: Collins & Harvill, Vol. 1, 1974, pp. 173–4

40A. Solzhenitsyn, *Letter to the Soviet leaders,* trans. Hilary Sternberg, London: Collins & Harvill, 1974, p. 43.

41 *The Gulag archipelago,* Vol. 1, p. 147.

42p. 161.

43p. 162. For a good treatment of ideology in *The Gulag archipelago,* see John B. Dunlop, *'The Gulag archipelago:* ideology or "point of view"', *Transactions of the Association of Russian–American Scholars,* no. 8, pp. 20–26.

44 *The Gulag archipelago,* Vol. 1, pp. 163–4.

45 *The Gulag archipelago,* trans. T. P. Whitney, London: Collins & Harvill, Vol. 2, 1975, p. 612.

46p. 615–16.

47p. 626.

48Vol. 1, p. 131.

49G. Nivat, *Sur Soljenitsyne,* Lausanne: Editions L'Age d'Homme, 1974, p. 167.

Chapter 6: Vladimir Maximov

1 *Tarusskie stranitsy,* Kaluga: Knizhnoe Izdatel'stvo, 1961, pp. 223–34.

2 *Oktyabr',* 10/62, pp. 89–119.

[3] V. Maksimov, *Sem' dnei tvoreniya,* Frankfurt am Main: Possev, 1971, pp. 15–16 (*The seven days of creation,* Harmondsworth: Penguin Books, 1977, p. 16. I quote my own translation, prepared before publication of the Penguin translation, by permission of the British and American publishers).

[4] p. 31 (31).

[5] pp. 441, 443 (408–9).

[6] pp. 35–40 (35–40).

[7] pp. 12–13 (13–14).

[8] p. 432 (399).

[9] p. 490 (453).

[10] pp. 119–25 (112–18).

[11] p. 137 (129).

[12] pp. 164–6 (153–6).

[13] p. 506 (468).

[14] p. 496 (459).

[15] V. Maksimov, *Karantin,* Frankfurt am Main: Possev, 1973, p. 12.

[16] p. 13.

[17] p. 229.

[18] p. 84.

[19] p. 86.

[20] p. 90.

[21] p. 91.

[22] p. 92.

[23] p. 350.

[24] p. 280.

[25] p. 354.

[26] Katerina Clark, '"Boy gets tractor" and all that: the parable structures of the Soviet novel', in R. Milner-Gulland et al., (eds), *Russian and Slavic literature,* Cambridge, Mass.: Slavica Publishers, 1976, p. 373.

[27] V. Maksimov, *Sobranie sochinenii,* Frankfurt am Main: Possev, 1974, Vol. 1, pp. 329–32.

Chapter 7: Vladimir Voinovich, Georgy Vladimov

[1] *Novyi Mir,* 2/63, p. 150.

[2] p. 197.

[3] Nadezhda Mandelstam, *Hope abandoned,* trans. Max Hayward, Harmondsworth: Penguin Books, 1976, pp. 24–5.

[4] *Novyi Mir,* 2/63, p. 162.

[5] pp. 170–1.

[6] p. 185.

[7] pp. 166, 172–4.

[8] p. 174.

[9] p. 186.

[10] *Novyi Mir,* 1/67, p. 89.

[11] p. 88.

[12] p. 88.

[13] p. 130.

[14]pp. 139-41.

[15]p. 152.

[16]p. 117.

[17]p. 87.

[18]p. 152.

[19]*The life and extraordinary adventures of Private Ivan Chonkin,* trans. R. Lourie, London: Jonathan Cape, 1977, pp. 20-1. (I quote this translation with my own modifications, by permission of the British and American publishers.) This passage is reminiscent of the prologue to Lermontov's *A hero of our times,* where the author parodies the official 'positive hero' of Nicholas I's Russia (I am grateful to Martin Dewhirst for pointing out this parallel to me).

[20]p. 3.

[21]pp. 217-18.

[22]p. 218.

[23]p. 3.

[24]p. 40.

[25]pp. 41-2.

[26]pp. 136, 138.

[27]pp. 145-6.

[28]pp. 80-1.

[29]p. 235.

[30]p. 271.

[31]pp. 64-5.

[32]Part 1, chapter 15.

[33]p. 106.

[34]p. 316.

[35]*Novyi Mir,* 7/61, p. 140.

[36]p. 155.

[37]p. 157.

[38]A. Terts, 'Lyudi i zveri', *Kontinent,* no. 5 (1975).

[39]*Grani,* no. 96 (1975), p. 21.

[40]p. 108.

[41]p. 121.

[42]p. 18.

[43]p. 33.

[44]p. 25.

[45]p. 66.

[46]p. 67.

[47]p. 101.

[48]p. 114.

[49]pp. 151-2.

Chapter 8: Vasily Shukshin

[1]V. Shukshin, 'Monolog na lestnitse', in V. Tolstykh (ed.), *Kul'tura chuvstv,* Moscow: Iskusstvo, 1968, p. 119.

[2]'Vasilii Shukshin: poslednie razgovory', *Literaturnaya Gazeta,* 13 November 1974, p. 8.

[3]*Zvezda,* 6/75, pp. 3–4.

[4]'Drugi igrishch i zabav', *Nash Sovremennik,* 9/74, pp. 2–11.

[5]'Obida', *Literaturnaya Rossiya,* 12 February 1971, pp. 18–19.

[6]'Svatovstvo', *Novyi Mir,* 7/70, pp. 42–8.

[7]'Van'ka Teplyashin', *Zvezda,* 2/73, pp. 3–7.

[8]'Vladimir Semënych iz myagkoi sektsii', *Literaturnaya Rossiya,* 30 March 1973, pp. 18–20.

[9]*Novyi Mir,* 9/67, pp. 88–94. (Donald M. Fiene (ed.), *Snowball Berry Red and other stories,* Ann Arbor: Ardis, 1979, pp. 21–30.)

[10]*Nash Sovremennik,* 4/73, pp. 105–6, 124.

[11]p. 88.

[12]pp. 104–5.

[13]pp. 126–7, 131–2.

[14]p. 133.

[15]p. 121.

[16]'Lyubaviny', *Sibirskie Ogni,* 6/65, pp. 3–39; 7/65, pp. 24–71; 8/65, pp. 28–102; 'Ya prishël dat' vam volyu', *Sibirskie Ogni,* 1/71, pp. 3–95; 2/71, pp. 3–122.

[17]*Sibirskie Ogni,* 8/65, pp. 70–1.

[18]p. 102.

[19]*Novyi Mir,* 11/64, pp. 64–72.

[20]V. Shukshin, *Tam, vdali,* Moscow: Sovetskii Pisatel', 1968, pp. 15–16.

[21]See Ronald Hingley's illuminating article on the subject of *vran'ë:* 'That's no lie, comrade', *Problems of Communism,* 2/62, pp. 47–55. Abram Terts, *Mysli vrasplokh,* New York: Rausen Publishers, 1966, p. 79.

[22]*Sibirskie Ogni,* 12/71, p. 12. (Fiene (ed.), p. 107. I quote my own version by permission of the publishers.)

[23]*Novyi Mir,* 9/67, pp. 94–7.

[24]pp. 97–100. (Fiene (ed.), pp. 131–5. I quote my own version by permission of the publishers.)

[25]*Nash Sovremennik,* 9/71, pp. 57–60.

[26]*Sibirskie Ogni,* 12/66, pp. 3–7.

[27]*Avrora,* 7/73, pp. 38–41.

[28]*Zvezda,* 9/71, pp. 24–30. (Fiene (ed.), pp. 87–96.)

[29]V. Shukshin, *Besedy pri yasnoi lune,* Moscow: Sovetskaya Rossiya, 1974, pp. 135–41. (Fiene (ed.), pp. 79–86.)

[30]*Zvezda,* 7/74, pp. 108–35. According to V. Korobov *(Vasilii Shukshin: tvorchestvo, lichnost',* Moscow: Sovetskaya Rossiya, 1977, p. 135), a first draft of this story was written as early as 1966 or 1967, and read to audiences then.

[31]*Nash Sovremennik,* 1/75, pp. 28–61.

[32]M. Geller, 'Vasilii Shukshin; v poiskakh voli', *Vestnik Russkogo Khristianskogo Dvizheniya,* no. 120 (1977), p. 166.

[33]*Literaturnaya Rossiya,* 19 January 1973, pp. 18–19.

[34]S. Le Fleming, 'Vasily Shukshin: a contemporary Scythian', in R. Milner-Gulland et al (eds), *Russian and Slavic literatures,* Cambridge,

Mass.: Slavica Publishers, 1976, pp. 449–66.

Chapter 9: Yury Trifonov

[1]Yu. Trifonov, *Studenty*, Moscow: Molodaya Gvardiya, 1951. A perceptive and amusing account of the novel can be found in Vera Dunham, *In Stalin's time: middleclass values in Soviet fiction,* 1976, *passim.*

[2]'Dom na naberezhnoi', *Druzhba Narodov,* 1/76, pp. 83–168.

[3]'Obsuzhdaem novye povesti Yu. Trifonova', *Voprosy Literatury,* 2/72, p. 65.

[4]*Novyi Mir,* 12/70, pp. 101–40.

[5]*Novyi Mir,* 8/71, pp. 53–107.

[6]*Novyi Mir,* 8/75, pp. 7–98.

[7]*Novyi Mir,* 8/71, p. 61.

[8]*Druzhba Narodov,* 1/76, p. 45.

[9]p. 103.

[10]pp. 154–5.

[11]p. 160.

[12]p. 164

[13]*Novyi Mir,* 12/70, p. 115.

[14]p. 105.

[15]p. 131.

[16]p. 124.

[17]p. 132.

[18]p. 104.

[19]p. 135.

[20]*Novyi Mir,* 8/71, p. 53.

[21]*Novyi Mir,* 12/69, p. 53.

[22]p. 56.

[23]p. 54.

[24]*Novyi Mir,* 8/75, p. 59.

[25]p. 95.

[26]p. 59.

[27]p. 97.

[28]p. 98.

[29]*Novyi Mir,* 8/71, p. 98.

[30]*Novyi Mir,* 12/70, p. 110.

[31]See Trifonov's own remarks on his literary method in *Voprosy Literatury,* 8/74, pp. 171–94, especially pp. 174–5.

Chapter 10: General Conclusions

[1]A. Solzhenitsyn, *The Gulag archipelago,* London: Collins & Harvill, 1975, Vol. 2, p. 609.

[2]R. Mathewson, *The positive hero in Russian literature,* 2nd ed., Stanford: Stanford University Press, 1975, p. 354.

3"Ideokraticheskoe soznanie i lichnost", *Samosoznanie: sbornik statei* (ed. P. Litvinov, M. Meerson-Aksenov, B. Shragin), New York: Khronika Press, 1976, pp. 117–52. D. Nelidov is a pseudonym.

4This may be said to be the underlying theme of Alexander Zinov'ev's novel (or philosophical treatise, or socio-political monograph, or however one should describe the genre), *Ziyayushchie vysoty*, Lausanne: L'Age d'Homme, 1976.

5*One word of truth* (the Nobel speech), London: Bodley Head, 1972, p. 15.

6A.Terts, *On Socialist Realism,* New York: Pantheon Books, 1960, p. 94.

7*Solzhenitsyn: a documentary record* (ed. Leopold Labedz), London: Allen Lane, 1970, p. 46.

8*Index on Censorship*, Vol. 7, no. 2 (March/April 1978), pp. 19–21.

9Voinovich's own account of the incident is in *Kontinent*, Vol. 5 (1975), pp. 51–98.

10See, for example, Yu. Mal'tsev, *Vol'naya russkaya literatura, 1955–75*, Frankfurt-am-Main: Possev Verlag, 1976, which is extremely useful for the information it gives on *samizdat* literature, but draws a rigid dividing line between that and published Soviet output, dismissing the latter as worthless. Likewise Rufus Mathewson, in the second edition of his *The positive hero in Russian Literature*, asserts that 'the opposition between directed and undirected writing is total' (p. 257).

11A. Solzhenitsyn, *Mir i nasilie,* Frankfurt am Main; Possev Verlag, 1974, p. 15.

12The literary establishment may have found a new way of dealing with embarrassingly controversial works: publishing them, and then surrounding them with critical silence. When the first part of Belov's novel *Kanuny* (see chapter 3 above) appeared in a journal, it was given a moderately favourable review by L. Emel'yanov in *Zvezda* (1972, no. 11); but Emel'yanov was then reprimanded, and no further reviews or critical articles on the novel appeared, even when it came out in full as a book in 1976. The same fate seems to have befallen Boris Mozhaev's *Muzhiki i baby* (Moscow: Sovremennik, 1976), which also deals sympathetically with the Russian village community of the late 1920s, and thus implicitly criticizes the way in which the subsequent forced collectivization of agriculture was carried out.

Bibliography

The lists of books and articles which follow are far from exhaustive. They are intended to help the interested reader to explore further the general themes and the individual authors discussed in this book.

Writings published or located while this book was in the press are listed in an Addendum beginning on p. 254.

The following abbreviations have been used:

LG – *Literaturnaya Gazeta*
LO – *Literaturnoe Obozrenie*
LR – *Literaturnaya Rossiya*
NM – *Novyi Mir*
NS – *Nash Sovremennik*
VL – *Voprosy Literatury*

General Bibliography

L. Anninskii, *Yadro orekha*, Moscow: Sovetskii Pisatel', 1965.

E. Auerbach, *Mimesis*, New York: Anchor Books, 1957; Oxford: Princeton University Press (paperback), 1969.

M. Bakhtin, *Voprosy literatury i estetiki*, Moscow: Khudozhest-vennaya Literatura, 1975.

K. Bjørnager and H. Dalgaard, *Portraet af et tiår: Sovjetprosa, 1965–1975*, Copenhagen: Berlingske Forlag, 1976.

Deming Brown, *Soviet Russian literature since Stalin*, Cambridge and New York: Cambridge University Press, 1978.

Edward J. Brown, *Russian literature since the revolution*, New York and London: Collier Books, 1969.

G. Clive, *The broken icon: intuitive existentialism in classical Russian fiction*, London: Collier-Macmillan, 1972; New York: Macmillan, 1972.

Terrence Des Pres, *The survivor: an anatomy of life in the death camps*, New York and London: Oxford University Press, 1976.

M. Dewhirst and R. Farrell (eds), *The Soviet censorship*, Metuchen, New Jersey: The Scarecrow Press, 1973.

Vera Dunham, *In Stalin's time: middleclass values in Soviet fiction*, Cambridge: University Press, 1976; New York (entitled *Stalinist fiction and Soviet society*): Cambridge University Press, 1976.

A. M. van der Eng-Liedermeier, *Soviet literary characters: an investigation into the portrayal of Soviet men in Russian prose, 1917–53*, The Hague: Mouton, 1959.

H. Ermolaev, *Soviet literary theories, 1917–34: the genesis of Socialist Realism*, Berkeley: University of California Press, 1963.

L. F. Ershov, *Satira i sovremennost'*, Moscow: Sovremennik, 1978.

——, *Satiricheskie zhanry russkoi sovetskoi literatury*, Leningrad: Nauka, 1977.

E. Etkind, *Zapiski nezagovorshchika*, London: Overseas Publications Interchange, 1977; New York (trans. entitled *Notes of a non-conspirator*): Oxford University Press, 1978.

M. Friedberg, *A decade of euphoria: western literature in post-Stalin Russia, 1954–64*, Bloomington: Indiana University Press, 1977.

X. Gasiorowska, *Women in Soviet fiction, 1917–64*, Madison: University of Wisconsin Press, 1968.

G. Gibian, *Interval of freedom: Soviet literature during the thaw, 1954–57*, Minneapolis: University of Minnesota Press, 1960.

Max Hayward and Leopold Labedz (eds), *Literature and revolution in Soviet Russia, 1917–62*, London: Oxford University Press, 1963; Westport, Ct.: Greenwood Press, repr. 1976.

Max Hayward and Edward L. Crowley (eds), *Soviet literature in the sixties*, New York: Frederick A. Praeger, 1964; London: Methuen, 1965.

M. Heller, *Le monde concentrationnaire et la littérature soviétique*, Lausanne: Editions L'Age d'Homme, 1974.

Ideinoe edinstvo i khudozhestvennoe mnogoobrazie sovestkoi-prozy, Moscow: Mysl', 1974.

Istoriya russkoi sovetskoi literatury, 2nd ed., Moscow: Vysshaya shkola, 1974.

Iz-pod glyb (sbornik statei), ed. A. Solzhenitsyn and I. Shafarevich,

Paris: YMCA Press, 1974 (available in English as *From under the rubble,* London: Collins & Harvill; New York: Little, Brown, 1975.

Priscilla Johnson (ed.), *Khrushchev and the arts: the politics of Soviet culture, 1962–64,* Cambridge, Mass. and London: MIT Press, 1965.

W. Kasack, *Lexikon der russischen Literatur ab 1917,* Stuttgart: Kröner Verlag, 1976.

Kontseptsiya cheloveka v estetike sotsialisticheskogo realizma, Moscow: Mysl', 1977.

V. A. Kovalev (ed.), *Russkii sovetskii rasskaz: ocherki istorii zhanra,* Leningrad: Nauka, 1970.

Kratkaya literaturnaya entsiklopediya, Moscow: Sovetskaya Entsiklopediya, 1962–75 (8 vols).

F. Kuznetsov, *Pereklichka epokh* (ocherki, stat'i, portrety), Moscow: Sovremennik, 1976.

——, *Za vsë v otvete: nravstvennye iskaniya v sovetskoi proze,* Moscow: Sovetskii Pisatel', 1975.

A. Lanshchikov, *Mnogoobrazie iskusstva,* Moscow: Moskovskii Rabochii, 1974.

P. Litvinov, M. Meerson-Aksenov, B. Shragin (eds), *Samosoznanie* (sbornik statei), New York: Khronika Press, 1976.

R. Lourie, *Letters to the future: an approach to Sinyavsky-Terts,* Ithaca and London: Cornell University Press, 1975.

Yu. Mal'tsev, *Vol'naya russkaya literatura, 1955–75,* Frankfurt am Main: Possev, 1976; New York: Atheneum, 1976 (paperback).

Nadezhda Mandelshtam, *Hope against hope,* New York: Atheneum, 1970; Harmondsworth: Penguin Books, 1975.

——, *Hope abandoned,* New York: Atheneum, 1973; Harmondsworth: Penguin Books, 1976.

Rufus Mathewson, *The positive hero in Russian literature,* 2nd ed. Stanford: Stanford University Press, 1975.

Zhores Medvedev, *Ten years after Ivan Denisovich,* London: Macmillan, 1973; New York: Alfred A. Knopf, 1973.

Mihajlo Mihajlov, *Russian themes,* London: Macdonald, 1968.

R. Milner-Gulland and M. Dewhirst (eds), *Russian writing today,* Harmondsworth: Penguin Books, 1977.

R. Milner-Gulland and others (eds), *Russian and Slavic literature,* Cambridge, Mass.: Slavica Publishers, 1976.

Czeslaw Milosz, *The captive mind,* New York: Vintage Books, 1953.

Helen Muchnic, *From Gorky to Pasternak: six modern Russian writers*, New York, Random House, 1963; London: Methuen, 1963.

A. Ninov, *Sovremennyi rasskaz: iz nablyudenii nad russkoi prozoi (1956–66)*, Leningrad: Khudozhestvennaya Literatura, 1969.

A. V. Ognev, *Russkii sovetskii rasskaz 50–70kh godov*, Moscow: Prosveshchenie, 1978.

A. Ovcharenko, *Novye geroi – novye puti: ot M. Gor'kogo do V. Shukshina*, Moscow: Sovremennik, 1977.

V. K. Pankov, *Vremya i kniga: problemy i geroi sovetskoi literatury, 1945–73gg.*, 2nd ed., Moscow: Prosveshchenie, 1974.

V. Perel'man, *Pokinutaya Rossiya*, 2 vols, Tel Aviv: Vremya i My, 1976.

Politicheskii dnevnik, 1964–70, 2 vols, Amsterdam: Herzen Foundation, 1972–75.

G. Pomerants, *Neopublikovannoe*, Frankfurt am Main: Possev, 1972.

R. Redlikh, *Stalinshchina, kak dukhovnyi fenomen*, 2nd ed., Frankfurt am Main: Possev, 1971.

T. F. Rogers, *'Superfluous men' and the post-Stalin 'thaw'*, The Hague: Mouton, 1972.

Russkaya sovetskaya literatura, Moscow: Uchpedgiz, 1963.

Russkie sovetskie pisateli, prozaiki: bibliograficheskii ukazatel', 7 vols, Moscow-Leningrad: various publishers, 1959–72.

M. Scammell (ed.), *Russia's other writers*, London: Longman, 1970.

H. G. Scott (ed.), *Problems of Soviet literature*, London: Martin Lawrence, no date.

B. Shragin, *Protivostoyanie dukha*, London: Overseas Publications Interchange, 1977.

E. A. Shubin, *Sovremennyi russkii rasskaz: voprosy poetiki zhanra*, Leningrad: Nauka, 1974.

E. Sidorov, *Vremya, pisatel', stil'*, Moscow: Sovetskii Pisatel', 1978.

M. Slonim, *Soviet Russian literature: writers and problems, 1917–77*, 2nd ed., New York and London: Oxford University Press, 1977.

Helen von Ssachno, *Der Aufstand der Person*, Berlin: Argon Verlag, 1965.

A. Steininger, *Literatur und Politik in der Sowjetunion nach Stalins Tod*, Wiesbaden: Otto Harrassowitz, 1965.

Gleb Struve, *Russian literature under Lenin and Stalin, 1917–53*, Norman: University of Oklahoma Press, 1971.

V. Surganov, *Chelovek na zemle*, Moscow: Sovetskii Pisatel', 1975.

H. Swayze, *Political control of literature in the USSR, 1946–59*,

Cambridge, Mass. and Oxford: Harvard University Press, 1962.

L. Terakopyan, *Pafos preobrazovaniya: zametki o sovremennoi derevenskoi proze*, Moscow: Khudozhestvennaya Literatura, 1974.

Abram Terts, *On Socialist Realism*, New York: Pantheon Books, 1960.

R. Tökés (ed.), *Dissent in the USSR: politics, ideology and people*, Baltimore and London: Johns Hopkins University Press, 1975.

R. Tucker (ed.), *Stalinism: essays in historical interpretation*, New York: Norton, 1977.

V nachale semidesyatykh: literatura nashikh dnei, Leningrad: Lenizdat, 1973.

V seredine semidesyatykh: literatura nashikh dnei, Leningrad: Lenizdat, 1977.

C. Vaughan James, *Soviet Socialist Realism: origins and theory*, London: Macmillan, 1973; New York: St Martin's Press, 1974.

Voprosy yazyka sovremennoi russkoi literatury, Moscow: Nauka, 1971.

G. Walker, *Soviet book publishing policy*, Cambridge and New York: Cambridge University Press, 1978.

Ian Watt, *The rise of the novel*, London: Chatto & Windus, 1957.

A. Yanov, *The Russian new right: right wing ideologies in the contemporary USSR*, Berkeley: Institute of International Studies, 1978.

Yazykovye protsessy sovremennoi russkoi khudozhestvennoi literatury: proza, Moscow: Nauka, 1977.

General Articles

F. Abramov, 'Lyudi kolkhoznoi derevni v poslevoennoi proze', *NM*, 4/54.

B. Anashenkov, 'Istselisya sam . . .', *VL*, 1/76.

L. Anninskii, 'Tochka opory: eticheskie problemy sovremennoi prozy', *Don*, 6–7/68.

L. Anninskii and V. Kozhinov, 'Moda na prostonarodnost' (kriticheskii dialog)', *Kodry*, 3/71.

L. Anninskii and L. Kryachko, 'Sut' poiska (dialog o proze molodykh)', *Oktyabr'*, 8/62.

V. A. Apukhtina, 'Khudozhestvennye iskaniya sovetskoi prozy 60-kh

222   BEYOND SOCIALIST REALISM

i 70-kh godov', *Vestnik Moskovskogo Universiteta* (filologiya), 5/77.

——, 'Zakonomernosti razvitiya sovremennoi sovetskoi prozy', *Nauchnye doklady vysshei shkoly* (filologicheskie nauki), 5/77.

M. Bakhtin, 'Epos i roman', in his *Voprosy literatury i estetiki*, Moscow: Khudozhestvennaya Literatura, 1975.

R. Beerman, 'Auf der Suche nach einem Sinn des Lebens: Notizen über die sowjetrussische Gegenswartsliteratur', *Osteuropa,* 9/77.

A. Bocharov, 'Kogda by zhizn' domashnim krugom (semeinyi syuzhet v sovremennoi sovetskoi proze)', *Druzhba narodov*, 7/75.

——, 'Vremya kristallizatsii', *VL*, 3/76.

A. Borshchagovskii, 'Poiski molodoi prozy', *Moskva*, 12/62.

Deming Brown, 'The art of Andrei Sinyavsky', *Slavic Review*, Vol. 29, no. 4 (December 1970).

——, 'Narrative devices in the contemporary Russian short story: intimacy and irony', *American Contributions to the Seventh International Congress of Slavists*, Vol. 2 (Literature and folklore), The Hague and Paris: Mouton, 1973.

——, 'Nationalism and ruralism in recent Soviet Russian literature', *Review of National Literatures*, Vol. 3, no. 1 (spring 1972).

——, 'The Očerk: suggestions towards a redefinition', *American Contributions to the Sixth International Congress of Slavists*, Vol. 2 (literary contributions). The Hague and Paris: Mouton, 1968.

Margaret M. Bullitt, 'Towards a Marxist theory of aesthetics: the development of Socialist Realism in the Soviet Union', *Russian Review*, Vol. 35, no. 1 (January 1976).

V. Chalmaev, 'Neizbezhnost'', *Molodaya Gvardiya,* 9/68.

'Cherty literatury poslednikh let', *VL*, 10/75.

M. Chudakova and A. Chudakov, 'Sovremennaya povest' i yumor', *NM*, 7/67.

Katerina Clark, '"Boy gets tractor" and all that: the parable structures of the Soviet novel', in R. Milner-Gulland et al. (eds.), *Russian and Slavic Literature*, Cambridge, Mass.: Slavica Publishers, 1976.

——, 'Little deeds and big deeds: literature responds to the First Five-Year Plan', in Sheila Fitzpatrick (ed.), *Cultural Revolution in Russia, 1928–31*, Bloomington: Indiana University Press, 1978.

——, 'Utopian anthropology as a context for Stalinist literature', in R. C. Tucker (ed.), *Stalinism: essays in historical interpretation*, New York: W. W. Norton, 1977.

I. Dedkov, 'Stranitsy derevenskoi zhizni (polemicheskie zametki), *NM*, 4/69.

——, 'Vozvrashchenie k sebe', *NS*, 7/75.

——, 'Chego trebuet vremya', *VL*, 8/75.

A. Dement'ev, 'O traditsiyakh i narodnosti', *NM*, 4/69.

M. Dewhirst, 'Soviet Russian literature and literary policy', in A Brown and M. Kaser (eds), *The Soviet Union since the fall of Khrushchev*, London: Macmillan, 1975; New York: Free Press, 1976.

N. V. Dragomiretskaya, 'O stilevykh traditsiyakh v sovremennoi sovetskoi prozc', *Izvestiya Akademii Nauk SSSR* (seriya literatury i yazyka), 6/77.

Victor Erlich, 'Post-Stalin trends in Russian literature', *Slavic Review*, Vol. 23, no. 3 (September 1964).

L. F. Ershov, 'Satiriko-yumoristicheskaya povest'', in *Sovremennaya russkaya sovetskaya povest'*, Leningrad: Nauka, 1975.

——, 'Sotsial'noe i nravstvennoe: po stranitsam prozy 70-kh godov', *Zvezda*, 10/76.

Edith R. Frankel, 'Literary policy in Stalin's last year', *Soviet Studies*, Vol. 28, no. 3. (July 1976).

——, 'Literature and politics under Khrushchev: the return of Tvardovsky to *Novyi Mir*, July 1958', *Russian Review*, Vol. 35, no. 2 (July 1976).

X. Gasiorowska, 'Happiness in recent Soviet fiction', *Russian Literature Triquarterly*, Vol. 9 (spring 1974).

——, 'Two decades of love and marriage in Soviet fiction', *Russian Review*, Vol. 34, no. 1 (January 1975).

——, 'Ungeschminkte Wirklichkeit: zum Verhältnis zwischen Mann und Frau im jüngeren sowjctischen Roman, *Osteuropa*, 1/78.

George Genereux, Jr, 'The Stalin prize novel and Soviet fiction', *Russian Literature Triquarterly*, Vols 5–6 (1973).

George Gibian, 'The urban theme in recent Soviet prose: notes towards a typology'; *Slavic Review*, Vol. 37, no. 1 (March 1978).

Max Hayward, 'The decline of Socialist Realism', *Survey*, Vol. 18, no. 1 (winter 1972).

——, 'Soviet literature, 1917–1962', in Max Hayward and Patricia Blake (eds), *Dissonant voices in Soviet literature*, New York: Pantheon Books, 1962. London: Allen & Unwin, 1965.

——, 'Themes and variations in Soviet literature', in M. M. Drachkovitch (ed.), *Fifty years of Communism in Russia*,

University Park, Pa.: Pennsylvania State University Press, 1968 and 1969.

G. Hildebrandt, 'Ein Beitrag zur sowjetischen Dorfprosa der Gegenwart', *Die Welt der Slawen*, Vol. 18 (1973).

J. Holthusen, 'Erzählung und auktorialer Kommentar im modernen russischen Roman', *Die Welt der Slawen*, Vol. 8 (1959).

——, 'Stilistik des "uneigentlichen" Erzählens in der sowjetischen Gegenwartsliteratur', *Die Welt der Slawen*, 3/68.

George Kline, 'Religious themes in Soviet literature', in R. H. Marshall, Jr (ed.), *Aspects of Religion in the Soviet Union*, Chicago and London: University of Chicago Press, 1971.

N. A. Kozhevnikova, 'O tipakh povestvovaniya v sovetskoi proze', in *Voprosy yazyka sovremennoi russkoi literatury*, Moscow: Nauka, 1971.

F. Kuznetsov, 'Byt' chelovekom: o nekotorykh nravstvennykh problemakh sovremennoi prozy', *Oktyabr'*, 2–3/75.

——, 'Sud'by derevni v proze i kritike', *NM*, 6/73.

——, 'Tsel' i smysl – chelovek (obraz sovremennika v sovremennoi literature)', *Moskva*, 9/77.

M. Kuznetsov, 'Sotsialisticheskii realizm i modernizm', *NM*, 8/63.

V. Lakshin, 'Pisatel', chitatel', kritik', *NM*, 4/65 and 8/66.

Philippa Lewis, 'Peasant nostalgia in contemporary Russian literature', *Soviet Studies*, Vol. 28, no. 4 (October 1976).

'Literatura i yazyk', *VL*, 6/67.

Yu. Mal'tsev, 'Russkaya literatura v poiskakh form', *Grani*, no. 98 (1975).

N. Mashovets, 'Obshchnost' tseli', *VL*, 5/76.

Klaus Mehnert, 'Humanismus in der jüngsten Sowjetliteratur?', *Abhandlungen der Akademie der Wissenschaften und der Literatur*, 1963, no. 1.

I. Motyashov, 'Otvetstvennost' khudozhnika' *VL*, 12/68.

Nadine Natov, 'Daily life and individual psychology in Soviet Russian prose of the 1970s', *Russian Review*, Vol. 33, no. 4 (October 1974).

V. V. Odintsov, 'Nablyudeniya nad dialogom v "molodezhnoi proze"', in *Voprosy yazyka sovremennoi russkoi literatury*, Moscow: Nauka, 1971.

A. Ovcharenko, 'Osnovnye tipy sotsialisticheskogo realizma', *Moskva*, 9/73.

——, 'Sovetskaya khudozhestvennaya proza 70kh godov', *Moskva*, 1–2/75.

M. Parkhomenko, 'Masshtabom nashei zhizni', *VL,* 5/76.

V. N. Pavlov, 'Spory o slavyanofil'stve i russkom patriotizme v sovetskoi nauchnoi literature, 1967–70gg', *Grani,* no. 82 (1971).

Yves Perret-Gentil, 'Der Kolchosbauer in der heutigen russischen Dorfliteratur', *Osteuropa,* 9/78.

A. Piatigorsky, 'Remarks on the metaphysical situation', in V. E. Maximov (ed.), *Kontinent 1,* London: André Deutsch, 1976; New York: Doubleday (Anchor paperback, 1976).

V. Pomerantsev, 'Ob iskrennosti v literature', *NM,* 12/53.

D. Pospielovsky, 'From Gosizdat to Samizdat and Tamizdat', *Canadian Slavonic Papers,* Vol. 20, no. 1 (March 1978).

V. I. Protchenko, 'Chelovek i ego trud v sovremennoi povesti o derevne', in *Problemy psikhologizma v sovremennoi literature,* Leningrad: Nauka, 1970.

——, 'Nekotorye voprosy razvitiya "derevenskoi prozy"', in *Problemy russkoi sovetskoi literatury 50–70 kh godov,* Leningrad: Nauka, 1976

——, 'Sovremennaya "derevenskaya proza" v literaturnoi kritike (real'nye dostizheniya i spornye otsenki)', *Russkaya Literatura,* 2/77.

——, 'Sovremennaya povest' o derevne', *Russkaya Literatura,* 4/70.

Ilma Rakusa, 'Die Emanzipation der Frau als Individualisierung-sprozess: zu einigen neueren Tendenzen der Sowjetliteratur,' *Studies in Soviet Thought,* Vol. 18, no. 2 (May 1978).

E. Reissner, 'Contemporary Russian Satire', *Survey,* Vol. 23, no. 3 (summer 1978).

V. Semënov, 'Rodniki b'yut iz glubin', *NS,* 2/69.

N. N. Shneidman, 'A new approach to old problems: the contemporary prose of Sergei Zalygin', *Russian Language Journal,* no. 106 (spring 1976).

——, 'The controversial prose of the 1970s: problems of marriage and love in contemporary Soviet literature', *Canadian Slavonic Papers,* Vol. 18, no. 4 (December 1976).

——, 'Soviet prose in the 1970s: evolution or stagnation?' *Canadian Slavonic Papers,* Vol. 20, no. 1 (March 1978).

E. Sidorov, 'Na puti k sintezu', *VL,* 6/75.

——, 'Prodolzhenie sleduet', *VL,* 6/76.

Gerry Smith, 'Underground songs', *Index on Censorship,* Vol. 7, no. 2 (March/April 1978).

Gene Sosin, 'Magnitizdat: uncensored songs of dissent', in R. L. Tökés (ed.), *Dissent in the USSR: ideology, politics and people,* Baltimore and Hemel Hempstead: Johns Hopkins University Press, 1975 and 1976.

'Soviet literature: a reappraisal', *Studies on the Soviet Union,* Vol. 8 (1969).

E. Starikova, 'Sotsiologicheskii aspekt sovremennoi "derevenskoi prozy"', *VL,* 7/72.

Jurij Striedter, 'Persönlichkeit und Kollektiv im Sowjetroman der Gegenwart', *Universitätstage,* 1961 ('Marxismus-Leninismus: Geschichte und Gestalt').

V. Surganov, 'Tugie uzly', *Znamya,* 2/71.

F. Svetov, 'O molodom geroe', *NM,* 5/67.

V. Tendryakov, 'V zashchitu polozhitel'nogo geroya', *NM,* 11/54.

Abram Terts, 'The literary process in Russia', *Kontinent 1,* London: André Deutsch, 1976; New York: Doubleday (Anchor paperback), 1976.

Albert Todd, 'The spiritual in recent Soviet literature', in Max Hayward and William Fletcher (eds), *Religion and the Soviet state,* New York: Frederick A. Praeger, 1969; London: Pall Mall, 1969.

A. Urban, 'Filosofichnost' khudozhestvennoi prozy', *Zvezda,* 9/78.

T. P. Whitney, 'Russian literature and Soviet politics', in his *The New Writing in Russia,* Ann Arbor: University of Michigan Press, 1964; London: Cresset Press, 1964.

A. Yanov, 'Dvizhenie molodogo geroya: sotsiologicheskie zametki o khudozhestvennoi proze 60kh godov', *NM,* 7/72.

Gleb Zekulin, 'Aspects of peasant life as portrayed in contemporary Soviet literature,' *Canadian Slavic Studies,* Vol. 1, no. 4 (winter 1967).

——, 'The contemporary countryside in Soviet literature: a search for new values', in J. R. Millar (ed.), *The Soviet Rural Community,* Urbana: Illinois University Press, 1971.

——, 'Efim Dorosh', in R. Milner-Gulland et al. (eds.), *Russian and Slavic Literature,* Cambridge, Mass.: Slavica Press, 1976.

I. Zolotusskii, 'Poznanie nastoyashchego', *VL,* 10/75.

Belov, Vasilii Ivanovich

Born 1932 in Vologda region. Worked on a kolkhoz in his youth, as agricultural labourer and carpenter. Published a few literary items in local newspapers, then 1959–64 studied at the Gor'kii Institute of World Literature. Returned to Vologda, where he has lived ever since. Member of the Party since 1956.

1. Books

Rechnye izluki, Moscow: Molodaya Gvardiya, 1964 ('Derevnya Berdyaika' and short stories).

Tisha da Grisha, Moscow: Sovetskaya Rossiya, 1966 ('Derevnya Berdyaika' and short stories).

Za tremya volokami, Moscow: Sovetskii Pisatel', 1968 ('Privychnoe delo' and short stories).

Plotnitskie rasskazy, Arkhangel'sk: Severo-Zapadnoe Knizhnoe Izdatel'stvo, 1968 ('Plotnitskie rasskazy' and short stories).

Sel'skie povesti, Moscow: Molodaya Gvardiya, 1971 ('Derevnya Berdyaika'; 'Privychnoe delo'; 'Plotnitskie rasskazy').

Den' za dnëm, Moscow: Sovetskii Pisatel', 1972 ('Bukhtiny vologodskie' and short stories).

Tseluyutsya zori, Moscow: Molodaya Gvardiya, 1975 ('Bukhtiny vologodskie'; 'Tseluyutsya zori' and short stories).

Kanuny, Moscow: Sovremennik, 1976 (parts 1 and 2 of the novel).

Gudyat provoda, Moscow: Sovetskaya Rossiya, 1978 (short stories).

2. Fictional work in journals

'Derevnya Berdyaika', *NS*, 3/61.

'Klavdiya'; 'Prezhnie gody'; 'Vechernie razgovory', *NS*, 1/62.

'Lyuba-Lyubushka', *Neva*, 1/63.

'Sel'skie rasskazy' ('Den' za dnëm'; 'Dozhinki'; 'Vovka-satyuk'), *NS*, 2/63.

'Koni', *NS*, 6/64.

'Za tremya volokami', *Sever*, 2/65.

'Tezki', *NS*, 4/65.

'Privychnoe delo', *Sever*, 1/66.

'Bobrishnyi ugor', *LR*, 19 May 1967.

'Mazurik', *NM*, 2/68.

'Sluchainye etyudy' ('Pis'mo'; 'Staryi da malyi'; 'Beskul'tur'e';

'Vesennyaya noch"; 'Kholmy'; 'Ne garyvali . . .'), *Sever*, 2/68.
'Plotnitskie rasskazy', *NM*, 7/68.
'Bukhtiny vologodskie', *NM,* 12/69.
'V trudnye gody', *Pod" ëm*, 2/71.
'Sluchainye etyudy' ('Prosvetlenie'; '"Dramma"'; 'Rybatskaya baika';
    'Kolybel'naya'), *NS*, 7/71.
'Kanuny' (Part 1 only), *Sever*, 4–5/72.
'Nad svetloi vodoi' (p'esa), *NS*, 1/73.
'Tseluyutsya zori', *Avrora*, 11/73.
'Malen'kie rasskazy' ('Moya zhizn"; 'Vospitanie po doktoru
    Spoku'), *Sever*, 7/74, 2–36.
'Utrom v subbotu (iz zapisnoi knizhki)', *Avrora*, 6/75.
'Koch', *Sever*, 1/76.
'Chok-Poluchok', *Druzhba Narodov*, 10/76.
'Svidanie po utram', *NS*, 1/77.

3. *Other writings*

'Literatura i yazyk', *VL*, 6/67 (answer to questionnaire).
'Derevnya i kino: zametki pisatelya', *Avrora*, 8/70.
'Zemlya. Lyudi. Literatura. (Kruglyi stol)', *Druzhba Narodov*, 9/70.
'Partiinost', vzyskatel 'nost', masterstvo', *Molodaya Gvardiya,* 6/71
    (contribution to discussion).

4. *Critical articles*

I. Borisova, 'Den' za dnëm', *NM,* 6/64.
V. Chalmaev, 'Glubinnoe techenie', *Izvestiya*, 20 February 1965.
E. Dorosh, 'Ivan Afrikanovich', *NM*, 8/66.
I. Borisova, 'Privychnoe delo – zhizn", *LG*, 3 December 1966.
L. Terakopyan, 'Prostye zaboty', *Druzhba Narodov*, 12/66.
O. Voitinskaya, 'Proza Vasiliya Belova', *Znamya*, 1/67.
B. Bursov, 'Puti k khudozhestvennoi pravde', *Zvezda*, 1/67.
F. Kuznetsov, 'K zrelosti', *Yunost'*, 5/67.
G. Brovman, 'Talant i napravlenie', *Don*, 7/67.
P. Glinkin, 'Zemlya i asfal't', *Molodaya Gvardiya*, 9/67.
V. Kamyanov, 'Ne dobrotoi edinoi . . .', *LG*, 22 November 1967.
L. Kryachko, 'Listy i korni', *LG*, 29 November 1967.

V. Kozhinov, 'Tsennosti istinnye i mnimye', *LG*, 31 January 1968.

V. Voronov, 'Eschë raz o tsennostyakh istinnykh i mnimykh', *LG*, 13 March 1968.

L. Anninskii, 'Tochka opory', *Don*, 6–7/68.

I. Dedkov, 'Stranitsy derevenskoi zhizni', *NM*, 3/69.

V. Kamyanov, 'Evklidu – Evklidovo', *VL*, 4/69.

V. Pertsovskii, 'Lyudi derevni', Zvezda, 9/69.

L. Anninskii, V. Kozhinov, 'Moda na prostonarodnost' (kriticheskii dialog), *Kodry*, 3/71.

E. Klepikova, 'Ot byta k eposu', *Avrora*, 9/71.

Yu. Seleznev, 'Sovremennost' traditsii', *NS*, 11/74.

T. V. Krivoshchanova, 'Rol' prozaicheskikh fol'klornykh zhanrov v tvorchestve Vasiliya Belova', *Vestnik Moskovskogo Universiteta* (filologiya), 4/76.

'S raznykh tochek zreniya (o rasskazakh V. Belova)', *LO*, 5/77 (a roundtable critical discussion: see a further contribution in *LO*, 10/77).

A. Pankov, 'Sovremennik na randevu', *NM*, 6/78.

Rasputin, Valentin Grigor'evich

Born 1937 in Irkutsk oblast'. Studied in the history-philology faculty of Irkutsk University, and began his career as a journalist in Siberia. His early stories and sketches were full of the romanticism of the *taiga;* but, especially from *Den'gi dlya Marii* onwards, focussed his attention more and more on individual psychology.

1. *Books*

Krai vozle samogo neba (ocherki i rasskazy), Irkutsk: Vostochno-Sibirskoe Knizhnoe Izdatel'stvo, 1966.

Chelovek s etogo sveta (rasskazy), Krasnoyarsk: Knizhnoe Izdatel'stvo, 1967.

Den'gi dlya Marii, Moscow: Molodaya Gvardiya, 1968 ('Den'gi dlya Marii' and short stories).

Poslednii srok, Novosibirsk: Zapadno-Sibirskoe Knizhnoe Izdatel'stvo, 1971 ('Poslednii srok' and short stories).

Vverkh i vniz po techeniya (ocherk odnoi poezdki), Moscow: Sovetskaya Rossiya, 1972.

Zhivi i pomni, Moscow: Sovremennik, 1975 ('Zhivi i pomni' and short stories).

Povesti, Moscow: Molodaya Gvardiya, 1976 ('Den'gi dlya Marii'; 'Poslednii srok'; 'Zhivi i pomni'; 'Proshchanie s Materoi').

2. *Fictional work in journals*

'Vasilii i Vasilisa', *LR,* 27 January 1967.

'Den'gi dlya Marii', *Angara,* 4/67 (there is another version in *Sibirskie Ogni,* 9/67).

(with V. Shugaev) 'Nechayannye khlopoty', *NS,* 5/69.

'Poslednii srok', *NS,* 7–8/70.

'Vniz po techeniyu', *NS* 6/72.

'Uroki frantsuzskogo', *LR,* 28 September 1973.

'Zhivi i pomni', *NS,* 10–11/74.

'Proshchanie s Materoi', *NS* 10–11/76.

(with V. Shugaev) 'Nechayannye khlopoty (istoriya, slyshannaya na Ust'-Ilime), *Angara,* Moscow: Sovremennik, 1977.

3. *Other writings*

'Byt' samim soboi' (beseda), *VL,* 9/76.

'Ne mog ne prostit'sya s Materoi' (beseda), *LG,* 16 March 1977.

'Vsë ostaëtsya lyudyam' (beseda), *Moskovskii Komsomolets,* 25 March 1977.

'Nagrada obyazyvaet', *LG,* 16 November 1977.

'Istiny Aleksandra Vampilova', *Sibir',* 4/77.

4. *Critical articles*

V. Trushkin, 'Poeziya prozy: o tvorchestve V. Rasputina', *Angara,* 1/68.

I. Vinogradov, 'Chuzhaya beda', *NM,* 7/68.

N. Tenditnik, 'Starukha Anna i eë deti', *Sibir',* 5/71.

V. Geideko, 'Preodolenie biografii', *Moskva,* 6/71.

N. Kotenko, 'Put' k cheloveku: zametki o proze V. Rasputina', *NS,* 1/72.

Yu. Seleznev, 'Ugol zreniya', *Molodaya Gvardiya,* 10/73.

F. Kuznetsov, 'Sud'ba Nastëny', *LO,* 3/75.

A. Bocharov, 'I net emu proshcheniya', *Oktyabr',* 6/75.

W. Kasack, 'Walentin Rasputin', *Osteuropa,* 7/75.

V. Vasil'ev, 'Radi istiny i dobra', *NS,* 6/76.

V. Shaposhnikov, 'Zhit' i pomnit'', *Komsomol'skaya Pravda,* 17 July 1976.

I. Bogatko, 'Pravo zhit' sredi lyudei', *LR,* 30 July 1976.

V. Kanashkin, 'Povest' otvorena zhizn'yu', *Don,* 10/76.

'Proza Valentina Rasputina', *VL,* 2/77 (a symposium with contributions by a number of critics).

E. I. Zakharova, 'Eto stanovitsya traditsiei (Valentin Rasputin v MGU), *Vestnik Moskovskogo Universiteta* (filologiya), 3/77

E. Umanskaya, 'Ne dozhidayas' poslednego sroka', *LO,* 4/77,

Yu. Petrovskii, 'Vrag yarkogo i smelogo (oblichenie meshchanstva v sovremennoi sovetskoi khudozhestvennoi literature)', *Zvezda,* 5/77.

L. Terakopyan, 'Blagodarnaya pamyat': povesti V. Rasputina', *Molodaya Gvardiya,* 6/77.

E. Starikova, 'Zhit' i pomnit': zametki o proze V. Rasputina', *NM,* 11/77.

V. Iverni, 'Smert'yu – o zhizni', *Kontinent,* no. 15 (1978).

B. Pankin, 'Proshchanie i vstrechi s Materoi', *Druzhba Narodov,* 2/78.

Tendryakov, Vladimir Fëdorovich

Born 1923 in Vologda region, in the family of a rural official. Fought at the front in the Second World War, and was wounded; then worked as a military instructor and Komsomol secretary in the schools of Kirov region. Came to Moscow in 1945, and studied first of all at the State Cinematographic Institute, then at the Gor'kii Institute of World Literature, from which he graduated in 1951. Worked for a time as an industrial correspondent before becoming a full-time writer. Member of the Party since 1948.

1. Books

Sredi lesov, Moscow: Sovetskii Pisatel', 1954 ('Sredi lesov'; 'Padenie Ivana Chuprova'; Nenast'e; 'Ne ko dvoru').

Ukhaby, Moscow: Molodaya Gvardiya, 1957 ('Tugoi uzel'; 'Ne ko dvoru'; 'Nenast'e; 'Padenie Ivana Chuprova'; 'Ukhaby').

Za begushchim dnëm, Moscow: Molodaya Gvardiya, 1960.

Povesti, Moscow: Moskovskii Rabochii, 1961 ('Za begushchim dnëm'; 'Ne ko dvoru'; 'Padenie Ivana Chuprova'; 'Ukhaby').

Izbrannye proizvedeniya v 2-kh tomakh, Moscow: Goslitizdat, 1963 (Vol. 1: 'Padenie Ivana Chuprova'; 'Ne ko dvoru'; 'Tugoi uzel'; 'Ukhaby'; 'Chudotvornaya'), (Vol. 2: 'Za begushchim dnem'; 'Troika, semërka, tuz'; 'Sud'; 'Chrezvychainoe').

Puteshestvie dlinoi v vek (nauchno-fantasticheskaya povest'), Vologda, Severo-Zapadnoe Knizhnoe Izdatel'stvo, 1965.

Svidanie s Nefertiti, Moscow: Molodaya Gvardiya, 1965.

Nakhodka, Moscow: Sovetskaya Rossiya, 1966.

Podënka – vek korotkii, Moscow Sovetskii Pisatel', 1969. ('Podënka – vek korotkii'; 'Chudotvornaya'; 'Chrezvychainoe'; 'Korotkoe zamykanie'; 'Onega').

Chrezvychainoe, Moscow: Sovremennik, 1972 ('Ne ko dvoru'; 'Chudotvornaya'; 'Chrezvychainoe'; 'Apostol'skaya komandi-rovka').

Perevërtyshi, Moscow: Sovremennik, 1974 ('Tri meshka sornoi pshenitsy'; 'Konchina'; 'Podënka – vek korotkii'; 'Sud'; 'Troika, semërka, tuz'; 'Vesennie perevërtyshi').

Grazhdane goroda solntsa, Moscow: Molodaya Gvardiya, 1977 ('Vesennie perevërtyshi'; 'Tri meshka sornoi pshenitsy'; 'Zatmenie').

Sobranie sochinenii, Moscow: Khudozhestvennaya Literatura, from 1978 (4 volume edition).

2. Fictional work in journals

'Sredi lesov', *God tridtsat' shestoi,* al'manakh 14, Moscow, 1953.

'Padenie Ivana Chuprova', *NM,* 12/53.

'Nenast'e', *NM,* 2/54.

'Ne ko dvoru', *NM,* 6/54.

'Ukhaby', *NS,* 2/56.

'Sasha otpravlyaetsya v put', *NM,* 2–3/56 (later republished under the title 'Tugoi uzel').

'Chudotvornaya', *Znamya*, 5/58.
'Za begushchim dnëm', *Molodaya Gvardiya*, 10–12/59.
'Troika, semërka, tuz', *NM*, 3/60.
'Sud', *NM*, 3/61.
'Chrezvychainoe', *Nauka i Religiya*, 7, 9, 10/61.
'Korotkoe zamykanie', *Znamya*, 3/62.
'Pis'mo, zapozdavshee na dvadtsat' let' (rasskazy radista), *NM*, 9/63.
'Svidanie s Nefertiti', *Moskva*, 10–12/64.
'Nakhodka', *Nauka i Religiya*, 1–2/65.
'Podenka – vek korotkii', *NM*, 5/65.
'Konchina', *Moskva*, 3/68.
'Apostol'skoe komandirovka', *Nauka i Religiya*, 8–10/69.
'Molilas' li ty na noch', Dezdemona?' (p'esa), *Sibir'*, 6/71.
'Tri meshka sornoi pshenitsy', *NS*, 2/73.
'Vesennie perevërtyshy', *NM*, 1/73.
'Noch' posle vypuska', *NM*, 9/74.
'Zatmenie', *Druzhba Narodov*, 5/77.
'Rasplata', *NM*, 3/79.

3. *Other writings*

'V zashchitu polozhitel'nogo geroya', *NM*, 11/54.
'V severnom krae (putevye zametki)', *Smena*, 2–3/54.
'Tyazhëlyi kharakter' (ocherk), *Partiinaya Zhizn'*, 1/55.
'Puteshestvie dlinoi v vek', *Nauka i Zhizn'*, 9–12/63.
'Kak ya pishu (otvet na anketu)', *VL*, 8/62.
'Den' na rodine' (ocherk)', *Nauka i Religiya*, 11/64.
'Vash syn i nasledstvo Komenskogo', *Moskva*, 11/65 (this article sparked off a lively discussion: see *Moskva* 1, 4, 10, 11/66).
'Otvetstvennost' khudozhnika (otvet na anketu)' *VL*, 1/66.
'Uchitel'' (K. G. Paustovskomu)', *LG*, 31 May 1967.
'Priroda tipichnogo (o literaturnom tvorchestve)', *LG*, 4 October 1967.
'O "svobode lichnosti" i svobode fal'sifikatsii (vpechatleniya ot poezdki v Angliyu)', *LG*, 22 November 1967.
'Priznanie' (under general rubric 'Trudy i dni sel'skogo uchitelya'), *Komsomol'skaya Pravda*, 22 February 1970.
'Novyi chas drevnego Samarkanda' (ocherk), *Druzhba Narodov*, 3/72.

'Plot' iskusstva', *NS*, 9/73.
'Bozheskoe i chelovecheskoye L'va Tolstogo', *Zvezda*, 8/78.

4. *Critical books and articles*

A. Chakovskii, 'Surovaya pravda', *LG*, 24 November 1953.
Yu. Surovtsev, 'Trudnye puti', *LG*, 27 July 1954.
V. Ovechkin, 'Kolkhoznaya zhizn' i literatura', *NM*, 12/55.
A. Berzer, 'Preodolevaya ukhaby', *Moskva*, 1/57.
I. Vinogradov, 'Optimisticheskaya tragediya Rod'ki Gulyaeva', *NM*, 9/58.
V. Chalmaev, 'Problema kharaktera v ocherkakh V. Tendryakova', in his *Ob ocherke*, Moscow: 1958.
J. Holthusen, 'Stilistik des "uneigentlichen" Erzählens in der sowjetischen Gegenwartsliteratur', *Die Welt der Slawen,* Vol. 13 (1968), no. 3.
Yu. Lukin, 'Kogo obvinyaet pisatel'?', *Pravda*, 28 March 1960.
F. Kuznetsov, 'Odin na odin s sovest'yu', *Izvestiya*, 12 May 1961.
B. Melov, 'Professional'nye nedobrozhelateli', *VL*, 5/61.
V. Litvinov, 'V. Tendryakov "staryi" i V. Tendryakov "novyi"', *Oktyabr'* 6/61.
D. Starikov, 'Paradoksy Vladimira Tendryakova', *Literatura i Zhizn'*, 15 April 1960 and 25 May 1962.
E. Starikova, 'Ispoved' obyknovennogo cheloveka', in her *Poeziya prozy*, Moscow: Sovetskii Pisatel', 1962.
L. Anninskii, 'Sovremennyi chelovek', *V Mire Knig*, 2/62.
I. Solov'eva, 'Problema i proza', *NM*, 7/62.
V. Pankov, 'Gumanizm v pokhode', *Moskva*, 10/62.
Yu. Burtin, 'O pol'ze obshchei idei', *Don*, 10/62.
B. Klyusov, *Na perednei linii* (ocherk tvorchestva V. Tendryakova), Minsk: Izdatel'stvo vysshego, srednego i spetsial'nogo obrazovaniya BSSR, 1963.
K. Mehnert, 'Humanismus in der jüngsten Sowjetliteratur?', *Abhandlungen der Akademie der Wissenschaften und der Literatur* (Klasse der Literatur), 1/63.
L. Kryachko, 'Tol'ko prelyudiya . . .', *LR*, 15 January 1965.
A. Makarov, 'Khudozhnik, iskusstvo, vremya', *LG*, 13, 16 February 1965 (see the author's reply in *LG*, 25 February 1965, and Makarov's further comment in *LG*, 2 March 1965).

J. Garrard, 'Vladimir Tendrjakov', *Slavic and East European Journal*, Vol. 9, no. 1 (spring 1965).

Ya. Bilinkis, 'Izobrazhenie zhizni', *Sever*, 5/65.

V. Kamyanov, 'Plyashut nad rekoi podënki', *LR*, 16 July 1965.

V. Surganov, 'Nastya vozvrashchaetsya k lyudyam', *LG*, 17 July 1965.

D. Nikolaev, 'Na istoricheskuyu pochvu', *VL*, 10/65.

O. Chaikovskaya, 'Priroda i vremya', *NM*, 10/65.

V. Pankov, 'Lykov, Slegov i drugie', *Znamya*, 10/68.

F. Kuznetsov, 'Pyat' povestei odnoi knigi', *LG*, 24 June 1970.

L. Antopol'skii, 'Prichashchenie v Krasnoglinke', *Druzhba Narodov*, 1/71.

V. Chalmaev, 'Uroki "del'nogo" napravleniya', *NS*, 12/73.

K. Lampert, 'The individual and the community in Vladimir Tendryakov', *Co-existence*, no. 11 (1974).

F. Kuznetsov, 'Dukhovnye tsennosti: mify i deistvitel'nost'', *NM*, 1/74.

V. K. Pankov, *Vremya i knigi* (problemy i geroi sovetskoi literatury), Moscow: Prosveshchenie, 1974.

N. Podzorova, 'Dar chelovechnosti', *Oktyabr'*, 10/74.

N. S. Rubtsov, *Tvorchestvo V. Tendryakova i sovremennaya russkaya sovetskaya povest'*, Moscow: Izdatel'stvo Moskovskogo Universiteta, 1975.

R. Hager, 'Die Evolution des literarischen Menschenbildes im Erzählschaffen Sergei Antonows, Jurij Nagibins und Vladimir Tendrjakows der 50er Jahre', *Zeitschrift für Slawistik*, 2/75.

V. Kardin, 'Igra v slova', *LG*, 1 October 1975.

V. Shubkin, 'Attestatsiya zrelosti', *LO*, 5/76.

V. Kamyanov, A. Gorlovskii, 'Mneniya o povesti V. Tendryakova "Zatmenie"', *LG*, 10 August 1977.

5. *English translations*

'Potholes', in C. P. Snow and Pamela Hansford Johnson (eds), *Stories from modern Russia: winter's tales 7*, New York: St Martin's Press, 1962 (also translated as 'Roads' in A. Yarmolinsky (ed.), *Soviet short stories*, New York: Doubleday-Anchor, 1960).

'Short Circuit', in T. P. Whitney (ed.), *The new writing in Russia*, Ann Arbor: University of Michigan Press, 1964; London: Cresset Press, 1964.

Solzhenitsyn, Alexander Isaevich

Born 1918 in Kislovodsk in the North Caucasus. He studied mathematics and physics at Rostov-on-Don University, then turned to literature as an extra-mural student, since he wanted to write a cycle of novels on the Russian revolution. He became an army officer in the war, and was arrested in 1945 for making critical remarks about Stalin in private letters. He was in prisons and labour camps 1945–53, and subsequently in exile, seriously ill with cancer, in Central Asia. Rehabilitated in 1957, he became a schoolmaster in Ryazan' where he quietly wrote *The First Circle, Cancer Ward* and *One day in the life of Ivan Denisovich*. With the publication of the latter in *Novyi Mir* in 1962, on Khrushchev's express approval, he became world-famous literally overnight, and the details of his life have since been the focus of international attention. Suffice it to mention here the confiscation of his manuscripts by the KGB in 1965, his letter to the 4th Writers' Union Congress in 1967 protesting against censorship and bureaucratic/police control of literature, his expulsion from the Writers' Union in 1969, and the award of the Nobel Prize for literature in 1971. In the autumn of 1973 the KGB discovered the manuscript of *The Gulag Archipelago*, whereupon Solzhenitsyn authorized its immediate publication in the west. In February 1974 he was expelled from the Soviet Union.

1. *Bibliographies*

F. d'Argent, 'Essai de bibliographie d'Alexandre Soljenitsyne', in G. Nivat and M. Aucouturier (see below, section 4).
L. Havrlant, 'A. I. Solzhenitsyn: selected bibliography, December 1962–October 1970', *Canadian Slavonic Papers*, Vol. 13 (1971), nos 2–3.
D. Fiene, *Alexander Solzhenitsyn: an international bibliography of writings by and about him, 1962–73*, Ann Arbor, Michigan: Ardis, 1973.
A. Artemova, 'Bibliografiya proizvedenii A. Solzhenitsyna', in *Sobranie sochinenii*, Vol. 6 (2nd ed., 1973 – see below, section 2).
J. B. Dunlop, 'A select Solzhenitsyn bibliography', in J. B. Dunlop, R. Haugh and A. Klimoff (see below, section 4).
M. Nicholson, 'A bibliography of responses in the official Soviet press from November 1962 to April 1973', in ibid.

M. Nicholson, 'Solzhenitsyn in 1976: a bibliographical reorientation', *Russian Literature Triquarterly*, Vol. 14 (winter 1976).

W. D. Buffington, 'A Solzhenitsyn bibliography', *Modern Fiction Studies*, Vol. 23, no. 1 (spring 1977).

W. Martin, *Alexander Solschenizyn: eine Bibliographie seiner Werke*, Hildesheim and New York: Georg Olms Verlag, 1977.

2. Books

The standard Russian edition of Solzhenitsyn's works (to date, but soon to be superseded) is *Sobranie sochinenii*, 6 vols, Frankfurt am Main: Possev, 1969–70. Revised and extended editions of Vols 5 and 6 were issued in 1971 and 1973 respectively. This whole collection, however, was put together from texts which had circulated in samizdat and had never been properly corrected by the author. For that reason, a completely revised collection, prepared by the author himself, is starting to appear, in 18 vols, published by the YMCA Press (Vermont and Paris). The 1969–70 collection also does not contain the following works:

Avgust chetyrnadtsatogo, Paris: YMCA Press, 1971.

Arkhipelag Gulag, 1918–1956: opyt khudozhestvennogo issledovaniya, 3 vols, Paris: YMCA Press, 1973–76.

Pis'mo vozhdyam Sovetskogo Soyuza, Paris: YMCA Press, 1974.

(joint editor with I. Shafarevich) *Iz-pod glyb*, Paris: YMCA Press, 1974.

Prusskie nochi (poema), Paris: YMCA Press, 1974.

Bodalsya telënok s dubom (ocherki literaturnoi zhizni), Paris: YMCA Press, 1975.

Lenin v Tsyurikhe, Paris: YMCA Press, 1975.

Rasskazy, Frankfurt am Main: Possev, 1976 (texts of the short stories, corrected by the author).

The original Russian text of *V kruge pervom* is in *Sobranie sochinenii*, vols 3 and 4. Solzhenitsyn has since added four chapters of a new version, which is to be in 96 rather than 87 chapters: these four can be found in *Vestnik Russkogo Khristianskogo Dvizheniya* nos 111 (1974), 112–13 (1974), 114 (1974), and in *Kontinent*, no. 1 (1974).

3. *Fictional work in journals*

'Odin den' Ivana Denisovicha', *NM,* 11/62.
Dva rasskaza: 'Matrënin dvor'; 'Sluchai na stantsii Krechetovka',
NM, 1/63.
'Dlya pol'zy dela', *NM,* 7/63.
'Zakhar-kalita', *NM,* 1/66.

4. *Books on Solzhenitsyn*

G. Lukacs, *Solzhenitsyn,* London: Merlin Press, 1970, revised ed.
1975; Cambridge, Mass.: MIT Press, 1970 and 1975 (revised ed.,
paperback).
L. Rzhevskii, *Prochten'e tvorcheskogo slova* (literaturovedcheskie
problemy i analizy), New York: New York University Press, 1970
(contains two articles on Solzhenitsyn).
G. Nivat and M. Aucouturier (eds), *Soljenitsyne,* Paris: L'Herne,
1971.
L. Rzhevskii, *Tvorets i podvig: ocherki po tvorchestvu Aleksandra
Solzhenitsyna,* Frankfurt am Main: Possev, 1972 (English ed.
University of Alabama Press, 1978).
Avgust chetyrnadtsatogo chitayut na rodine (sbornik statei i
otzyvov), Paris: YMCA Press, 1973.
E. Markstein and F. Ingold (eds), *Über Solschenizyn: Aufsätze,
Berichte, Materialien,* Darmstadt und Neuwied: Luchterhand
Verlag, 1973.
Zh. Medvedev, *Ten years after Ivan Denisovich,* London: Macmillan,
1973; New York: Alfred A. Knopf, 1973.
P. Daix, *Ce que je sais de Soljenitsyne,* Paris: Seuil, 1973.
G. Nivat, *Sur Soljenitsyne,* Lausanne: Editions l'Age d'Homme,
1974.
L. Labedz (ed.), *Solzhenitsyn: a documentary record,* enlarged ed.,
Harmondsworth: Penguin Books, 1974; Bloomington, Ind.:
Indiana University Press, 1973.
J. B. Dunlop, R. Haugh, A. Klimoff (eds), *Alexander Solzhenitsyn:
critical essays and documentary materials,* 2nd ed., London and
New York: Collier-Macmillan, 1975.
K. Feuer (ed.), *Solzhenitsyn: a collection of critical essays,* Englewood
Cliffs, NJ and Hemel Hempstead: Prentice-Hall, 1975 and 1976.

C. Moody, *Solzhenitsyn*, 2nd revised ed., New York: Barnes & Noble and Harper & Row (paperback), 1975; Edinburgh: Oliver & Boyd, 1976.

O. Clément, *The spirit of Solzhenitsyn*, London: Search Press, 1976.

R. Gul', *Solzhenitsyn: stat'i*, New York: Most, 1976.

R. Medvedev, *Political essays*, Nottingham: Spokesman Books, 1976; Short Hills, NJ: Enslow, 1977.

V. Carpovich, *Solzhenitsyn's peculiar vocabulary: a Russian-English glossary*, New York: Technical Dictionaries, 1976.

S. Carter, *The politics of Solzhenitsyn*, London: Macmillan, 1977; New York: Holmes & Meier, 1977.

F. Barker, *Solzhenitsyn: politics and form*, London: Macmillan, 1977; New York: Barnes & Noble, 1978.

5. *Critical articles*

V. Lakshin, 'Ivan Denisovich, ego druz'ya i nedrugi', *NM*, 1/64.

T. G. Vinokur, 'O yazyke i stile povesti A. I. Solzhenitsyna "Odin den' Ivana Denisovicha"', *Voprosy kul'tury rechi*, 6/65.

M. Glenny, 'Alexander Solzhenitsyn', *Studies in Comparative Communism*, Vol. 2 (1969), no. 1.

Deming Brown, '"Cancer Ward" and "First Circle"', *Slavic Review*, Vol. 28 (1969), no. 2.

Edward J. Brown, 'Solzhenitsyn's cast of characters', *Slavic and East European Journal*, Vol. 15 (1971), no. 2.

R. Luplow, 'Narrative style and structure in "One day in the life of Ivan Denisovich"', *Russian Literature Triquarterly*, Vol. 1. (1971).

Canadian Slavonic Papers, Vol. 13 (1971), nos 2–3, is devoted to articles on Solzhenitsyn.

Dorothy Atkinson, 'Solzhenitsyn's heroes as Russian historical types', *Russian Review*, Vol. 30 (1971), no. 1.

Helen Muchnic, 'Aleksandr Solzhenitsyn', in her *Russian writers: notes and essays*, New York: Random House, 1971.

V. I. Grebenshchikov, 'The infernal circles of Dante and Solzhenitsyn', *Transactions of the Association of Russian-American Scholars in the USA*, Vol. 6 (1972).

J. B. Dunlop, '"The Gulag Archipelago": ideology or "point of view"', ibid, Vol. 8 (1974).

Modern Fiction Studies, Vol. 23 (1977), no. 1 is devoted to articles on Solzhenitsyn.

V. Krasnov, '"Mnogogolosost'" geroev v romane Solzhenitsyna "V kruge pervom"', *Grani*, Vol. 103 (1977).

V. Lakshin, 'Solzhenitsyn, Tvardovskii i "Novyi Mir"', *Dvadtsatyi Vek*, Vol. 2 (1977).

D. Pike, 'A camp through the eyes of a peasant: Solzhenitsyn's "One Day in the Life of Ivan Denisovich"', *California Slavic Studies*, Vol. 10 (1977).

6. *English translations*

The main English editions of Solzhenitsyn's works are as follows:

One day in the life of Ivan Denisovich, trans. R. Parker, London: Gollancz, 1963; Harmondsworth: Penguin Books, 1970; trans. M. Hayward and R. Hingley, New York: Frederick A. Praeger, 1963 and Bantam Books, 1970.

For the good of the cause, trans. D. Floyd and M. Hayward, New York: Frederick A. Praeger, 1964; London: Pall Mall, 1964.

The first circle, trans. M. Guybon, London: Collins & Harvill, 1968 and Fontana, 1970; trans. T. P. Whitney, New York: Harper & Row, 1968 and Bantam Books, 1976.

Cancer ward, trans. N. Bethell and D. Burg, London: Bodley Head, 1968, 1969, new ed. 1970; Harmondsworth: Penguin Books, 1971; New York: Farrar, Straus & Giroux and Bantam Books, 1969.

The love-girl and the innocent (drama), trans. N. Bethell and D. Burg, London: Bodley Head, 1969; Harmondsworth: Penguin Books, 1971; New York: Farrar, Straus & Giroux, 1970 (available in paperback).

Stories and prose poems, trans. M. Glenny, London: Bodley Head, 1970 and Penguin, 1973; New York: Farrar, Straus & Giroux, 1971 (paperback, 1974).

August 1914, trans. M. Glenny, London: Bodley Head, 1972; Harmondsworth: Penguin Books, 1974; New York: Bantam Books, 1969 and Farrar, Straus & Giroux, 1972.

One word of truth (Nobel speech on literature, 1970), trans. T. P. Whitney, London: Bodley Head, 1972; New York (entitled *The Nobel lecture on literature*): Harper & Row, 1972.

Candle in the wind (drama), trans. K. Armes and A. Hudkins, London: Bodley Head and Oxford University Press, 1973;

Harmondsworth: Penguin Books, 1976; New York: Bantam Books, 1974.

Letter to the Soviet leaders, trans. Hilary Sternberg, London: Collins & Harvill, 1974; New York: Harper & Row, 1974 (paperback, 1975).

The Gulag archipelago, 1918–1956: an experiment in literary investigation, Vols 1 and 2, trans. T. P. Whitney, New York: Harper & Row, 1974 and 1975 (available in paperback); London: Collins & Harvill, 1974 and 1975, and Fontana, 1975 and 1976; Vol. 3, trans. H. T. Willetts, New York: Harper & Row, 1978 (available in paperback); London: Collins & Harvill, 1978 and Fontana, 1979.

(joint ed. with I. Shafarevich) *From under the rubble*, trans. M. Scammell, London: Collins & Harvill, 1975: New York: Little, Brown, 1975.

Matryona's House and other stories, Harmondsworth: Penguin Books, 1975.

Lenin in Zurich, trans. H. T. Willetts, London: Bodley Head, 1976 and Penguin Books, 1978; New York: Farrar, Straus & Giroux, 1976 and Bantam Books, 1977.

A warning to the western world, London: Bodley Head, 1976; New York (entitled *A warning to the west*): Farrar, Straus & Giroux, 1976 (available in paperback).

Prussian nights (narrative poem), trans. R. Conquest (bilingual ed.), London: Collins & Harvill, 1977; New York: Farrar, Straus & Giroux, 1977 (available in paperback).

Maximov, Vladimir Emel'yanovich

Born 1932 in a workers' family in Moscow. In 1933 his father was arrested, and Maximov spent much of his childhood in children's homes and approved schools. He trained as a stonemason, and worked on collective farms and building sites in various parts of the country. His first literary works were poetry, but it was not until he published a story in *Tarusskie Stranitsy* (see below) in 1961 that he attracted attention. His early stories were about criminals and outcasts, and proved to be extremely controversial. He was twice committed for compulsory psychiatric treatment. He was for a short time on the editorial board of the journal *Oktyabr'*. In June 1973 he was expelled from the Union of Soviet Writers for publishing *The Seven Days of Creation* abroad. In February 1974 he left the Soviet Union and settled in Paris. He is now chief editor of the émigré journal *Kontinent*.

1. *Books*

Zhiv chelovek (povest'), Moscow: Molodaya Gvardiya, 1964.
Zhiv chelovek (povest' i rasskazy), Magadan: Knizhnoe Izdatel'stvo, 1965.
Sem' dnei tvoreniya, Frankfurt am Main: Possev, 1971.
Karantin, Frankfurt am Main: Possev, 1973.
Proshchanie iz niotkuda, Frankfurt am Main: Possev, 1974.
Sobranie sochinenii, Vols 1–5, Frankfurt am Main: Possev, 1974–6.

2. *Fictional work in journals*

'My obzhivaem zemlyu', *Tarusskie Stranitsy*, Kaluga: Knizhnoe Izdatel'stvo, 1961.
'Zhiv chelovek', *Oktyabr'*, 10/62.
'Pozyvnye tvoikh parallelei' (p'esa), *Oktyabr'*, 2/64.
'Shagi k gorizontu' (rasskazy: 'Iskushenie'; 'Sashka'; 'Dusya i nas pyatero'), *Oktyabr'*, 9/64.
'Stan' za chertu', *Oktyabr'*, 2/67 (republished as a play in *Novyi Zhurnal,* nos 116–17 (1974)).
(All these early stories are extensively reworked and republished under the title 'Saga o Savve' in *Sobranie sochinenii*, Vol. 1.)
'Chetverg. Pozdnii svet', *Grani*, no. 80 (1971) (later appeared as part of *Sem' dnei tvoreniya*).
'Kovcheg dlya nezvanykh (glavy iz romana)', *Kontinent*, no. 9 (1976) and no. 14 (1977); *Vestnik Russkogo Khristianskogo Dvizheniya*, no. 124 (1978).

3. *Other writings*

'Vladimir Maximov's visa (an interview in London)' *Encounter*, Vol. 42, no. 6 (June 1974).

4. *Critical articles*

L. Ivanova, 'Eshchë raz o zle i dobre', *Znamya,* 3/63.

A. Berzer, 'Pobedil chelovek', *NM*, 4/63.

V. Bushin, 'Spor veka', *Zvezda*, 4/63.

V. Pertsovskii, 'Osmyslenie zhizni: o tvorchestve prozaikov Yu. Kazakova, V. Konetskogo i V. Maksimova', *VL*, 2/64.

L. Anninskii, 'Bremya pravdy', *Teatr*, 10/65.

'Kto on – geroi sovremennogo rasskaza', *VL*, 10/65.

E. Krasnoshchekova, 'Nravstvennyi konflikt v sovremennoi povesti', in *Zhanrovo-stilevye iskaniya sovremennoi sovetskoi prozy,* Moscow: Nauka, 1971.

N. Antonov, 'Gody bezvremenshchiny (o romane *Sem' dnei tvoreniya)', Grani,* nos 89–90 (1973).

N. Antonov, 'Krest i kamen' (o romane *Karantin)', Grani,* nos 92 3 (1974).

V. Iverni, 'Postizhenie (o tvorchestve V. Maksimova)', *Vestnik Russkogo Khristianskogo Dvizheniya,* no. 126 (1978).

L. Rzhevskii, 'Triptikh V. E. Maksimova', *Grani,* no. 109 (1978).

V. Iverni, 'Postizhenie (o tvorchestve V. Maksimova), *Vestnik Russkogo Khristianskogo Dvizheniya,* no. 126 (1978).

5. *English translations*

The seven days of creation, London: Weidenfeld & Nicolson, 1975; Harmondsworth: Penguin Books, 1977; New York: Alfred A. Knopf, 1975.

Farewell from nowhere, trans. M. Glenny, London: Collins & Harvill, 1978; New York: Doubleday, 1979.

Voinovich, Vladimir Nikolaevich

Born 1932 in Stalinabad (now Dushanbe) in Tadzhikistan: his mother was a schoolteacher, his father a journalist. He trained as a carpenter. Served in the army, 1951–5, and published some verse, but was not accepted when he applied to the Gor'kii Institute of World Literature in 1956 and 1957. He worked as a carpenter, then taught evening classes in the Virgin Lands region of Kazakhstan. In 1960 he found a job with Moscow Radio, where he composed a cosmonauts' song that won him wide popularity. At about the same time his first story was accepted for publication in *Novyi Mir*. His works published in that journal made him popular, though controversial. His real difficulties with the authorities came, however, when he protested against the writers' trials of 1966–68 and against the expulsion of Solzhenitsyn from the Writers' Union. The publication abroad of Part One of *Chonkin* (in 1969) caused further difficulties, even though he dissociated himself publicly from it. In 1974, he was expelled from the Writers' Union, and since then nothing of his has been published in the Soviet Union.

1. *Books*

My zdes' zhivëm, Moscow: Sovetskii Pisatel', 1963.
Povesti, Moscow: Sovetskii Pisatel', 1972 ('My zdes' zhivëm'; 'Dva tovarishcha'; 'Vladychitsa').
Stepen' doveriya (povest' o Vere Figner), Moscow: Politizdat, 1973.
Zhizn' i neobychainye priklyucheniya soldata Ivana Chonkina (parts 1 and 2), Paris: YMCA Press, 1975.
Ivan'kiada (ili rasskaz o vselenii pisatelya Voinovicha v novuyu kvartiru), Ann Arbor: Ardis, 1976.
Putëm vzaimnoi perepiski, Paris: YMCA Press, 1979 (includes some new autobiographical fragments, and an unpublished short story, 'V krugu druzei').

2. *Fictional work in journals*

'My zdes' zhivëm', *NM*, 1/61.
Dva rasskaza ('Khochu byt' chestnym'; 'Rasstoyanie v polkilometra'), *NM*, 2/63.
'V kupe', *NM*, 2/65.
'Dva tovarishcha', *NM*, 1/67.
'Vladychitsa', *Nauka i Religiya*, 4–5/69.
'Zhizn' i neobychainye priklyucheniya soldata Ivana Chonkina' (part 1), *Grani*, no. 72 (1969).
'Putëm vzaimnoi perepiski', *Grani*, nos 87–88 (1973).

3. *Other writings*

'Zhizn', kak ona est' (otvety na anketu)', *Literatura i Zhizn*', 9 December 1962.

'Pisatel', geroi, molodëzh' (soveshchanie molodykh pisatelei), *Moskovskii Komsomolets*, 11 December 1964.

'V redaktsiyu *Literaturnoi Gazety'*, *LG*, 14 October 1970.

'O ritme khudozhestvennoi prozy (otvet na anketu)', *VL*, 7/73.

'Otkrytoe pis'mo predsedatelyu VAAPa', *Posev*, 11/73.

'Zayavlenie V. Voinovicha v sekretariat moskovskogo otdela Soyuza Pisatelei RSFSR', *Russkaya Mysl*', 28 March 1974.

'Dissident wider Willen' (Interview with Thomas Rothschild), *Die Zeit*, 17 January 1975.

'Otkrytoe pis'mo predsedatelyu KGB Yu.V. Andropovu', *Arkhiv Samizdata*, no. 2151.

'Proisshestvie v Metropole', *Kontinent*, no. 5 (1975).

4. *Critical articles*

V. Tendryakov, 'Svezhii golos – est'!', *LG*, 25 February 1961.

V. Kardin, 'Vechnye voprosy – novye otvety', *VL*, 3/61.

S. Rassadin, 'O nastoyashchem i pokhozhem', *Yunost*', 4/62.

G. Brovman, 'Grazhdanstvennost' avtora i geroya', *Moskva*, 6/63.

M. Sinel'nik, 'Preodolenie', *LG*, 4 October 1967.

V. Ya. Grechnev, 'Vybor geroya i kharakter konflikta', in V. A. Kovaleva and V. V. Timofeeva, *Sovetskaya literatura i novyi chelovek*, Leningrad: Nauka, 1967.

Deming Brown, 'Narrative devices in the contemporary Russian short story: intimacy and irony', *American Contributions to the 7th International Congress of Slavists*, Vol. 2: *Literature and Folklore*, The Hague and Paris: Mouton, 1973.

N. Muravina, 'Vladimir Voinovich – zhizn' i neobychainye priklyucheniya soldata Ivana Chonkina', *Vestnik Russkogo Khristianskogo Dvizheniya*, no. 115 (1975).

O. Grotte, 'Dissident ponevole', *Russkaya Mysl*', 27 February 1975.

N. Korzhavin, 'Stolknovenie stikhii', *Posev*, 8/75.

V. Iverni, 'Komediya nesovmestimosti', *Kontinent*, no. 5 (1975).

Yu. Vishnevskaya, 'Novyi roman Vladimira Voinovicha', *Russkaya Mysl*', 22 May 1975.

——, 'Biografiya pisatelya V. Voinovicha', *Russkaya Mysl*', 17 July 1975.

——, 'V. N. Voinovich (bio-bibliograficheskaya spravka)', *Radio Svoboda*, RS 242/75.

D. Shtok, 'Vybor puti: o tvorchestve Vladimira Voinovicha', *Grani*, no. 104 (1976).

G. Hosking, 'The good soldier Chonkin', *Times Literary Supplement*, 23 January 1976.

M. A. Szporluk, 'Vladimir Voinovich: the development of a new satirical voice', *Russian Literature Triquarterly*, no. 14 (1976).

E. Reissner, 'Satire in der russischen Gegenwartsliteratur', *Osteuropa* Vol. 28, no. 3 (March 1978) (in English in *Survey*, no. 104, (1978)).

5. *English translations*

'I'd be honest if they'd let me', in *Four Soviet masterpieces*, New York: Bantam Books, 1965.

'In the compartment', in M. Dewhirst and R. Milner-Gulland (eds), *Russian writing today*, Harmondsworth: Penguin Books, 1977.

'A distance of half a kilometer', *Chicago Review*, Vol. 29, no. 2 (autumn 1977).

The life and extraordinary adventures of Private Ivan Chonkin, trans. R. Lourie, New York: Farrar, Straus & Giroux, 1977 and Bantam Books, 1978; London: Jonathan Cape, 1977 and Penguin Books, 1979.

The Ivankiad (or the tale of the writer Voinovich's installation in his new apartment), trans. D. Lapeza, New York: Farrar, Straus & Girou, 1977 (available in paperback); London: Jonathan Cape, 1978.

'Incident at the Metropol' in *Kontinent 2*, London: André Deutsch, 1978.

Vladimov, Georgii Nikolaevich

Born 1931 in Khar'kov, son of a schoolteacher. Studied law at Leningrad University, but began his career as a literary critic, before publishing his first major literary work in *Novyi Mir* in 1961. In 1967 he circulated a memorandum to the 4th Writers' Union Congress demanding public discussion of Solzhenitsyn's letter on censorship.

After that (and the appearance abroad of *Faithful Ruslan*), he had his ups and downs with the literary authorities, but appeared to be returning to favour, when suddenly, in October 1977, he resigned from the Writers' Union, calling it a 'police apparatus', and became secretary of the Moscow Branch of Amnesty International.

1. *Books*

Bol'shaya ruda, Moscow: Sovetskaya Rossiya, 1962.
Vernyi Ruslan, Frankfurt-am-Main: Possev, 1975.

2. *Fictional work in journals*

'Vse my dostoiny bol'shego', *Smena*, 13/60.
'Bol'shaya ruda', *NM*, 7/61.
'Tri minuty molchaniya', *NM*, 7–9/69.
'Vernyi Ruslan', *Grani*, no. 96 (1975).

3. *Other writings*

'Pisatel', geroi, mododëzh' (soveshchanie molodykh pisatelei), *Moskovskii Komsomolets*, 11 December 1964.
(with F. Kuznetsov) 'Dialog o proze', *LG*, 18 February 1976.
M. Popovskii, 'Interv'yu s moskovskim pisatelem Georgiem Vladimovym', *Vol'noe Slovo*, vypusk 29 (1978).

4. *Critical articles*

L. Anninskii, 'Gibel' Pronyakina', *Ural*, 1/62.
E. Starikova, 'Zhizn' i gibel' shofëra Pronyakina', *Znamya*, 1/62.
S. Rassadin, 'O nastoyashchem i pokhozhem', *Yunost'*, 4/62.
A. A. Kots, 'Khudozhestvennoe svoeobrazie prozy G. Vladimova', *Uchënye Zapiski Permskogo Universiteta*, no. 241 (1970).
L. Anninskii, 'Sol' vody', *Yunost'*, 6/70.
A. Terts, 'Lyudi i zveri', *Kontinent*, no. 5 (1975).
V. Chernyavskii, 'Gibel' geroev', *Grani*, no. 106 (1977).

5. *English translations*

'The real stuff', *Soviet Literature Monthly*, 3/63.
'The great ore', in *Four Soviet masterpieces*, New York: Bantam Books, 1965.

Shukshin, Vasilii Makarovich

Born 1929 in the Altai Territory. Finished seven years' schooling, and worked for a time on collective farms and building sites. He served in the navy, where he first participated in amateur theatrical performances. Studied at the All-Union State Institute of Cinematography under Mikhail Romm, where he began the triple career as actor, film director and writer which occupied him for the rest of his life. His great ambition was to make a film about the peasant rebel of the 17th century, Sten'ka Razin, and he seems to have been given permission to go ahead with this shortly before his death of a heart attack in October 1974. Member of the Party since 1955.

To indicate in the following bibliography all the original publications of Shukshin's stories would take up more space than is available. They are given in my bibliography, published in Donald M. Fiene (ed.), Vasily Shukshin: *Snowball Berry Red and other stories,* Ann Arbor, Michigan: Ardis, 1978.

1. *Books*

Sel'skie zhiteli, Moscow: Molodaya Gvardiya, 1963.
Zhivët takoi paren' (kinotsenarii), Moscow: Iskusstvo, 1964.
Lyubaviny (roman), Moscow: Sovetskii Pisatel', 1965.
Tam, vdali (povest' i rasskazy), Moscow: Sovetskii Pisatel', 1968.
Zemlyaki, Moscow: Sovetskii Pisatel', 1970.
Kharaktery, Moscow: Sovremennik, 1973.
Ya prishël dat' vam volyu (roman), Moscow: Sovetskii Pisatel', 1974.
Besedy pri yasnoi lune, Moscow: Sovetskaya Rossiya, 1974.
Brat moi, Moscow: Sovremennik, 1975.
Izbrannye proizvedeniya, 2 vols, Moscow: Molodaya Gvardiya, 1975.
Kinopovesti, Moscow: Iskusstvo, 1975.

Do tret'ikh petukhov (povesti i rasskazy), Moscow: Izvestiya, 1976.
Okhota zhit' (rasskazy), Kazan': Tatarskoe Knizhnoe Izdatel'stvo, 1977.
Lyubaviny (roman), Novosibirsk: Zapadno-sibirskoe Knizhnoe Izdatel'stvo, 1978.

2. *Other writings*

'Kak ya ponimayu rasskaz', *Literaturnaya Rossiya,* 20 November 1964.
Contribution to 'Literatura i yazyk', *VL,* 6/67.
'Monolog na lestnitse', in V. Tolstykh (ed.), *Kul'tura Chuvstv,* Moscow: Iskusstvo, 1968.
'Nasushchnoe, kak khleb (problemy kul'tury i byta sela)', *Sovetskaya Kul'tura,* 18 January 1969.
'Stepan Razin – legenda i byl'', *LG,* 4 November 1970.
'Vasilii Shukshin: poslednie razgovory', *LG,* 13 November 1974 (most of this material appears in English in 'Vasily Shukshin's last interview', *Soviet Literature,* 4/75).
'Ot prozy k fil'mu', in *Kinopanorama (sovetskoe kino segodnya),* Moscow: Iskusstvo, 1975.
'Nenapisannaya avtobiografiya', *Smena,* 19/75.
'Milaya moya rodina', *LO,* 12/75.

3. *Critical and other articles*

V. Yavinskii, 'Pisatel', aktër, rezhissër', *Altai,* 1/68.
V. Kantorovich, 'Novye tipy, novyi slovar', novye otnosheniya', *Sibirskie Ogni,* 9/71.
M. Chudakova, 'Zametki o yazyke sovremennoi prozy', *NM,* 1/72.
V. Chalmaev, 'Poryv vetra (molodye geroi i novelisticheskoe iskusstvo V. Shukshina)', *Sever,* 10/72.
L. Emel'yanov, 'Edinitsa izmereniya: zametki o proze V. Shukshina', *NS,* 10/73.
I. Solov'ëva, V. Shitova, 'Svoi lyudi – sochtëmsya', *NM,* 3/74.
'Zhiznennyi material, poisk khudozhnika, avtorskaya kontseptsiya (obsuzhdaem "Kalinu krasnuyu", kinopovest' i fil'm V. Shukshina)', *VL,* 7/74 (partially reproduced in English in 'Reality and the writer's vision', *Soviet Literature,* 9/75).

N. Leiderman, 'Trudnaya doroga vozvysheniya (o novykh proiz-vedeniyakh V. Shukshina)', *Sibirskie Ogni*, 8/74.

L. Mikhailova, 'Pronitsatel'nost' talanta', *LO*, 1/75.

F. Kuznetsov, 'S vekom naravne', *NM*, 2/75.

I. Dedkov, 'Poslednie shtrikhi', *Druzhba Narodov*, 4/75.

D. M. Fiene and B. M. Peskin, 'The remarkable art of Vasily Shukshin', *Russian Literature Triquarterly*, Vol. 11 (1975).

A. Ovcharenko, 'Rasskazy Vasiliya Shukshina', *Don*, 1/76.

A. Lanshchikov, 'Razmyshleniya o "Kaline krasnoi"', *Volga,* 3/76.

Yu. Tyurin, '"Kalina krasnaya", kinopovest' i fil'm', *Moskva*, 4/76.

L. Annenskii, 'Put' Vasiliya Shukshina', *Nedelya*, 15/76 (reproduced in *Sever*, 11/76).

L. Belova, 'Tri rusla odnogo puti (o tvorchestve V. Shukshina)', *Voprosy Kinoiskusstva*, Vol. 17 (1976).

V. F. Gorn, 'Pereizdaniyam V. Shukshina – podlinno nauchnyi uroven'', *VL*, 1/77.

V. Korobov, 'Pisatel', aktër, rezhissër Shukshin', *Smena,* 1–5/77.

Yu. Seleznev, 'Fantasticheskoe v sovremennoi proze', *Moskva*, 2/77.

V. F. Gorn, 'Zhivoi yazyk Vasiliya Shukshina', *Russkaya Rech'* 2/77.

Viktor Nekrasov, 'Vasya Shukshin', *Novoe Russkoe Slovo*, 27 February 1977 (reproduced in his 'Vzglyad i nechto', *Kontinent*, Vol. 12 (1977)).

G. Belaya, 'Antimiry Vasiliya Shukshina', *LO*, 5/77.

V. Kaverin, 'Rasskazy Shukshina', *NM*, 6/77.

M. Geller, 'Vasilii Shukshin: v poiskakh voli', *Vestnik Russkogo Khristianskogo Dvizheniya*, Vol. 120 (1977) (reproduced in English in D. M. Fiene (ed.), *Shukshin: Snowball Berry Red and other stóries*, Ann Arbor, Michigan: Ardis, 1978).

V. A. Kuz'muk, 'Svoeobrazie geroya rasskazov Vasiliya Shukshina', *Vestnik Moskovskogo Universiteta* (filologiya), 2/78.

A. Pankov, 'Kharaktery i rezkaya kritika nravov (o tvorchestve V. Shukshina)', *Sibirskie Ogni*, 4/78.

I. Strelkova, 'So smekhom mnogoe ponimaetsya . . . (yumor v proizvedeniyakh V. Shukshina i V. Belova), *NS*, 4/78.

V. Solov'ev, 'Vasilii Shukshin: maniya pravdoiskatel'stva', *Vremya i My*, Vol. 34 (1978).

One critical and biographical book on Shukshin has appeared:

V. I. Korobov, *Vasilii Shukshin: tvorchestvo, lichnost'*, Moscow: Sovetskaya Rossiya, 1977.

4. *English translation*

D. M. Fiene (ed.), *Snowball Berry Red and other stories*, Ann Arbor: Ardis, 1979.

Trifonov, Yurii Valentinovich

Born 1925 in Moscow, the son of a party official who had taken a prominent part in the revolutions of 1905 and 1917, but who was arrested and executed in 1937. Received his schooling in Tashkent, worked from 1942 in Moscow aircraft factories, and studied at the Gor'kii Literary Institute, 1944–49. Reached fame with his first novel, *Studenty*, which received a Stalin Prize in 1950.

1. *Books*

Studenty, Moscow: Molodaya Gvardiya, 1951 (subsequent editions, Moscow: Moskovskii Rabochii, 1956; Moscow: Sovetskii Pisatel', 1960).
Pod solntsem (rasskazy), Moscow: Sovetskii Pisatel', 1959.
Utolenie zhazhdy, Moscow: Sovetskii Pisatel', 1963.
Kostry i dozhd' (rasskazy), Moscow: Sovetskaya Rossiya, 1964.
Otblesk kostra, Moscow: Sovetskii Pisatel', 1966.
Kepka s bol'shim kozyr'kom (rasskazy), Moscow: Sovetskaya Rossiya, 1969.
Rasskazy i povesti, Moscow: Khudozhestvennaya Literatura, 1971 ('Obmen').
Dolgoe proshchanie, Moscow: Sovetskaya Rossiya, 1973 ('Obmen'; 'Predvaritel'nye itogi'; 'Dolgoe proshchanie'; 'Beskonechnye igry').
Neterpenie (povest' ob Andree Zhelyabove), Moscow: Politizdat, 1974.
Prodolzhitel'nye uroki, Moscow: Sovetskaya Rossiya, 1975 (collection of critical and reflective articles).
Drugaya zhizn', Moscow: Sovetskii Pisatel', 1976.
Izbrannye proizvedeniya v dvukh tomakh, Moscow: Khudozhestvennaya Literatura, 1978 ('Obmen'; 'Predvaritel'nye itogi'; 'Dolgoe proshchanie'; 'Drugaya zhizn''; 'Neterpenie').

Povesti, Moscow: Sovetskaya Rossiya, 1978 ('Obmen'; 'Predvaritel'nye itogi'; 'Dolgoe proshchanie'; 'Drugaya Zhizn''; 'Dom na naberezhnoi').

2. *Fictional work in journals*

'Studenty', *NM*, 10–11/50.
'Pod solntsem (tsikl rasskazov)', *Znamya*, 2/59.
'Utolenie zhazhdy', *Znamya*, 4–7/63.
'Otblèsk kostra', *Znamya*, 2–3/65.
Dva rasskaza ('Vera i Zoika'; 'V letnii polden''), *NM,* 12/66.
Dva rasskaza ('Samyi malen'kii gorod'; 'Golubinaya gibel''), *NM*, 1/68.
'Pobeditel' (rasskaz)', *Znamya*, 7/68.
'V gribnuyu osen' (rasskaz)', *NM*, 8/68.
'Obmen', *NM*, 12/69.
'Beskonechnye igry', *Prostor*, 7/70.
'Predvaritel'nye itogi', *NM,* 12/70.
'Dolgoe proshchanie', *NM*, 8/71.
'Neterpenie', *NM*, 3–5/73.
'Drugaya zhizn'', *NM*, 8/75.
'Dom na naberezhnoi', *Druzhba narodov*, 1/76.
'Starik', *Druzhba narodov*, 3/78.

3. *Other writings*

'Mayak skvoz' gody', *LG*, 1 November 1967.
'Otblesk istorii – o knige, kotoraya budet', *LR*, 7 March 1969.
(with others) 'Rasskaz segodnya – ob izmenivsheisya fakture rasskaza', *VL*, 7/69.
(with others) 'Rabochii klass i literatura', *Druzhba narodov*, 3/70.
'Vechnozelënoe puteshestvie', *VL*, 12/71.
'Neskonchaemoe nachalo' (under the general rubric 'Kak my pishem'), *LR*, 21 December 1973.
'Sovremennost' – splav istorii i budushchego', *LG,* 19 June 1974.
(with others) 'Na polkakh folianty . . . (o roli starykh knig v zhizni i tvorchestve)', *LG*, 27 July 1974.
'V kratkom – beskonechnoe (interv'yu pisatelya)', *VL,* 8/74.

'Voobrazit' beskonechnost' (beseda), *LO,* 4/77.

'Knigi, kotorye vybirayut nas', *LG,* 10 November 1976.

4. *Critical articles*

V. Roslyakov, 'Utolennaya zhazhda', *Moskva,* 10/63.

F. Kuznetsov, 'Nastuplenie novoi nravstvennosti', *VL,* 2/64.

L. Anninskii, 'Pisatel' za rabochim stolom,' *Vechernyaya Moskva,* 11 July 1964.

I. Kramov, 'Sud'ba i vremya', *NM,* 3/67.

V. Gusev, 'Usloviya vstrechi', *LG,* 4 February 1970.

E. Babaev, 'Rasskazy romanista', *NM,* 9/70.

Yu. Andreev, 'V zamknutom mirke', *LG,* 3 March 1971.

A. Gorlovskii, 'A chto v itoge?', *LR,* 19 March 1971.

V. Bednenko and O. Krinitskii, 'Prezhdevremennye itogi', *Molodaya Gvardiya,* 10/71.

V. Pertsovskii, 'Proza vmeshivaetsya v spor', *VL,* 10/71.

'Obsuzhdaem novye povesti Yu. Trifonova', *VL,* 2/72.

G. Brovman, 'Izmereniya malogo mira', *LG,* 8 March 1972.

L. Anninskii, 'Neokonchatel'nye itogi', *Don,* 5/72.

N. Ravich, 'Podvig Andreya Zhelyabova', *LG,* 26 September 1973.

V. Oskotskii, 'Nravstvennye uroki "Narodnoi Voli"', *LO,* 11/73.

A. Lanshchikov, 'Geroi i vremya', *Don,* 11/73.

V. Sakharov, 'Flamandskoi shkoly pëstryi sor . . .', *NS,* 5/74.

A. Khort, 'Vysokaya temperatura', *LR,* 28 June 1974.

V. Kardin, 'Proroki v svoem otechestve', *Druzhba Narodov,* 8/74.

V. Pertsovskii, 'Ispytanie bytom', *NM,* 11/74.

X. Gasiorowska, 'Two decades of love and marriage in Soviet fiction,' *Russian Review,* Vol. 34, no. 1 (January 1975).

A. Bocharov, 'Voskhozhdenie', *Oktyabr',* 8/75.

V. Solov'ëv, 'O lyubvi i ne tol'ko o lyubvi', *LO,* 2/76.

V. Dudintsev, 'Stoit li umirat' ran'she vremeni', *LO,* 4/76; 'Velikii smysl – zhit'', *LO,* 5/76.

I. Sozonova, 'Vnutri kruga', *LO,* 5/76.

N. Il'ina, 'Iz rodoslovnoi russkoi revolyutsii', *Neman,* 12/76.

N. Tyul'pinov, 'Otblesk drugoi zhizni', *Zvezda,* 2/77.

N. N. Shneidman, 'Iurii Trifonov and the ethics of contemporary Soviet city life', *Canadian Slavonic Papers,* Vol. 19, no. 3 (September 1977).

T. L. Rybal'chenko, 'Zhanrovaya struktura i khudozhestvennaya ideya (povest' Yu. Trifonova 'Predvaritel'nye itogi'), *Problemy Metoda i Zhanra*, 1977, vypusk 4.

A. Bocharov, 'Strast' bor'by i igrushechnye strasti', *LO*, 10/78.

E. Reissner, 'Auf der Suche nach der verlorenen Wahrheit: Jurij Trifonows jüngster Roman *Der Alte*', *Osteuropa*, 2/79.

5. *English translations*

Students, Moscow: Foreign Languages Publishing House, 1953.

'Thirst aquenched', *Soviet Literature*, 1/64.

'The exchange', *Russian Literature Triquarterly*, no. 5 (1973).

'The present – an alloy of history and future', *Soviet Literature*, 2/75.

The long goodbye (three novellas), trans. Helen P. Burlingame and Ellendea Proffer, New York: Harper & Row, 1978 (includes also translations of 'The exchange' and 'Taking stock').

ADDENDA

General

G. Belaya, 'Vechnoe i prekhodyashchee: chelovek i priroda v interpretatsii sovremennoi prozy', *LO*, 2/79.

A. Bocharov, 'Ternistye puti khudozhestvennoi pravdy', *Oktyabr'*, 8–9/79.

A. El'yashevich, 'Literatura semidesyatykh (monologi i dialogi)', *Zvezda*, 3/79.

Ronald Hingley, *Russian writers and Soviet society, 1917–78*, London: Weidenfeld & Nicolson; New York: Random House, 1979.

V. Pertsovskii, 'Pokoryayas' techeniyu', *VL*, 4/79.

Belov

'That's how it is', *Soviet Literature*, 1/69 (translation of *Privychnoe delo*).

Rasputin

'Money for Maria', *Soviet Literature*, 4/69.
'The French lesson', *Soviet Literature*, 1/75.
N. Podzorova, 'Ravnozvuchie: zlobodnevnoe i vechnoe v proze V. Rasputina', *NS*, 10/78.
N. Yanovskii, 'Zaboty i trevogi Valentina Rasputina', *Sever*, 2/79.

Tendryakov

'A topsy-turvy spring', *Soviet Literature*, 12/73.
Three, Seven, Ace and other stories, trans. D. Alger et al., London: Harvill Press, 1973.

Maximov

Kovcheg dlya nezvanykh, Frankfurt-am-Main: Possev, 1979.
'Saga o nosorogakh', *Kontinent*, no. 19 (1979).
V. Maramzin, 'Russkii roman Vladimira Maksimova "Proshchanie iz niotkuda"', *Ekho*, no. 1 (1978).

Voinovich

In plain Russian, trans. R. Lourie, New York: Farrar, Straus & Giroux, 1979 (translation of the collection *Putëm vzaimnoi perepiski*).
Pretendent na prestol (*novye priklyucheniya soldata Ivana Chonkina*), Paris: YMCA Press, 1979.

Vladimov

Faithful Ruslan, trans. M. Glenny, London: Jonathan Cape; New York: Simon & Schuster, 1979.

Shukshin

'Ya rodom iz derevni', *NS* 7/79 (translation of a 1974 interview with an Italian journalist, Carlo Benedetti).
I want to live, Moscow: Progress, 1973 (translations of short stories).
'The red guelder rose' and other short stories, *Soviet Literature*, 9/75.
L. Emel'yanov, 'Vtoroe prochtenie', *NS*, 7/79.
G. Kapralov, 'Bor'ba za cheloveka nikogda ne konchaetsya: Shukshin v zhizni, knigakh, teatre, kino', *Neva*, 2/79.
'Obsuzhdaem roman V. Shukshina *Ya prishel dat' vam volyu* i spektakl' moskovskogo teatra imeni Vakhtangova *Stepan Razin*', *LO*, 3/79.

Trifonov

The impatient ones, Moscow: Progress, 1978.
B. Pankin, 'Po krugu ili po spirali? O povestyakh Yu. Trifonova', *Druzhba Narodov*, 5/77.

Index